SUBLIME LADY OF IMMORTALITY

SUBLIME LADY OF IMMORTALITY

Teachings on Chimé Phakmé Nyingtik

by

Jamyang Khyentse Wangpo
Jamgön Kongtrul Lodrö Taye
Jamyang Khyentse Chökyi Lodrö
Dilgo Khyentse Rinpoche
& Tulku Orgyen Tobgyal

Translated by *Gyurme Avertin*

With contributions from
Patrick Gaffney, Han Kop, and Adam Pearcey

Edited by *Janine Schulz*

Rangjung Yeshe
PUBLICATIONS

Namthar Limited
An imprint of Rangjung Yeshe Publications
55 Mitchell Blvd, Suite 20
San Rafael, CA 94903 USA

www.rangjung.com
www.all-otr.org

1 3 5 7 9 8 6 4 2

FIRST PAPERBACK EDITION PUBLISHED IN 2021
PRINTED IN THE UNITED STATES OF AMERICA
DISTRIBUTED TO THE BOOK TRADE BY:
PGW/INGRAM

ISBN 9781735707 (paperback)

Title: *Sublime Lady of Immortality.* Foreword by H.H. Sakya Gongma Trichen.

Other titles: *'chi med 'phags ma'i snying thig las phrin las ye shes snang ba | 'chi med 'phags
ma'i snying tig las rgyun gyi rnal 'byor phyag rgya gcig pa | dris lan mdor bsdus skor las chi med
'phags ma'i snying tig gi bsnyen sgrub las brtsams pa'i dris lan cung zad |*
'Jam-dbyangs mKhyen-brtse dBang-po.

*dgongs gter 'phags ma'i snying thig gi bsnyen sgrub ji ltar
bya ba'i zin bris zla zer bdud rtsi'i thig le |*
'Jam-mgon Kong-sprul bLo-gros mTha'-yas.

*chi med 'phags ma'i snying thig gi rgyun gyi rnal 'byor phyag rgya gcig dang 'brel ba'i bskyed
rdzogs kyi khrid mdor bsdus |* 'Jam-byangs mKhyen-brtse Chos-kyi bLo-gros.

'chi med 'phags ma'i snying thig gi bsnyen sgrub las gsum gyi bzlas dmigs |
Dil-mgo mKhyen-brtse Rin po che.

BISAC: RELIGION / Buddhism / Sacred Writings. | RELIGION / Buddhism / History.
| RELIGION / Buddhism / Tibetan.

This book is dedicated towards the long life of Dzongsar Jamyang Khyentse Rinpoche and Neten Chokling Rinpoche, the current holders of the unique and sublime lineage of Chimé Phakmé Nyingtik.

May the Three Deities of Long Life shower their blessings upon them, so their lives remain forever youthful and firm, free of any obstacles.

May their vision for the dharma unfold with ever-growing benefit and success, exactly as they wish.

And may they continue to grace us with their teachings, practice and the blessings of their unchanging wisdom minds.

CONTENTS

His Holiness
The Gongma Trichen
SUPREME HEAD OF THE SAKYAPA ORDER
OF TIBETAN BUDDHISM

FOREWORD

Chimé Phakmé Nyingtik is a very important treasure teaching from Jamyang Khyentse Wangpo. It is one of my personal practices, and I do its short sadhana every day. It is a very precious teaching and a great blessing, and from my own experience even people who are terminally ill can survive through its practice.

Gyurme Avertin is an experienced Tibetan/French/English translator and an expert in the Chimé Phakmé Nyingtik practice. For the past twelve years, he has been translating sadhanas, explanatory texts and oral commentaries related to the subject. I am very pleased that he has composed this remarkable book, comprising a selection of works that encompass the very essence of this exceptional practice.

I pray that this excellent presentation of the Chimé Phakmé Nyingtik may be a source of inspiration and guidance to all students who undertake its practice in earnest and that it may lead them swiftly to complete liberation.

The Sakya Trichen

5ᵗʰ January 2021

DOLMA PHODRANG

192 Rajpur Road, P.O. BOX Rajpur, 248009 Dehradun, U.K. India
+91-135-2734081 · sakyadolmaphodrang@gmail.com

I

TRANSLATOR'S INTRODUCTION

The Heart Essence of the Sublime Lady of Immortality is one of the most famous and revered termas of Jamyang Khyentse Wangpo. Thanks to its power and blessings, all his greatest students, such as Jamgön Kongtrul Lodrö Taye and the 14th and 15th Karmapas, were able to remove obstacles to their long lives and activities. According to prophecy, had it not been for this practice, the life of Jamgön Kongtrul would have been fraught with obstacles and much shorter. More recently, it was the main practice of Jamyang Khyentse Chökyi Lodrö, Dudjom Rinpoche, Dilgo Khyentse Rinpoche and Trulshik Rinpoche. It is also the heart practice of His Holiness Sakya Gongma Trichen Rinpoche.

The Heart Essence of the Sublime Lady of Immortality or *Chimé Phakmé Nyingtik* is a Secret Mantra Vajrayana practice. As such, to benefit from this book and the practice, it is essential that you first receive the Chimé Phakmé Nyingtik empowerment. If you have yet to receive the empowerment and reading transmission, it's best to keep this book on your shrine as an object of veneration until you receive them. The empowerment is a must, not an option. According to the *Mirror of the Heart of Vajrasattva* tantra, "In the Secret Mantra Vehicle, there can be no accomplishment without empowerment; it is like a boatman with no oars".

I came up with the idea of producing a book that focuses exclusively on the Chimé Phakmé Nyingtik at the end of 2020, after I heard that Dzongsar Khyentse Rinpoche had asked many of his students to practise the Chime Phakmé Nyingtik throughout the Iron Ox Year (2021). When I realised that, I began to think that it would be a good idea to compile all the commentaries and teachings on the *Heart Essence of the Sublime Lady of Immortality* that I have worked on over the years into one book and then dedicate it to the long lives of both Dzongsar Khyentse Rinpoche and Neten Chokling Rinpoche.

Fifteen years ago, a teaching on the *Chimé Phakmé Nyingtik* was the first sadhana teaching that I translated live—well, let's say that I attempted to translate it. One evening, about twenty practitioners locked themselves into a shrine room with Tulku Orgyen Tobgyal to receive teachings on the

Heart Essence of the Supreme Lady of Immortality and dragged me along with them. Since then, I have often translated Tulku Orgyen Tobgyal's Chimé Phakmé Nyingtik teachings. Over the years, I have also translated and revised Jamgön Kongtrul Lodrö Taye's *Retreat Manual* and the sadhana. The last time I worked on the sadhana was a Chimé Phakmé Nyingtik drupchen in Bir, during which I once again checked the text thoroughly with Khenpo Yeshe Dorje. Khenpo is the abbot of Chokling Monastery in Bir, Northern India, and is famous for his ritual knowledge. I also consulted Yongdzin Khen Rinpoche, Yeshe Gyaltsen, who was the tutor of Yangsi Dilgo Khyentse Rinpoche and a staunch Chimé Phakmé Nyingtik practitioner. When Yongdzin Khen Rinpoche couldn't answer my questions, we asked Tulku Orgyen Tobgyal himself, who has Dilgo Khyentse Rinpoche's personal copy of the text of the sadhana that is more accurate than the version commonly used by Tibetans, and he clarified a number of questions in consultation with that text.

Although I have always tried to retranslate and upload the most significant of Orgyen Tobgyal's oral teachings to his website,[1] many dharma friends have urged me to produce a compilation of the Chimé Phakmé Nyingtik teachings as a physical book. This is another reason I have compiled this book. My goal was to produce as definitive a set of teachings as possible. I have therefore included as many of the relevant texts by the great masters of this lineage as I could find. So in addition to Jamgön Kongtrul's *Retreat Manual,* I translated Jamyang Khyentse Wangpo's answers to questions about the Chimé Phakmé Nyingtik that had formed the basis of the *Retreat Manual.* Han Kop and Adam Pearcey, with the help of Alak Zenkar Rinpoche, Khenpo Sonam Tsewang and Ven. Tenzin Jamchen (Sean Price), produced—on very short notice—a translation of Jamyang Khyentse Chökyi Lodrö's practice instructions. Dilgo Khyentse Rinpoche's two-page visualization guide is also included, most of which he copied from Jamyang Khyentse Wangpo. That really is a gem of a text and has been wonderfully translated by Patrick Gaffney. It might be a good piece to keep on your table as you do a retreat. All these teachings, everything you find in this book, reveal the profound views, powerful meditations, sacred conduct and ultimate goals of the Vajrayana teachings of Tibetan Buddhism.

I hope this book will provide beginning and advanced practitioners with the information they need to practise the Chimé Phakmé Nyingtik. It contains instructions and commentaries by the great masters of this lineage, as well as advice from the oral lineage given by Tulku Orgyen Tobgyal. Not only do these teachings represent all the information necessary for practising the Chimé Phakmé Nyingtik and clarify a number of points that apply to all sadhana practices, but Tulku Orgyen Tobgyal is also a great coach and motivator, so these pages are also a source of enthusiasm and confidence in the different aspects of these practices, which is an invaluable source of inspiration while on retreat. So even if you don't practise the Chimé Phakmé Nyingtik, you can benefit from reading this book. Orgyen Tobgyal's presentations of kyerim practice based on the Chimé Phakmé Nyingtik in particular is packed with practical instructions passed down from the great siddhas of this lineage.

CHIMÉ PHAKMÉ NYINGTIK: REVELATION AND TRANSMISSION

White Tara was Jamyang Khyentse Wangpo's main yidam. Just before dawn, one morning early in 1855, Jamyang Khyentse Wangpo had a vision of White Tara, the Wish-Fulfilling Wheel. She appeared in the sky before him, and her ten-syllable mantra OM TARE TUTTARE TURE SOHA resounded everywhere. She then dissolved into him, and he became indivisible from Tara's enlightened body, speech and mind; in that moment he had a profound experience of primordial wisdom. When he arose from that state Shri Singha, Vimalamitra and Guru Rinpoche, the three masters who had attained the vidyadhara level of power over life, appeared in front of him. Joyfully, they gave him an empowerment, then melted into light; and the moment they dissolved into him, his ordinary consciousness dissolved within the expanse of the dharmadhatu, and the combined blessings of the three great masters made it possible for the entire Chimé Phakmé Nyingtik—all the tantras, empowerments, pith instructions and sadhanas—to enter his wisdom mind as clearly and distinctly as a reflection in a mirror.

The following day Khyentse Wangpo began to transcribe the sadhana, with the help of Vimalamitra, who gave him repeated blessings and even checked the manuscript after Jamyang Khyentse Wangpo had written it. In

Jamyang Khyentse Wangpo's autobiography, he stated that he had not transcribed the entire Chimé Phakmé Nyingtik cycle—these details can only have been known to the tertön himself. He transcribed only the root sadhana known as the Chimé Phakmé Nyingtik, the sadhana and instruction cycle of the lama known as *Vima Ladrup* (*The Sadhana of Vimalamitra*) and that of White Amitayus and Ushnisha Vijaya.

For five years Jamyang Khyentse Wangpo practised these teachings in complete secrecy. Tertöns are often instructed to keep termas secret for several years before transmitting them to the prophesied recipients. Then at Dokhoma near the Derge capital, he gave the empowerment and teachings of the Chimé Phakmé Nyingtik to Chokgyur Dechen Lingpa. The following night he dreamt that his mother gave him the heart of a dakini who had lost her life for the crime of having revealed what should be kept secret to those not bound by oath. In an age when social media announces very publicly the dates and times of tantric empowerments and teachings, for someone to have died for failing to keep the Vajrayana secret sounds a little extreme. However, Orgyen Tobgyal and other lamas have pointed out that our lack of secrecy is why, even after many years of practice, today's practitioners show no signs of realization. Basically, their samayas are being compromised before they even start.

Having transmitted the Chimé Phakmé Nyingtik to Chokgyur Lingpa, Jamyang Khyentse Wangpo then gave it to the 14th Karmapa, Tekchok Dorje. He also gave it to Jamgön Kongtrul Rinpoche, who was then instrumental in spreading the Chimé Phakmé Nyingtik teachings. He compiled thirteen of the cycle's twenty-seven texts based on the original terma, such as Ushnisha Vijaya practice, lineage prayer, short tsok, fire offering and the *Retreat Manual*, the translation of which can be found in Chapter 6 of this book. Later, Jamyang Khyentse Wangpo transmitted these teachings to his students, such as Tertön Sogyal, Shechen Gyaltsab Pema Namgyal, Karmapa Khakhyab Dorje, Dodrupchen Jigme Tenpe Nyima and Kathok Situ Chökyi Gyatso, among many others, all of whom took it as one of their main practices. Kathok Situ gave the empowerments and instructions to Jamyang Khyentse Chökyi Lodrö. It was such an important practice for Chökyi Lodrö that his biography tells us that he went to receive the empowerment ten times, then gave it all to Dilgo Khyentse Rinpoche. After completing the required practices seven times in retreat, Dilgo Khyentse Rinpoche gave everything to Dzongsar Khyentse Rinpoche, Neten Chokling Rinpoche and Tulku Orgyen Tobgyal, among others.

THE CONTENTS OF THIS BOOK

Tulku Orgyen Tobgyal gave the teachings presented in this book between the summer of 1996 and the end of July 2015. In 1996, the first Chimé Phakmé Nyingtik group practice took place at Lerab Ling. After His Holiness Sakya Gongma Trichen's divination said that to remove obstacles to Sogyal Rinpoche's life, an annual long-life ceremony or tenshuk (see Appendices 4 and 5) should be performed based on a Chimé Phakmé Nyingtik drupchen, Tulku Orgyen Tobgyal taught the Chimé Phakmé Nyingtik every year during those drupchens. He also gave detailed teachings at Tulku Pema Wangyal's and later Dzongsar Khyentse Rinpoche's requests to some students who were in retreat. Tulku Orgyen Tobgyal's instructions on every aspect of the practice are always clear and characteristically direct, and he based all his teachings on instructions he had received directly from Dilgo Khyentse Rinpoche.

The book presents Orgyen Tobgyal's teachings in order from the most essential to the most elaborate. As the subject is always the Chimé Phakmé Nyingtik, there is of course a certain amount of repetition. But with each teaching Orgyen Tobgyal's explanations deepen many of the most crucial points further and further. Hopefully this structure will make it possible for all levels of practitioner to benefit from this book. As your experience and understanding progresses, you may prefer to study each teaching in succession. Or you may prefer to focus on a specific teaching, perhaps in preparation for a retreat or to help you establish a daily practice. Sometimes you will find that the most appropriate teaching is short and sweet; at other times it will be rather more detailed.

I decided not to edit all Tulku Orgyen Tobgyal's teachings together or to eliminate repetitions, because he always thinks very deeply about which points to include in each teaching. Sometimes he just lists these points for the sake of completeness, but he always emphasizes those that are most important for the practitioner. This approach makes even his most essential teachings complete because he always tells beginners how and where to begin and makes more experienced practitioners aware of what they must not omit at any cost.

You will not find instructions about how to do the rituals in this book, how to chant, use a bell and dorje, perform mudras, make tormas and so on, all of which you will be taught by your own teacher. Neither are the practices included as separate texts. If you need copies of the practice texts, you will find them on the Lotsawa House website.[2] The other translations I mention by Khenpo Sonam Phuntsok of Dzongsar Shedra (Chauntra) and Steve Cline are excellent renderings of all the practices necessary for a Chimé Phakmé Nyingtik drupchen and include most of the practice texts of this cycle. Their compilation is called *The Great Accomplishment Ritual of the Heart Essence of Deathless Ārya Tārā* and is freely available as a pdf to those who have received the empowerment and maintain the samayas.[3]

Finally, I have not used Sanskrit diacritics. It's not that I find diacritics inelegant, quite the opposite, and they certainly give an air of authority to a book. However, I have chosen not to use them because for years, a number of my dharma friends have complained about how unreadable they make a text. Even if a key to the pronunciation of each squiggle and dot is provided, "It is simply too complicated for simple practitioners! Please think of those of us who can't even learn English, let alone Tibetan or Sanskrit." (These friends of mine are French.)

Sakya Pandita was a great scholar and well versed in Sanskrit. Once, as he passed through a dense forest, he heard the Vajrakilaya mantra. He looked around to see who was chanting it and realised it was coming from everywhere, the rivers, the rocks and everywhere. "A great practitioner must live near here," he thought. But then he heard a mistake. Whoever was chanting this mantra was mispronouncing a word and was chanting "om bendza chili chilaya". As he emerged into a small clearing, Sakya Pandita bumped into the yogi and very respectfully drew the yogi's attention to his mispronunciation.

The yogi instantly raised his phurba, recited "om bendza chili chilaya", mistake and all, then struck a rock. His phurba sank into the rock as though it were butter. The yogi then turned to Sakya Pandita and said, "Please, do the same with 'kili kilaya'!" But Sakya Pandita could not.

Mantras said with a Tibetan accent seem to retain their effectiveness, and termas are the words of Guru Rinpoche which tertöns faithfully transcribe. This is why Tibetan masters say that a terma text must never be changed or tampered with. Even if there appears to be a mistake in the order, the words or the spelling, even the spelling of the mantras which can include both Sanskrit and Tibetan, nothing should be changed. I have therefore used approximate phonetic transcription of the mantras in an attempt to preserve the tertön's pronunciation passed down by the great masters of this lineage. It is of course ideal to pronounce the Sanskrit syllables correctly and a number of practitioners have adopted that approach. However, I would like to offer the alternative, in case people cannot read diacritics and end up mispronouncing the mantras. Besides, as Tulku Orgyen Tobgyal says on several occasions in these pages, Jamyang Khyentse Wangpo says that it is better to visualize the syllables of the mantra in the script of our country, because they are part of our bodies, inside the channels. Since diacritics are not in English-speaking countries, one may wonder how then should one visualize the mantra syllables.

THE TEACHINGS
Chapter 1: The History and Background of the Chimé Phakmé Nyingtik Teachings

This is the teaching Tulku Orgyen Tobgyal gave the day before the elaborate empowerment of Chimé Phakmé Nyingtik that Dzongsar Khyentse Rinpoche gave at Lerab Ling on 19 August 1996. During his teaching about the five perfections that form the basis for how we receive an empowerment, he narrated the history of the Chimé Phakmé Nyingtik teachings. This introduction is important if you wish to practice the Chimé Phakmé Nyingtik. To inspire faith in both the teaching and the teacher, Orgyen Tobgyal went on to talk at length about Jamyang Khyentse Wangpo and Jamyang Khyentse Chökyi Lodrö, and both biographies can be found on the Lotsawa House website,[4] so that students may realise the incredible qualities of the master who was about to empower them.

Chapter 2: Long-Life Practice

In this teaching, given on a rainy summer's afternoon, 26 July 1998, Tulku Orgyen Tobgyal spoke about how and why those who follow this tradition should do long-life practices. Then at the request of Dzongsar Khyentse Rinpoche and Sogyal Rinpoche, he focused on longevity sadhana practices, specifically the Chimé Phakmé Nyingtik. The teaching turned out to be a crash course on how to do the Chimé Phakmé Nyingtik and included a brief, very pithy but complete instruction on kyerim practice, which is central to all sadhana practices. It is the shortest instruction Rinpoche has ever given on this subject and a very good starting point for beginners.

Chapter 3: Daily Chimé Phakmé Nyingtik in a Nutshell

During a ten-day Chimé Phakmé Nyingtik drupchen presided over by Dzongsar Khyentse Rinpoche and Chokling Rinpoche, Tulku Orgyen Tobgyal gave this teaching on the *Single Mudra,* the daily Chimé Phakmé Nyingtik practice. The drupchen took place at Tulku Orgyen Tobgyal's home in Bir, India, and one of its purposes was to consecrate the new temple he had built in his back garden. This teaching came about after some Taiwanese participants asked Tulku Orgyen Tobgyal to give them a short, essential instruction that would help them make the most of their Chimé Phakmé Nyingtik daily practice.

Chapter 4: An Explanation of *Single Mudra,*
the Daily Practice from the Chimé Phakmé Nyingtik

On 26 July 2006, Orgyen Tobgyal deepened his explanation of the daily practice and talked about how to do a retreat based on the *Single Mudra,* which according to Jamyang Khyentse Wangpo is acceptable for the approach phase but not for the accomplishment and activity phases, for which we must rely on the longer sadhana.[5] Orgyen Tobgyal would have preferred to base his teaching on doing a retreat using the longer sadhana, but there wasn't enough time. About twenty determined practitioners had waited until the end of Orgyen Tobgyal's stay at Lerab Ling to ask him how to do a Chimé Phakmé Nyingtik retreat. Rinpoche started telling them how to do a retreat based on the daily sadhana, but ran out of time and had to complete the teaching from his bed in Paris two days later.

Chapter 5: *The Sweet Ambrosia of Immortality*

Jamyang Khyentse Chökyi Lodrö's Chimé Phakmé Nyingtik instruction manual is called *The Sweet Ambrosia of Immortality*. It clearly explains how to practice the Chimé Phakmé Nyingtik and includes unique instructions on the preliminary practices that serious practitioners should do before starting the Chimé Phakmé Nyingtik. His instructions on the kyerim and dzogrim phases are based on *Single Mudra*, the daily practice text. As Jamyang Khyentse Chökyi Lodrö explains, the instructions are not his own invention; he is repeating the words of Jamyang Khyentse Wangpo—the tertön who discovered this terma—that he received through the lineage.

Chapter 6: *A Drop of Moonlight Nectar*

A Drop of Moonlight Nectar: Notes on How to Do the Approach and Accomplishment Practices of the Chimé Phakmé Nyingtik Mind Treasure, the retreat manual by Jamgön Kongtrul, explains how to practise the approach and accomplishment practices in the Chimé Phakmé Nyingtik and includes everything a practitioner ought to know before doing retreat.

Chapter 7: Chimé Phakmé Nyingtik: Presentation of *A Drop of Moonlight Nectar*

Tulku Orgyen Tobgyal gave this explanation about how to do a Chimé Phakmé Nyingtik retreat based on Jamgön Kongtrul Lodrö Taye's *Retreat Manual* on 3 September 1996, at Bois Bas near Saint-Léon-sur-Vézère in the Dordogne to an audience of nine three-year retreatants.

Chapter 8: Explanation of *Activities for Uncovering Primordial Wisdom*, the Root Sadhana of the Chimé Phakmé Nyingtik

From 22 to 24 April 2011, Tulku Orgyen Tobgyal taught how to do a Chimé Phakmé Nyingtik retreat by explaining the root sadhana in detail at Deer Park, Bir, in the north of India, at Dzongsar Khyentse Rinpoche's request.

Although unfortunately the recordings for the second day are patchy, student's notes were used to complete the teaching which Orgyen Tobgyal then further clarified.

Chapter 9: How to Direct the Practice of Chimé Phakmé Nyingtik for Someone Else

In May 2009, Tulku Orgyen Tobgyal gave a series of teachings on Yumka Dechen Gyalmo. Just before one teaching, the Rigpa sangha asked him if he would include an explanation about how to direct their practice for the long life of Sogyal Rinpoche. He agreed but felt that for the sake of auspiciousness, it would better if he talked about long-life practice first, which he did on 13 May 2009.

Chapter 10: Origins of Chimé Phakmé Nyingtik Drupchen

Many of us had not realised how uniquely qualified Tulku Orgyen Tobgyal is to explain the authenticity of practising the Chimé Phakmé Nyingtik as a drupchen until he spoke about the origins of this tradition during such a drupchen at Lerab Ling on 29 July 2015.

Chapter 11: The Chimé Phakmé Nyingtik Torma

Towards the end of the annual Chimé Phakmé Nyingtik drupchen at Lerab Ling, on 21 July 2015, Rinpoche explained a meditation specific to this practice. Over the years he said that he had given all the instructions necessary for us to practise the Chimé Phakmé Nyingtik, except for one very important one: the torma meditation.

Appendix 1: *Brief Answers to Questions on Chimé Phakmé Nyingtik, Beginning with Approach and Accomplishment*

This is the translation of Jamyang Khyentse Wangpo's answers to questions about the Chimé Phakmé Nyingtik. It appears in an appendix rather than in the middle of the text because Jamgön Kongtrul copied and pasted most of it into the *Retreat Manual* verbatim. In those days there was no such thing as copyright. Most people felt it was far better to repeat the words of one's master precisely than to try to write something original. The text has been included for completeness and so that practitioners can refer directly to it when necessary, and it does also include a little information that doesn't appear in the *Retreat Manual*.

Appendix 2: *The Visualization for the Mantra Recitation of the Phases of Approach, Accomplishment and Activity of Chimé Phakmé Nyingtik*

This is the translation of Dilgo Khyentse Rinpoche's visualization guide for the three phases of approach, accomplishment and activity. In this case, Dilgo Khyentse Rinpoche mostly plagiarised texts by Jamyang Khyentse Wangpo and Jamgön Kongtrul. Again, I included it for completeness so that practitioners will have all the material they need and because it can be very handy to have this text with you during recitation sessions to help actualise the practice.

Appendix 3: Vajrasattva Mantra Recitation from *The Confession and Fulfillment of Vima Ladrup*—Jamgön Kongtrul Lodrö Taye

In his commentary *The Sweet Ambrosia of Immortality*, Jamyang Khyentse Chökyi Lodrö explains that before completing the approach and accomplishment of the Chimé Phakmé Nyingtik on retreat, it would be good to do preliminary practices that he explains. For the confession Chökyi Lodrö's advice is to do a short prayer extracted from the *Vima Ladrup* root terma and which Jamgön Kongtrul Lodrö Taye included in *The Confession and Fulfillment* liturgy for the *Vima Ladrup*. For those eager to practise these preliminaries, I have added this prayer with the kind permission of Steve Cline who translated the text with Khenpo Sonam Phuntsok, slightly adapting their translation.

Appendix 4: The Meaning of Sundok and Tenshuk: The Traditional Long-Life Ceremony

The long-life ceremony that Tulku Orgyen Tobgyal and his monks do annually at Lerab Ling is based on a text by Jamyang Khyentse Wangpo. The ceremony always includes a sundok and tenshuk, and on 19 July 2015 at

Lerab Ling, Orgyen Tobgyal taught on both. Strictly speaking neither practice is exclusive to the Chimé Phakmé Nyingtik, but this teaching has been
included because Chimé Phakmé Nyingtik drupchens often provide the
framework for ceremonies for the long lives of masters.

Appendix 5: Advice for Offering a Short Tenshuk

Orgyen Tobgyal recorded this teaching in New Delhi on 11 January 2015 and
it is included because it deepens the teaching presented in Appendix 4. In
2015 Rigpa wanted to do a slightly simpler version of the practice and to ensure that the potency and authenticity were preserved asked Tulku Orgyen
Tobgyal for his advice.

Appendix 6: Setting up the Mandala of Chimé Phakmé Nyingtik According to *A Drop of Moonlight Nectar* by Jamgön Kongtrul Lodrö Taye

How a Chimé Phakmé Nyingtik shrine is set up by Ane Chökyi Drolma,
Lerab Ling's head chopön.

ACKNOWLEDGEMENTS

I must begin by expressing the tremendous sense of gratitude all of us feel
for Tulku Orgyen Tobgyal's teachings and to Dzongsar Khyentse Rinpoche,
Sogyal Rinpoche and Tulku Pema Wangyal Rinpoche for creating the perfect circumstances in which the teachings could take place. The translation
into English of Tulku Orgyen Tobgyal's teachings have been possible by the
unfailing kindness of our sponsors and specifically the generous support of
the Khyentse Foundation. I would also like to thank Markus Schmidt for
preparing the recordings; Rigpa's exceptional transcription team, particularly Anette Cyran, for transcribing the teachings; and Janine Schulz for her
brilliant editing that brings alive Tulku Orgyen Tobgyal's verve. I am very
grateful to Han Kop and Adam Pearcey who, under the Jamyang Khyentse
Chökyi Lodrö Sungbum translation project, produced in a very short time
a much-needed translation of Chökyi Lodrö's practice manual; to Patrick

Gaffney for allowing us to use his beautiful translation of Dilgo Khyentse Rinpoche's text and to Ane Chökyi Drolma for sharing the results of her research.

For the production of the book, I am also indebted to Regina Marco, Sherab Gyaltsen, Ven. Tenzin Jamchen (Sean Price), Philip Philippou, Marcia B. Schmidt and the team at Rangjung Yeshe Publications for their advices and support, and Steve Cline whose suggestions brought about significant improvements during the final stages of preparation; to Kay Henry for the copyediting; to Ane Tsöndru for her excellent proofreading; to the talented Tara di Gesu for the cover image and Peter Fry for the elegant cover design. This book and its free distribution to about five hundred Chimé Phakmé Nyingtik practitioners around the world has been possible thanks to the enthusiasm and generous financial support of a few dharma friends, some of whom preferred to remain anonymous, who have devotion for the dharma and the great masters, such as Dzongsar Khyentse Rinpoche and Neten Chokling Rinpoche, and who wish to dedicate this publication to the long lives of the masters, the preservation and expansion of the dharma and the well-being and ultimate happiness of all sentient beings.

—Gyurme Avertin, Valle de Bravo, January 2021

CHAPTER 1:

The History and Background of the Chimé Phakmé Nyingtik Teachings

by Tulku Orgyen Tobgyal

The Vinaya teachings report that the Bhagavan Buddha said, "Gather with friends to talk about the dharma." And the tantras say,

> If you do not explain its history,
> You run the risk of people not trusting
> The great, secret, ultimate teaching.[6]

When the great, secret, ultimate teaching is given, if its history is not explained, those receiving the teaching will not trust it. As the lack of trust can be a problem, the tantras say that both to inspire our minds and kindle our trust, the origin and background of the teaching must always be taught first.

First of all, you should know there are two ways the right circumstances come together. One is to create the auspicious conditions, and the other is that the conditions arise spontaneously and are not created. On this occasion all the right conditions have manifested spontaneously, as all five perfections have come together naturally to create a situation that's quite exceptional in this world. Since everything arises interdependently, interdependent circumstances are of the utmost importance. As the perfectly enlightened Buddha said,

> Not even one thing exists
> That has not dependently arisen.[7]

It is because of interdependence that all things, all phenomena, in both samsara and nirvana, the good and the bad, appear and exist. Today interdependent circumstances have naturally come together for this empowerment, and I would like to tell you how I think that's happened.

PERFECT PLACE

Sogyal Rinpoche came to Europe many years ago and has taught all over the continent, particularly in France. In France he found this place, Lerab Ling, which has been blessed by the two great Holinesses—Dudjom Rinpoche and Dilgo Khyentse Rinpoche. Their blessings make it an extremely sacred place.

About a year ago the incarnation of the all-knowing lord Jamyang Khyentse Chökyi Lodrö, Dzongsar Khyentse Rinpoche, made a prophecy. He said that if in a special place—like Lerab Ling—a Chimé Phakmé Nyingtik fire ceremony was performed, it would be extremely beneficial for the spread of the buddhadharma generally, for specific teachings and for the long life of Sogyal Rinpoche, his work and his students.

PERFECT TIME

The time is also excellent. We have gathered here during the summer which is a time of growth and the increase of longevity, merit and so forth. Everything grows—branches, grass, trees, forests. It's a time when beings naturally feel uplifted and want to celebrate.

PERFECT TEACHER

On top of that, as an expression of exceptional merit, Jamyang Khyentse Rinpoche's incarnation, Thubten Chökyi Gyatso, in other words Dzongsar Khyentse Rinpoche, came to France to do a drupchen in the Dordogne, where he was joined by the incarnation of Chokgyur Lingpa, Neten Chokling Rinpoche, who brought with him the right number of monks. So all the right circumstances have come together naturally without having to be arranged or organised.

These two great incarnations of Jamyang Khyentse Wangpo and Chokgyur Dechen Lingpa are also the incarnations of the dharma king Trison Deutsen and his middle son Damdzin Murub Tsenpo. For thirteen generations, the incarnations of these two great tertöns have maintained a connection as close as that of a father and son.

> Especially, you awakened the residual karmic link of father
>   and son,
> With Jamgon Khyentse Wangpo.
> I supplicate you who, mingling your minds into one,
> Opened hundreds of doors for wondrous coincidences.[8]

When the karmic connection between father and son was awakened, the minds of Jamyang Khyentse Wangpo and Chokgyur Dechen Lingpa merged as one. As a result, in Tibet they were able to spread once more the treasury of dharma known as the seven transmissions in a way that no other tertön could.

Along with these two great incarnations of the father and son, the wisdom consort of Dorje Chang Jamyang Khyentse Chökyi Lodrö herself is also here, which is so remarkable that I can hardly believe it myself. Many termas include prophecies about her, saying she is the incarnation of Shelkar Dorje Tso, the embodiment of all wisdoms and of all objects of devotion and reliance. So for Khandro Tsering Chödrön to be here is quite extraordinary.

As if that weren't enough, the great Dzogchen teacher and light for the whole world, Nyoshul Khen Rinpoche, Jamyang Dorje—omniscient Gyalwa Longchenpa in the flesh—is also here.

PERFECT TEACHING

These are the conditions in which, over the next two days, the mandala of Jamyang Khyentse Wangpo's mind terma known as the Chimé Phakmé Nyingtik will be opened. The Chimé Phakmé Nyingtik will be the basis of our drupchö practice and fire puja.

The ripening empowerment in the elaborate abhisheka of the Chimé Phakmé Nyingtik includes preparatory practices and a main section. There are three kinds of empowerment in the Chimé Phakmé Nyingtik: simple, medium-length and elaborate.

Of course, all the Buddha's teachings are imbued with tremendous blessings, but the blessings of Secret Mantra Vajrayana are especially powerful,
particularly the Mahayoga approach which emphasizes kyerim practice and
is the approach followed in the Chimé Phakmé Nyingtik. The Chimé
Phakmé Nyingtik is a Mahayoga practice that condenses the special yidam
deity of the three great vidyadharas of India—Shri Singha, Vimalamitra
and Guru Rinpoche—and it was received by Jamyang Khyentse Wangpo in
the form of a mind terma. So the Chimé Phakmé Nyingtik is an extremely
blessed practice.

When and how did Jamyang Khyentse receive the Chimé Phakmé Nyingtik? At the age of thirty-five Jamyang Khyentse Wangpo the Great was
in his residence—the Joyful Grove of Immortal Accomplishment—at his
monastic seat of Dzongsar Tashi Lhatse. As he focused intensively on the
practice of Tara, he had a vision of the wisdom body of the three great
masters—Shri Singha, Guru Rinpoche and Vimalamitra. Then like filling
a vase to its brim, they gave him all the Chimé Phakmé Nyingtik tantras,
including the empowerments, all the transmissions, pith instructions and
sadhanas. So the entire root and branch teachings and practices of the
Chimé Phakmé Nyingtik entered Jamyang Khyentse Wangpo's wisdom
mind as a result of the combined blessings of these three great masters. It
was as if the teachings had been perfectly reproduced in his mind like a
photograph.

At first when Khyentse Wangpo deciphered the terma, he wrote down
just the sadhana of Chimé Phakmé Nyingtik. Then he began to practise it
and receive its extraordinary power and blessings. Vimalamitra appeared to
him again and again, blessed him and proofread the text he had written.
Khyentse Wangpo then transmitted the final draft to Terchen Chokgyur
Dechen Lingpa, the Karmapa Tekchok Dorje, Jamgön Kongtrul and so on.
Having kept these teachings secret for five years, this was how he gradually
transmitted them.

The great Jamgön Kongtrul himself had a very long life, having taken
the practice of Chimé Phakmé Nyingtik as his special yidam. Many termas
had predicted that Jamgön Kongtrul would face many obstacles and that
his life wouldn't be very long. However, by practising the approach and ac-

complishment of Chimé Phakmé Nyingtik, he was able to live his life to the full and to accomplish many great works, like the five great treasures, without any obstacles. Jamgön Kongtrul himself said that this was only possible thanks to the power and blessings of Chimé Phakmé Nyingtik.

So Jamyang Khyentse Wangpo, his student Jamgön Kongtrul, both the fourteenth and the fifteenth Karmapas—Tekchok Dorje and Khakhyab Dorje—Shechen Gyaltsab, Tertön Sogyal, Dodrupchen Rinpoche Jigme Tenpe Nyima, Drubwang Shakya Shri and all his other students focused on the practice of Chimé Phakmé Nyingtik and took it as their yidam.

Therefore, Chimé Phakmé Nyingtik is extraordinarily blessed. You could say the warmth of the blessings of the dakinis has never cooled, that it is still hot with dakinis' blessings.

Our root teacher Jamyang Khyentse Chökyi Lodrö himself received this elaborate empowerment about ten times from those great masters. He wrote in his journal that he practised the approach, accomplishment and activity extensively three times. He also maintained the daily practice. The Chimé Phakmé Nyingtik was also Dilgo Khyentse Rinpoche's main heart practice and he completed the entire retreat seven times. There was a prophecy that one of the Khyentse incarnations would live a very long life. Dilgo Khyentse Rinpoche once said, "Perhaps it's me, since I have now lived for more than eighty years." His Holiness the Dalai Lama is an example of one of today's great Rimé masters who received the empowerment of the Chimé Phakmé Nyingtik from Dilgo Khyentse Rinpoche and practises it according to his instructions. His Holiness Sakya Trichen says that this Chimé Phakmé Nyingtik is his main practice, that he has done many retreats and practises it continuously. He attributes his success, his long life and the removal of many obstacles to the practice of Chimé Phakmé Nyingtik. Similarly the Chimé Phakmé Nyingtik is the special yidam of all Sarma and Nyingma teaching holders.

This incredibly blessed and powerful practice of Chimé Phakmé Nyingtik is what you are about to receive. The preparatory steps will take place tomorrow and the main empowerment next day. This is the perfect teaching.

PERFECT ASSEMBLY

Those of us who are here have gathered because of our past karma and our aspirations. We would not be able to be here had we not accumulated vast amounts of merit during numerous past lives. Only those with a past connection to this teaching could be here today, without that connection they could not have come. So each and every one of you should rejoice and recognize that you've accomplished the potential offered by this precious human birth.

So one point I wanted to make is that it's extremely difficult for these five great perfections to come together in this world.

CHAPTER 2:

Long-Life Practice

by Tulku Orgyen Tobgyal

Generally, it can be said that all the sentient beings living in this world are the product of delusions and that those delusions are the result of our karma. Basically, we don't actually die; mind does not die. However, mind is supported by a physical body which is created by our delusions, and that body will live a short or a long life. Either way, because we have a body, that body will at some point die. A body that is born must die. Mind is supported by a physical form, so we must have a body. When mind and body separate, the body becomes a corpse, inanimate physical matter. So although mind is always mind, when mind and body are separated, the body will no longer be a body.

In every sentient being can be found what we call buddha nature, or sugatagarbha. It is thanks to the fact that we have this nature that beings are capable of enlightenment. So the basis of enlightenment for sentient beings is buddha nature. Enlightenment, buddha, is very special; but if there were no basis for enlightenment, it wouldn't be possible for anyone to become a buddha. In that case the length of our lives, long or short, would be entirely irrelevant.

At the same time we must have a physical body to follow the path that leads to buddhahood. It is taught that of the six classes of beings, the human body is the supreme basis from which to attain enlightenment. In the *Way of the Bodhisattva*, Shantideva said,

> So take advantage of this human boat.
> Free yourself from sorrow's mighty stream!
> This vessel will be later hard to find.
> The time that you have now, you fool, is not for sleep![9]

This verse means that the human body is like a boat that's extremely useful for crossing water. So the boat—of the human body—is very important.

But we aren't often reborn with a human body, so when we are we must take care to make the most of it and avoid going to sleep.

The sutras describe about how the precious human birth is endowed with the eight freedoms and ten advantages which shows how important this human body is. The sutras also explain how difficult it is to find such a body using many examples, quotations and quantifications. Guru Rinpoche said,

> As the first of all activities,
> The vidyadhara should achieve longevity!

And,

> If life is long, it can be virtuous,
> And the purpose of this life and the next can be achieved.

It's good to live a long life because then you are able to fully accomplish the purpose of this and future lives. How do we prolong life? With great compassion and many skilful methods, the victorious ones have taught a variety of ways of extending life, both common and supreme. The common methods include "extracting the essence" (*rasayana*) and using medicinal substances, as well as special breath and yogic exercises, all of which have a positive impact. Uncommon or supreme methods include deity meditation, mantra recitation and dzogrim practice.

Since longevity is so important, in every terma that Guru Rinpoche hid to be rediscovered by the tertöns, there is some form of long-life practice. Some tertöns revealed as many as five or six practices, others two or three. Therefore, many long-life sadhanas exist.

Guru Rinpoche himself did a long-life practice in Maratika Cave, where he saw the actual face of the protector Amitayus who granted him an empowerment with his vase. Guru Rinpoche was then blessed with an immutable vajra body which will last until the end of the kalpa.

When our human bodies are destroyed and our consciousnesses transferred to another field, we call it "death"; and when we emerge from our mother's womb, we call it "birth". In between birth and death, we live "long lives" or "short lives". In one year, there are three hundred and sixty-five days or twelve months. If someone lives for one hundred years, they are generally considered to have had a very long life. Although each day slips by easily and quickly, in one hundred years there are actually only thirty-six thousand five hundred days. See for yourself, work it out on a calculator! Then work out how many days there are in sixty years: twenty-one thousand nine hundred.

As you can see it's very important for dharma practitioners to have a long life. But from a dharma perspective it doesn't really matter how long worldly people who don't practise live. Worldly people are quite naturally, absolutely convinced that they also need long lives. But as a dharma practitioner you can see that a worldly life is full of negative activities. You can also see that it's probably better for worldly people not to live for too long; this train of thought also exists in the teachings. Every day that a person who doesn't practise dharma remains in this world results in the further accumulation of vast amounts of negative actions, the karma of which will ripen and be experienced in future lives. So the negativity accumulated by spending a single year as a human being in this world can only lead to rebirth in the hell realms where the suffering is extremely intense and where you have to remain for a very long time.

As the Victorious One has great compassion and many skilful means at his command, he has taught the supreme methods for prolonging life. Medical treatments, extracting essences, maintaining good health, breathing and physical exercises are all ordinary methods and they are common to most cultures. Even termas, for example, teach us how to prepare long-life pills from medicinal ingredients and explain breathing techniques and physical exercises for lengthening life spans.

Once we have a body, we breathe in and out twenty-one thousand times every twenty-four hours. It's said that once we've exhausted our allotted number of breaths, we die. One of the signs of the approach of death is that our breath gets shorter, so to remedy that the teachings suggest various methods, like vase breathing. Similarly, the formation of the body depends on the five elements. This is why there are methods for lengthening a body's life using the five elements. These are some of the common methods that have now become well-known throughout the world. Many people have taken advantage of them, and as a result live for quite a long time.

Even if we don't mix both the ordinary and the supreme methods for prolonging life, by practising these methods we will lengthen our life spans.

However, when we do long-life practices, the ordinary and the supreme methods are brought together. By practising both methods we will attain both ordinary and supreme accomplishments. So we can lengthen life through both ordinary and extraordinary meditation by, for example, gathering ordinary medicinal substances to make long-life pills and at the same time practising the extraordinary deity meditation. During deity meditation we spend a lot of time in samadhi, and by doing so we bless the medicinal substances. This is how we bring together the ordinary and supreme methods.

Some breathing practices and physical exercises can be found in both Buddhist and non-Buddhist traditions. However, the practices found in tantric Buddhism are different. For example, while tantric breathing exercises rely on the breath, obviously they also involve the clear visualization of the three channels, five chakras and the deities residing within them. These are the special or extraordinary elements that are brought into tantric practice. We recite mantras to invoke the wisdom mind of the wisdom deities, and the breathing practice involves the vase-retention practice using the three syllables OM AH HUNG. When we breath in, we visualize the syllable OM; when we retain the breath, we visualize the syllable AH; and when we breathe out, we visualize HUNG. So these long-life practices involve extraordinary methods.

The special point you need to understand here is that all long-life sadhanas accomplish ordinary and supreme accomplishments. Therefore, we achieve the ordinary siddhi of longevity and the supreme siddhi at the same time. We first lengthen our lives, which in the best-case scenario will eventually lead us to the supreme accomplishment of rainbow body. At the very least during our eighty- or ninety-year life, we will attain realization as vast as space and the ability to accomplish benefit for ourselves and others. Thus, long-life practice can provide us with the opportunity to become good dharma practitioners.

Turning to how long we live, from the Buddhist point of view whether we live a long or short life depends on our karma; basically, the length of life is determined by karma. For example, if you protect and save life, you will have a long life, but killing and always being angry causes a life to be short.

Anyway, everyone should have a long-life practice, and it must bring together both the ordinary and supreme methods. This means that you must be taught how to do such a long-life practice. There's no need to teach you the ordinary methods because you already know them, and everyone I meet seems to have something to say about this. "Take walks," they say. "Take exercise, don't eat meat and eat lots of vegetables and fruit." Americans add, "Take a lot of vitamins!" whereas Canadians and Europeans are less keen on vitamins. They say, "Spend more time in the countryside, communing with nature."

Sogyal Rinpoche said I should explain the long-life practice called Chimé Phakmé Nyingtik because according to him you have all received the empowerment. Chimé Phakmé Nyingtik is the practice of the mandala of deities that surround White Tara in union with Amitayus. I explained the history of this cycle thoroughly two years ago.[10]

When we practise whichever sadhana we're doing, first we always take refuge and generate the mind of enlightenment. Next all the negative forces that might obstruct deity meditation in the main part of the practice must be sent far away. You do this in the longer sadhana with an elaborate obstacle-elimination practice and in the shorter sadhana through the mantra recitation. This is followed by the descent of blessings and blessing the offerings which come together in the Chimé Phakmé Nyingtik.

I. ENLIGHTENED BODY: VISUALIZATION
OF THE DEITY MANDALA
A. The Three Samadhis

In the main part of the practice at the point when we meditate on the deity, we must establish the structure of the three samadhis. This is done in the same way for all ritual practices: the samadhi of suchness, the samadhi of great compassion and the causal samadhi. It is impossible to do this kind of practice without them.

The samadhi of suchness is emptiness meditation. The second samadhi, the samadhi of great compassion, is compassion meditation. This means we meditate on emptiness and on our great compassion for all beings who fill the whole of space. The third samadhi is the causal samadhi. This is where the outer environment and all the beings it contains—in other words the support and the supported, the palace and the deities—arise from the union of emptiness and compassion as the seed syllable which is their cause. So the third samadhi is the meditation on the seed syllable.

The instructions specify that you establish the structure of the three samadhis. If you try to practise without the three samadhis, you really don't know much about kyerim. If you want to do kyerim practice, you must understand, experience and realise the three samadhis. First you must establish a good intellectual understanding of what they are, and then you must think about and try to experience them. Unless you develop a good realization of these three samadhis, you will not be able to practise kyerim. The three samadhis are not specific to long-life practices, they are an integral part of Mahayoga kyerim practice. But in Dzogchen there are some generation stage practices that don't use them.

For beginners if you don't know how to establish the structure of the three samadhis, well then the path of kyerim will not bring about fruition. For details about the three samadhis and the reasoning behind these practices, we rely heavily on the sacred texts which offer extensive explanations. When Khenpo Petse gave the explanation based on the *Secret Essence Tantra* last year, he must have explained all this.[11] But even if you have already received the detailed teachings, you must also receive and practise the pith instructions from the great masters which pull together all the instructions you've received. You will then be able to practise their essence. Without the pith instructions the detailed explanations in the sacred texts aren't very useful. The teachings on the three samadhis, for example, fill an entire volume, and a whole volume of teaching is far too much to bring to mind in an instant when you meditate.

At the beginning of all rituals there are instructions about how to actualise kyerim and meditate on the three samadhis. Some of these instructions have four lines, one line for each samadhi; some have one verse for each samadhi; some have just one line for all three and some only have a mantra and no verse in Tibetan. As it is said, "Secret Mantra is recitation and meditation." This means that when you do a Secret Mantra Vajrayana ritual, you say the words with your mouth while your mind meditates on their meaning. We generally say things out loud so others can hear us, but when we do a sadhana, it is not like that. The reason we say the words out loud during sadhana practice is to help us concentrate—and to help our minds meditate. Just giving voice to the words can be done just as easily with a machine as it can with our own voices, but since we are not machines we must combine recitation with meditation.

For example, when a Vajrakilaya practice text says that the deity has six arms and three faces, we say those words at the same time that we imagine all those arms and faces in our mind's eye. Just to say "three faces" without actualising that picture in your mind is of no use whatsoever. I only have one head and no matter how many times I repeat that I want three heads, unless I bring to mind and meditate on myself as a deity with three heads, I will always only have one head.

Because the three samadhis are so crucial, I'll try to explain them essentially according to the practice instructions.

1. The Samadhi of Suchness

If you have been introduced to rigpa by your teacher and have recognized the nature of your mind, then the samadhi of suchness is simply to abide by that recognition. You don't have to do anything other than rest your mind in that samadhi—just leave the mind unaltered.

If you haven't recognized the nature of mind, to use Dzogchen terminology and which other approaches describe as "seeing emptiness", then it's not possible truly to meditate—your practice will be limited. So what should you do? As you recite the words that actualise the samadhi of suchness, gaze into the sky and consider your body is merging with space. Look at the thought that is present in your mind and let the mind rest as it looks at itself. In that instant mind doesn't see anything. Neither does it think, "I am not seeing anything."

If you cannot practise like that either, just think, "All phenomena are emptiness." That's all you can do. But of course merely to think or say to yourself, "This is emptiness" is not the same as having determined that "This is emptiness" is the truth. The first two methods require that you recognize the view of emptiness which you then bring into your own experience. But in this third method you just entertain the thought, "All things are emptiness", you don't bring emptiness itself into your practice.

2. The Samadhi of Great Compassion

Here you see how all sentient beings have failed to realise emptiness and are therefore deluded. In reality there is no delusion but sentient beings are caught up in their own dualistic perceptions, and it's these perceptions that delude them. So cultivate compassion for all deluded beings. Your compassion must be extremely vast, not small-scale compassion. And it shouldn't be limited to one or two people, rather it should be immense, great compassion for all sentient beings wherever they may be.

Actually, this compassion arises from the power (*tsal*) of emptiness and reaches every corner of space. It arises naturally like heat rising from fire or a rainbow appearing in the sky. If it doesn't happen naturally, you have no choice but to cultivate compassion deliberately, for example by thinking about, ". . . all these poor sentient beings who pervade the whole of space."

3. The Causal Samadhi

Based on the previous two samadhis, the coming together of the two elements of emptiness and compassion, the third or causal samadhi arises. When you practise Arya Tara, the causal samadhi takes the form of the seed syllable TAM. So here you meditate on a white syllable TAM. When it comes to the shape of the letters you visualize, although some lamas have said they should take the form of the Indian script known as Lantsa, Jamyang Khyentse Wangpo said it wasn't necessary. He said people could visualize the syllables in their own script since the Vajrayana teachings say the syllables, which develop in the chakras when the aggregates, elements and sense sources of the body are formed, appear in the native script of your country. So Tibetans can visualize the mantras in Tibetan, Chinese can visualize Chinese characters, Indians can visualize Indian script and so on.

B. Visualization of the Deity Mandala

When you practise kyerim meditation, you should visualize the external world as a pure buddha realm such as the Heaven of Great Bliss (Skt. Sukhavati). And you should visualize all sentient beings as male and female deities and all houses and buildings as palaces.[12] In the middle of the deity's palace the causal syllable TAM descends to rest on a lotus and moon-disc seat. It then transforms into Arya Tara who is visualized as she appears in the thangka, inseparable from your own mind.

Jamyang Khyentse Wangpo said that the difference between the visualization you create and the thangka is that in your visualization the Lord of Dance, Amitayus,[13] is bright red. This is a secret instruction, and it's because it's a secret instruction that traditionally Amitayus' colour is not shown in a thangka.

Now you meditate on the jnanasattva. At Tara's heart again on a lotus and moon-disc seat sits the jnanasattva Amitayus, white in colour. The form of this Amitayus is the same as the most commonly known Amitayus except that he is white. White Tara is the samayasattva, the samaya deity, and the Amitayus in her heart is the jnanasattva, the wisdom deity.

If you do an elaborate Chimé Phakmé Nyingtik practice, during kyerim you will have to visualize many deities such as the Taras seating in the four directions who pacify, enrich, magnetise and subjugate and the four Gatekeeper Taras standing at the four gates. But for the shorter daily sadhana, you only have to visualize the three main deities, the three deities of long life: Jetsun Tara, Amitayus and Ushnisha Vijaya. However, you don't have to visualize other deities of the mandala.

Visualize the samadhisattva in the heart of the jnanasattva. In this practice the samadhisattva is a white syllable TAM which the text says sits on a lotus, sun and moon-disc seat and is surrounded by the syllables of the mantra mala. As you visualize the deities, also visualize at your three centres the three syllables that embody the vajra body, speech and mind of all the sugatas—white OM, red AH and dark blue HUNG. Or if you are doing a more elaborate practice, visualize Akshobhya, Amitabha and Amoghasiddhi. Whichever you do, it is important that you consider them to be vajra body, vajra speech and vajra mind.

Next you extend an invitation to the jnanasattvas. From the syllables of the three vajras rays of light stream out to the pure buddha fields such as Akanishtha to invite the jnanasattvas who look very similar to the samaya deities that you have already been visualizing. Innumerable wisdom beings appear and pour into you, just as water pours into water. Think to yourself, "Samayasattva and jnanasattva have merged indivisibly, they are now one taste."

Invite them by saying the four mantras DZA, HUNG, BAM and HO and performing the four mudras of hook, noose, chain and bell. DZA emanates the Hook goddesses who invite the wisdom deities. HUNG invokes the Noose goddesses who receive the wisdom deities as they arrive, and the wisdom deities merge indivisibly with the samaya deities. From BAM the Chain goddesses appear who please the wisdom deities and ensure that they remain with the samaya deities. Finally, HO emanates Bell goddesses who welcome the wisdom deities to remain, continually and joyfully. With SA-MAYA TISHTALEN ask them to stay, and with AH LA LA HO ATIPUHO PRATITSA HO do prostrations. Now make the outer, inner and secret offerings, after which you must offer praise.

These are the stages you go through to create a visualization or kyerim, and this is deity meditation. Actually, kyerim practice boils down to clarity, stable vajra pride and remembering the purity.

Clarity

"Clarity" is to be able to see the deities in your mind's eye and maintain a detailed awareness of those deities. This means you should be able to see the bodies, clothing and attributes of the principal deities and their retinues clearly and distinctly, as clearly as a reflection of the sun or the moon on the surface of a clear, still lake.

Vajra Pride

"Vajra pride" relates to how we differentiate between ourselves and the deity. When we follow the Mahayoga approach, we must abandon the kind of grasping that considers one to be better than the other.

All of us have the ground which is our buddha nature, but right now it's masked by adventitious obscurations. Once these obscurations have been removed, it'll become clear that your nature is exactly the same as the bud-dhas. Basically, you will see that there is no difference between your mind and the mind of the buddhas, or between you and the yidam deity. So you must maintain the kind of stable vajra pride that knows there is no differ-ence if you could only purify your obscurations. If instead of stable vajra pride you start out with the dualistic notion that the deity is good and you are bad, then the practice will not work.

Remembering the Purity

To practise "remembering the purity" elaborately, you must remember that every detail of the visualization such as each deity's face, hand, colour, hand implement, attribute and palace feature corresponds to specific pure qualities. If you practise more essentially, think, "All meaningful aspects—deities, mantras, mandala and so on—are simply an expression of mind and have no reality. They are nothing but the ground's primordial purity (*kadak*), the wisdom of the dharmakaya." To think in this way is remembering the purity.

Maintaining a clear visualization of the deities and stable vajra pride are both aspects of kyerim practice, whereas remembering the purity is dzogrim practice. So to practise kyerim and dzogrim at the same time, you must bring these three together. You do this by placing a thangka—as the samaya support—in front of you, then you look at it. Focus on the painting with your eyes as you use your mind to concentrate on what your eyes can see. Don't get distracted and do this for a long time. Then close your eyes to check if you can see the image in your mind's eye. If you can, then slowly start to train your mind to manipulate the image by sometimes making it larger, sometimes smaller and so on.

II. ENLIGHTENED SPEECH: MANTRA RECITATION

Reciting the mantra corresponds to enlightened speech. We have been visualizing ourselves as Arya Tara. Arya Tara is white in colour and in union. At Tara's heart is the jnanasattva, white Amitayus. At Amitayus' heart is the syllable TAM surrounded by the mantra mala. TAM emanates rays of light that shoot out of your fontanelle and transform into countless white Ushnisha Vijayas. Each Ushnisha Vijaya holds a vase in her left hand and a hook in her right hand. With her hook she gathers into her vase the essence of the elements (fire, air, space, earth and water) along with the life force, merit and strength of all beings, gods and rishis who have accomplished so many mantras that they can live for thousands of years. The way they collect the life force is similar to the way bees collect pollen. Bees extract pollen without causing flowers any harm at all. In the same way extracting the essence of all life force and merit through samadhi brings no harm to others. Some Ge-lugpa lamas have suggested that the visualizations used in various Nyingma long-life and wealth practices actually steal the life and merit from other beings. But all this method does is gather the accomplishments of long-life and wealth through meditation practice, it doesn't involve stealing anything or causing any kind of harm. It's like making use of the light of the sun and the moon to see by, which by no stretch of the imagination could be described as stealing!

We also visualize the Ushnisha Vijayas gathering all the wisdom, love, power, compassion and blessings from the victorious ones who have been freed from samsara—in other words the buddhas—and who dwell in an in-calculable number of buddha fields. We also visualize their sons, the bodhi-sattvas and arhats and so on. Their wisdom, love and so on appear in the form of rays of light, the nature of which is longevity, and the Ushnisha Vijayas pour all this into their vases. Longevity, merit and strength increase as does the wisdom of great bliss. Truly, to receive the supreme and ordi-nary accomplishments, you must have complete confidence that you have received them.

What is the nectar of great bliss? What's it like? The nectar of great bliss is found in the god realms and is so potent that if it were sprinkled over a dry, dead tree, that tree would immediately burst into life sprouting leaves, fruit and flowers. If this nectar were given to an ordinary man, he would suddenly have the strength of a hundred elephants. And if it were given to an old woman, she would instantly regain the vitality of youth. As you med-itate on this nectar, make sure it has all these kinds of quality and features. It is white like the moon, but at the same time it's as bright as the sun.

Recite the ten-syllable mantra as you repeat this meditation again and again. As you recite the mantra, you should also practise the vajra recitation, which involves the retention of breath or vase breathing. If you cannot do vajra recitation, then you must recite the mantra out loud.

When you practise the daily sadhana, focus on reciting the ten-syllable mantra OM TARE TUTTARE TURE SOHA. Then recite a smaller number of combined mantras, OM TARE TUTTARE TURE HRIH DROOM BENDZA JNANA AYUKE SOHA. Then do about one hundred of each of the dharanis of Amitayus, OM AMARANI DZIWANTIYE SOHA, and Ushnisha Vijaya, OM AMRITA AYURDADE SOHA.

After that follow the usual sequence: recite the mantra of the vowels and consonants, the mantra of dependent origination and the hundred-syllable mantra, followed by a brief offering and praise. Then go through the process of dissolution in which the visualized deity dissolves in the completion phase of dzogrim and arises again very vividly. Finally, do the prayers of aspiration, dedication and auspiciousness.

That was a very short, extremely essential way of presenting the daily Chimé Phakmé Nyingtik sadhana. This is unlike the time I received Chimé Phakmé Nyingtik teachings from Dilgo Khyentse Rinpoche when he taught every evening for more than a month! If you put into practise what I've just said, your practice will qualify as basic practice which is just one step ahead of not knowing how to practise at all. This practice of Chimé Phakmé Nyingtik brings extraordinary blessings. I have given this short explanation because Dzongsar Khyentse Rinpoche—who gave all of us the empowerment—asked me to.

CHAPTER 3:

Daily Chimé Phakmé Nyingtik in a Nutshell

by Tulku Orgyen Tobgyal

INTRODUCTION

Of all the teachings that Jamyang Khyentse Wangpo received through the seven methods of transmission, the Chimé Phakmé Nyingtik is said to be the most profound. Not only does it bring about a long life but a life that is free of obstacles. It also causes wisdom to blossom and is said to bestow the most blessings.

The Chimé Phakmé Nyingtik was the heart practice of Jamyang Khyentse Wangpo's student, Jamgön Kongtrul Lodrö Taye, and of the fourteenth, fifteenth and sixteenth Karmapas: Tekchok Dorje, Khakhyab Dorje and Rigpe Dorje. Other great Kagyupa masters like the previous Situ Rinpoche, Situ Pema Wangchuk Gyalpo, also practised it, as does the present Sakya Trichen who has said of this practice, "This is my sole yidam", and most Nyingma lamas.

The Chimé Phakmé Nyingtik cycle contains a tantra and associated sadhanas as well as individual lama sadhanas for accomplishing Guru Rinpoche, Shri Singha and Vimalamitra. Dzogchen is referred to throughout.[14] It's also the cycle that contains the longer sadhana we've been practising during this drupchen for which Jamgön Kongtrul Lodrö Taye wrote a retreat manual, a self-empowerment[15] and a fire offering practice.[16] The text we're using to guide us through the drupchen[17] was put together by Jamyang Khyentse Chökyi Lodrö. But today we'll look at the daily practice.

This short sadhana was written by Jamyang Khyentse Wangpo to fulfill Jamgön Kongtrul Lodrö Taye's request for a daily Chimé Phakmé Nyingtik text. The long sadhana describes nine deities, but in the daily practice we only meditate on the main deity which is why it's called the "*Single Mudra*" practice.

You've asked me to tell you how to do the Chimé Phakmé Nyingtik as a daily practice. First, you must receive an empowerment. There are three ways of giving the Chimé Phakmé Nyingtik empowerment: the elaborate ritual, the medium-length ritual and the simple blessing. You must receive at least one of them.[18]

Next you must practise the path. Actually, if you were to follow the traditional approach, first you would do a retreat based on the longer sadhana. The instructions specify that you should spend twenty-one days on the approach practice, seven on the accomplishment and one day on the activity phase. So if you add the first afternoon and final morning, a Chimé Phakmé Nyingtik retreat will last thirty-one days. Usually only after completing a retreat would you start to practise the daily sadhana. However, you can do the daily sadhana even if you haven't done a retreat.

If you just do the daily practice, you don't need to offer tormas, offerings or long-life pills, although of course it's always better to have them. For a retreat you will need supports and samaya substances for your practice, in this case include a thangka and a kapala containing pills made from the longevity substances mentioned at the beginning of the longer sadhana. I've been asked if these substances are difficult to obtain. No, they're not. We have them here in Bir in large quantities.

If you're practising the path of Chimé Phakmé Nyingtik, it's said to be better to do the practice early in the morning, but it's also fine to do it at any time. Before you begin the practice, you must turn your mind inwardly, look at your mind and motivate yourself with the fervent wish to practise the kyerim and dzogrim of Chimé Phakmé Nyingtik for the sake of all sentient beings. First you must think about this. Then recite the invocation prayers to ward off any obstacles to your practice by doing whichever prayer you are familiar with, the Seven Line Prayer for example.

I. THE PRELIMINARIES

Immediately the lama appears in the sky before you in the form of White Tara Wish-Fulfilling Wheel in union with Amitayus Lord of the Dance.[19]

She is surrounded by all the deities of the mandala, lamas, yidams, dakinis, dharma protectors and so on. Once you have created this visualization in your mind, take refuge by repeating the words of the text three times,

> Homage!
> Until we attain enlightenment, I and all living beings
> Take refuge with unwavering devotion
> In you, Guru Wish-Fulfilling Wheel, who is
> The very essence of the Three Jewels!

Then with the objects of refuge as your witnesses, generate bodhichitta. The way you benefit sentient beings is by realising the unborn nature of things which is when your service to them becomes truly far-reaching.

At this point the longer sadhana includes the seven-branch offering, but the daily practice doesn't and you recite HUNG HUNG HUNG instead. The sound of the HUNGs becomes a huge number of wrathful deities who eliminate all obstructing forces which are destroyed by the sound of HUNG. Of course, the real obstructing forces are our thoughts. In fact, just thinking about the meaning of HUNG has the power to chase away all other thoughts.

Now you say BENDZA JNANA RAKSHA AH HUNG to establish the protective sphere. What is a protective sphere? It is your mind which is by nature empty, so negative influences and obstructing forces cannot harm it. In fact, none of the five primary elements like space or earth can affect it.

Having arranged the offerings, recite the mantra OM AH HUNG SARWA PUDZA MEGHA SAMAYE HUNG to bless them. If you don't have actual offerings, don't recite this mantra. Add the Sky Treasury mudra and mantra OM NAMA SARWA TATAGATE BAYO BISHO MUGEBE SARWA TAKAM UTGATE SAPARANA IMAM GAGANA KAM SOHA to multiply the offerings and render them inexhaustible like the offerings made by Samantabhadra.

If you just want to make a small offering, prepare the traditional seven offering bowls plus amrita and rakta. If you don't have a torma, use some food instead.

II. THE MAIN PRACTICE

Up to this point you have been practising the preliminaries. Now we come to the actual practice which is meditation on the deity and kyerim practice, the generation stage or creation meditation.

A. Visualization of the Deity
1. Meditation on the Samayasattva
The Three Samadhis

To meditate on the deity start by reciting the mantra OM MAHA SHUNYATA JNANA BENDZA SOBHAVA EMAKO HANG and establish that everything is emptiness which is sometimes called "great emptiness". Then follow the text.

First purify the entire world and all beings within it into the state of emptiness. It is mind that purifies everything into emptiness and mind itself is empty right from the start. Mind is empty, it isn't made empty. It's empty naturally and always has been. When there is delusion, mind is simply deluded, but even so mind is empty. This is an important point. Next, when a thought arises as the natural display of emptiness, you must meditate on compassion for all sentient beings who are themselves merely the play of emptiness. These are the first two samadhis—the samadhi of suchness and the samadhi of universal manifestation, or great compassion. The dynamic energy of compassion, or rather of the indivisible unity of emptiness and compassion, manifests in the form of the causal syllable TAM which you can visualize as Tibetan script, Chinese, Indian or any other script.

The three samadhis appear in the text as follows: "The luminous space of suchness" is the first samadhi, the second samadhi is "in which arises the power of all-illuminating compassion" and the third samadhi is "their union is the causal samadhi, a white TAM . . .". When you practise kyerim, these three samadhis must be brought to mind right at the beginning. The next part of the text which begins "appearing like a rainbow from the sky" is very straightforward. One important point though is that those who don't know much about the palaces of deities should just remember that the palace you visualize isn't an ordinary house. It doesn't obstruct anything and has no substance so you can see in from the outside and out from the inside, and it's made of precious, pure crystal. Everything about it defies the imagination.

In a nutshell, the important points here are:

—Having accomplished the meditation on the three samadhis, you meditate on the outer environment.
—Meditate on the palace.
—Meditate on the lotus, sun and moon disc seat.
—Visualize the descent of the syllable TAM which comes to rest on that seat.
—Meditate on the deities.

The rest of this section is very clear. Everyone can understand what's meant by "one head, two hands and so on", so I don't need to explain it to you.

Clear Visualization

As you meditate on yourself as the deity, it is important to hold the image of that deity in your mind as clearly as possible. A thangka is a samaya support for practice. Look at the picture in the thangka, then close your eyes and the picture will appear in your mind. You then check the details of that mental image and repeat the process until you can hold a clear image of the deity in your mind. Once you can do that, play with the image by visualizing it as being very big, then very small and so on. This is what thangkas are drawn for. Eventually though that mental image will not be like a painting, hologram or mere drawing but vivid and clear. This aspect of deity practice is called "clear visualization" which means that you should visualize as clearly as you can. However, if you can't visualize clearly, don't imagine that your practice is therefore useless, because it isn't. Simply thinking about the deity is already extremely beneficial.

Vajra Pride

Mind is what meditates on the deity. Primordially your mind is the buddha, mind is buddha nature. The teachings tell us that delusion is adventitious which means that originally it wasn't there, it came later. Because delusion came later, it can be eliminated. Had it been primordial, we wouldn't be able to get rid of it. This is why we practise, thinking, "I am the deity." It's not a trick! You're not fooling yourself or trying to convince yourself of something that's not true. So recognize that you are the deity—we are all buddhas— and steadfastly maintain the vajra pride of being the deity. The sun is always in the sky. When clouds mass overhead you cannot see the sun, but the moment they've passed you can see it perfectly.

Remembering the Purity

Buddhas and sentient beings are nothing more than the natural radiance of mind which is by nature empty. So the delusion of thinking, "I am a buddha" is nothing more than the play of the natural radiance of an empty mind. The buddha—the deity—is also empty. Therefore, remember the purity. Remember that the appearance of the deity—Jetsun Drolma's face, hands and so on—are nothing more than the play of emptiness.

These are the three most important elements of the practice—clear visualization, vajra pride and remembering the purity. As you practise sometimes focus on the clarity of your visualization, sometimes concentrate on maintaining vajra pride and sometimes remember the purity. In other words we practise kyerim by alternating between these three aspects of practice.

2. Inviting and Absorbing the Jnanasattva

Until now you have been meditating on yourself as the deity, and this visualized deity is called "the samayasattva" or samaya being. Next we invite the jnanasattvas, the wisdom deities.

First, though, you must actualise the three vajras. Human beings have three aspects known as body, speech and mind. At this point you are visualizing yourself as the deity with the deity's face, hands and so on. Deities also have three aspects which we call the three vajras: enlightened body, enlightened speech and enlightened mind. Here you visualize the three vajras at your forehead, throat and heart. Usually vajra body appears as Vairochana, vajra speech as Amitabha and vajra mind as Akshobhya, but here the text says you mark your three places with the three seed syllables OM AH HUNG which radiate rays of light inviting the jnanasattvas, the wisdom deities.

In reality the wisdom deity and the samaya being are not separate. However, although mind thinks "they are not different", it still hangs on to the idea that the wisdom deity must be somehow distinct from the samaya being. As long as it makes that separation, you will need to invite the wisdom deity. Once samayasattva and jnanasattva are indivisible, you won't need to extend the invitation. The words of the invitation prayer are easy to understand so follow the text until DZA HUNG BAM HO.

Taking Their Seats

After the invitation at SAMAYA TISHTALEN you ask the deities to take their seats and remain in this place. However, the wisdom deity doesn't take a seat, she simply merges indivisibly with the samaya being like water poured on water.

Paying Homage

Then you pay homage. AH LA LA HO! expresses amazement at the enlightened body, speech and mind of the deity. AH TI PU HO means "I pay homage", and PRATI TSA HO means "I acknowledge and receive homage". "Ultimate prostration" is to rest in the realization of the indivisibility of the deity and yourself.

Offerings

Emanate offering deities who then present you with the outer offerings that are made up of the seven offerings of refreshing and cleansing waters, incense, flower, lamp, scented water and food, plus music. You also offer the five inner offerings of beautiful forms, sounds, fragrance, taste and touch. Amrita, rakta and torma are the secret offerings, and SARWA DHARMADHATU EMAKO HANG indicates the ultimate offering, the offering of suchness.

In the longer sadhana the offerings are presented in individual verses that describe each in detail. Here in the daily practice there's just one verse for all the offerings, plus the individual mantras of each kind of offering.

Praise

The next verse, "OM! You were born from the tears . . ." is the offering of praise. If you want to practise these three sections of homage, offering and praise, you can. However, you can also skip them. In that case having invited the wisdom deity, jump to the mantra recitation section after reciting the mantra SAMAYA TISHTALEN.

3. Focusing the Mind on the Form of the Deity
Clarity, Confidence and Purity: Essence of Kyerim and Dzogrim

The really important points for this practice are the clarity of the visualization, vajra pride and remembering the purity. Of these three a strong sense of being the deity is crucial. Trust that you look like the deity with the absolute confidence that you're not trying to fool yourself, that it's not an invention and that ultimately the deity is indivisible from your mind. "This is who I am!" If you do not trust in this way, you will not accomplish the practice; but if you do, you will.

The two other aspects on which you meditate—clarity of visualization and vajra pride—are also the play of emptiness and must be dissolved back into emptiness. When you dissolve your visualization (kyerim) back into emptiness, it's called dzogrim. As the text advises, when you tire of practising like this, recite the mantra.

Focusing the Mind on the Enlightened Body of the Deity

We have spoken about the three main aspects of kyerim practice—clear visualization, vajra pride and remembering the purity—and you must meditate on each of them in turn. They are the essence of kyerim and are crucial to kyerim practice. At first you won't be able to do all three at once, but as you become more familiar with the practice you'll be able to bring them all together. When you reach the point where you have established a clear visualization and vajra pride, immediately remember the purity. This is how you begin to hold all three aspects in your mind at the same time.

For a Vajrayana practitioner, whether man or woman, the Mantrayana samaya is to perceive the nature of everything as the deity which means that when you think, "Everything is the deity", you automatically meditate on your yidam deity with the three aspects of clear visualization, vajra pride and remembering the purity. In other words there's never a time when you don't meditate on the deity. Vajrayana practitioners should try to maintain an awareness of the deity every moment! If you only have an instant in which to practise, you should still try to maintain that awareness. It's challenging at first because you aren't yet familiar with the practice. Once you get used to it though, it'll become easier. Things you're very familiar with are easy to picture in your mind.

For example, if you think of your father, that thought immediately awakens in your mind a picture of all his features and you can easily hold a visualization of his eyes, ears, nose and so on in your mind. Not only do you visualize him clearly, but it happens instantly. This will be true when you think of your father or anyone you know well or live with. Just to hear their name makes the image of that person pop up clearly in your mind. So you must bring the deity to mind again and again until you become completely familiar with it.

The result of practising in this way is that the temporary obscurations that conceal the ground of the buddha nature present in all of us will diminish as they are purified, and your buddha nature will manifest more and more. This concludes what I wanted to say about generating the enlightened body of the deity.

B. The Mantra Recitation:
The Enlightened Speech of the Deity

Next is the enlightened speech of the deity which corresponds to, "I am the sublime Tara: in my heart . . ." Actualise the meaning of the words as you read them.

In drupchens or empowerments you must meditate on a self- and a front visualization, and the front visualization separates out of the self-visualization. You visualize yourself as the mandala of the deity while generating another mandala in the sky before you that's identical to the self-visualization. However, in this daily practice you don't need to do that. Just visualize yourself as the deity.

As I'm sure most of you know, when you meditate on a deity—any deity—the body of that deity isn't made of flesh, blood, lungs, liver and so on. It isn't like the bodies of ordinary human beings but empty and luminous, an illusory appearance. In this practice, at White Tara's heart is Amitayus, the jnanasattva or wisdom being. The sadhana text just says, "In my heart is the jnanasattva Amitayus", which means at the heart of the main deity. It continues, "Brilliant white and holding a long-life vase in the mudra of meditation." He is, "Beautiful with his silk and jewelled ornaments." He sits, "In vajra posture on a lotus and moon disc seat" and is "shining and resplendent amidst brilliant rays of light." Since the main deity Tara Wish-Fulfilling Wheel is a buddha, she has all the qualities of a buddha. These are qualities that are inconceivable to us like the thirty-two major and eighty minor marks and so on. According to the teachings this is why the emanation and reabsorption of light is necessary in visualization practice, but we won't be discussing how that works here.

In the centre of Amitayus' heart is a lotus, a flower. On the seat provided by this flower rests sun and moon discs in the middle of which is TAM, encircled by the revolving mantra mala.

There are four main mantras in the Chimé Phakmé Nyingtik, one for each of the three deities of long life and one for all three combined. The mantra that circles the seed syllable will be the mantra of the deity you're focusing on at that point and is arranged counterclockwise so that it can turn clockwise.

"Reciting the mantra evokes his wisdom mind . . ." This means that you should focus your mind on the mantra. By focusing on the mantra mala you accomplish the recitation of the mantra. When your mind is aware of a mantra—OM TARE TUTTARE TURE SOHA for example—the recitation is accomplished.

As the mantra mala revolves around the seed syllable, it emanates rays of white light that ". . . burst out through the tip of the jewel on the ushnisha on the crown of my head." Amitayus is visualized at your heart centre, and at first the wisdom light shines out of Amitayus' ushnisha, the infinite protuberance on a buddha's head. It then goes up and out through the top of your own head in the form of White Tara. It then manifests in the form of countless Ushnisha Vijayas—Namgyalma in Tibetan—white, with one face, two hands and holding a long-life vase and an iron hook.

"She radiates light and rays of light and limitless forms of herself, streaming out like particles of dust in sunbeams." Once the rays of light are streaming out of your visualized body, they transform into an infinite number of different sized Ushnisha Vijayas. As they fill the whole of space, ". . . they gather and bring back the quintessence of samsara and nirvana." "Samsara" refers to the six realms of existence, and "nirvana" refers to completely enlightened buddhas—all the buddhas in an infinity of universes. The "inanimate universe" refers to the four primary elements, earth, water, fire and air, while "animate" means the sentient beings in the inanimate universes, in other words all living beings.

The Ushnisha Vijayas gather the very essence of everything in samsara and nirvana in the form of great bliss. The great bliss appears in the form of white nectar that moves like quicksilver, is radiant with light and is marked with the symbols of great bliss. The power of this nectar is such that if it's scattered on a dead tree, the tree will immediately burst into life and become laden with leaves, flowers and fruit. If scattered on a sixty year old man, he will suddenly have the vigour of a sixteen year old and his life span will be the same as that of the sun and the moon.

This quicksilver-like nectar is drawn back in through your three doors which are your body, speech and mind. "Absorb into the bindus of my body, speech and mind . . ." Here, body, speech and mind correspond to the enlightened body, speech and mind at our three centres—forehead, throat and heart. The nectar is absorbed into your three centres,

> Granting me the siddhi of immortal life,
> And intensifying the wisdom of great bliss.

I believe there is a translation of this text, so this should be clear for you.[20] As the nectar is absorbed you receive the siddhi of immortal life. Great bliss, the great mudra (*mahamudra*) and the great perfection (*dzogpachenpo*) are intensified. The text says you should now recite the mantra OM TARE TUTTARE TURE SOHA, then OM AMARANI DZIWANTIYE SOHA, followed by OM AMRITA AYURDADE SOHA, and you should recite a few more of the first mantra. If you're short of time you can skip the other two mantras, but if you want to recite them, please do.

Then recite OM TARE TUTTARE TURE HRIH DROOM BENDZA JNANA AYUKE SOHA which is the mantra of the three main deities and which must be recited when you direct your practice for longevity. These are the points that concern the mantra recitation.

At the end of the session recite the vowel and consonant mantra and the mantra of the essence of dependent origination. The vowel mantra is A AA, I II, U UU, RI RII, LI LII, E EE, O AU, ANG AH. The consonant mantra is KA KHA GA GHA NGA, CHA CHHA JA JHA NYA, T'A TH'A D'A DH'A N'A, TA THA DA DHA NA, PA PHA BA BHA MA, YA RA LA WA SHA ZHA SA HA KSHA. And the mantra of the essence of dependent origination is OM YE DHARMA HETU PRABHAWA HETUN TESHAN TATHAGATO HYAVADAT TESHAN TSA YO NIRODHA EVAM VADE MAHA SHRAMANAH SOHA. We recite these three mantras to purify any lack of clarity or unintended additions or omissions in our practice. If you have time, recite these mantras three times, but if you're in a hurry you can just say them once. The instructions also say that here we should make a brief offering and praise. The prayers of offering and praise don't appear in the Tibetan text, but they have been added to the English version so you just need to follow the text. Then recite the hundred-syllable mantra. If you have a thangka or a statue, you must perform the consecration. This concludes the instructions on enlightened speech.

Summary: Enlightened Body and Speech

To summarize, we practise the aspect of the enlightened body by visualizing ourselves as White Tara in union with white Amitayus at her heart. At Amitayus' heart we visualize the seed syllable TAM standing on a sun and moon disc seat that rests on a blossoming lotus. These are what we call the "three nested sattvas". The three sattvas are White Tara, Amitayus and the syllable TAM, and they appear one inside the other.

White Tara's consort, the male deity Avalokiteshvara,[21] the Lord of the Dance, is the natural radiance of Tara herself. Commentaries say he is white with a slight tinge of red, but in the thangka that belonged to Jamgön Kongtrul and that has instructions on the back written in Jamyang Khyentse

Wangpo's own handwriting, he is red. I know this because I own the thang-ka. This is the enlightened body meditation. When you do the daily prac-tice, you don't need to visualize the entire retinue of deities.

For the mantra meditation visualize each mantra in succession revolving around the seed syllable: OM TARE TUTTARE TURE SOHA around TAM, then OM AMARANI DZIWANTIYE SOHA around HRIH, then OM AMRITA AYURDADE SOHA around DROOM, then OM TARE TUTTARE TURE HRIH DROOM BENDZA JNANA AYUKE SOHA around TAM.

As you focus your mind on this visualization also imagine that as the man-tra revolves, it emanates light which fills Amitayus completely. The light then streams out of the top of his head and fills Tara. Once Tara is completely full of light, rays stream out of the top of her head and manifest in the form of an infinite number of Ushnisha Vijayas (Namgyalmas) who are white and hold long-life vases in their left hands and iron hooks in their right. Each Ushnisha Vijaya gathers nectar with her iron hook and collects it in her vase. This is how to direct the practice as you follow the words of the sadhana.

The mantra activity you visualize, very briefly, is of rays of light that ema-nate from the syllables of the mantra, accomplish the activities, then immedi-ately return and dissolve back into the self-visualization as nectar. The nectar enters your three doors (body, speech and mind) by dissolving into your three places (forehead, throat and heart). As it does so you blaze, magnificent and resplendent, and receive the blessings as I've just described.

The mantra you must recite more than any other is OM TARE TUT-TARE TURE SOHA. Recite fewer of the two other mantras, the mantra of Amitayus and the mantra of Ushnisha Vijaya. Also recite the combined mantra. If you wish to direct the practice for long life, accumulate more of the combined mantra. Here in the drupchen as we direct the practice for longevity, we accumulate three times more of the combined mantra than of the others.

After the main mantras recite the vowel and consonant mantras and the mantra of the essence of dependent origination as I've described. Then recite the verses of offering and praise and the hundred-syllable mantra.

In terms of what kind of mala to use, a crystal mala is good for this prac-tice. This was the instruction on enlightened speech.

III. THE CONCLUSION
Dissolution: The Enlightened Mind of the Deity

Ah! The samayasattva, rigpa's natural display
With its attributes like the face and hands, dissolves into
all-pervading space.

The deity and all her aspects that we have just been visualizing are nothing more than rigpa's natural display. The entire environment melts into light and dissolves into the palace. The palace melts into light and dissolves into the deity which melts into light starting at both the lotus seat on which she sits and the top of her head and works towards the centre of her body. White Tara dissolves into Amitayus who melts into light and dissolves into the samadhisattva, the syllable TAM. TAM melts into light from top and bottom like Tara and disappears so there's nothing left. Everything that was visualized is now empty like space. Rest in that state.

"Once again like a rainbow appearing from the sky", you arise as the play of great wisdom. This means that the deity manifests once more. This concludes the instructions on the aspect of enlightened mind.

Now you say OM AH HUNG because the deity has appeared again, and we must invoke the three aspects of enlightened body (OM), enlightened speech (AH) and enlightened mind (HUNG). As I told you earlier, Vajrayana practitioners must constantly maintain the awareness of the deity and meditate as if they themselves are Jetsun Tara.

Of course at the end of the practice session you dedicate and add the relevant verses of auspiciousness although Jamyang Khyentse Wangpo didn't include them in his daily practice. This is how to do this daily practice of Chimé Phakmé Nyingtik.

Summary and Conclusion

At the beginning of the practice, you invoke the masters of the lineage with the appropriate prayers. Then meditate on refuge and bodhichitta by reciting the prayers as many times as you like, three, one or whatever. What's important is that you really pay attention to the meaning of the words and actualise it. Say HUNG three times to eliminate all obstacles and obstructing forces. With the mantra BENDZA JNANA RAKSHA AH HUNG, generate the protective sphere. If you make offerings, recite OM AH HUNG SARWA PUDZA MEGHA SAMAYE HUNG to bless them followed by the Sky Treasury mantra and mudra. If you don't make physical offerings, you don't need to do these mantras and mudra.

The mantra OM MAHA SHUNYATA . . . is the beginning of the meditation on the deity as I explained above. Then comes the section of paying homage, offering and praise. They are good to do but you can also skip them. The practice text says, "If you wish, occasionally, to perform a concise homage, offering and praise." So if you wish you can, if you don't you don't have to. What you absolutely must do is follow the practice faithfully up until SAMAYA TISHTALEN, then if you want to skip paying homage, offerings and praise, you can jump to "I am the sublime Tara: at my heart . . ." Next you accumulate the mantras for as long as you can, then you do the offering and praise. If you want a short offering and praise, just use the short prayer we're doing during the drupchen, "Assembly of wisdom deities . . ."[22] This concludes the practice of the enlightened speech of the deity.

The enlightened mind starts with, "Ah! The samayasattva, rigpa's natural display . . ." After the dissolution you rest in meditation. As in this kind of practice we must bring together kyerim and dzogrim, at this stage we do dzogrim meditation. All phenomena are perfect and complete within the nature of mind. "Dzogrim" means completion stage.

When you reach enlightenment, you'll continue to manifest for the sake of sentient beings, and similarly here we arise once again as the deity and make an auspicious connection by appearing again, like a rainbow in the sky.

At the beginning we generated bodhichitta, didn't we? During the practice we maintain our awareness. At the end we dedicate. So the "three authentics", also known as the "three noble principles", are complete: good at the beginning, good in the middle and good at the end. Now I hope you'll be able to do this practice.

Resources: Orgyen Tobgyal's Teachings on
Chimé Phakmé Nyingtik

Dzongsar Khyentse Rinpoche instructed me quite strongly to teach this practice. Last April here in Bir, I taught everything I know about it in great detail.[23] I relied on many important sources like the terma text,[24] Jamgön Kongtrul's retreat instructions[25] and the presentation of the four nails by Dza Patrul Rinpoche.[26] I also drew points from the *Lamrim Yeshe Nyingpo*.[27] Nowadays as the usual method of study is to listen to recordings, you are welcome to listen to those teachings.

I received these teachings many times from Dilgo Khyentse Rinpoche. He practised the Chimé Phakmé Nyingtik every day without fail and always recited the combined mantra of the three main deities OM TARE TUTTARE TURE HRIH DROOM BENDZA JNANA AYUKE SOHA one thousand times. He never missed a single day!

I've explained the daily practice at Lerab Ling and I went over each word of the practice for those who were going into three-year retreat. So you may want to listen to those teachings too.

CHAPTER 4:

An Explanation of *Single Mudra*, the Daily Practice from the Chimé Phakmé Nyingtik

by Tulku Orgyen Tobgyal

SINGLE MUDRA

This text, *Single Mudra*, is the daily practice from Jamyang Khyentse Wangpo's mind treasure, the Chimé Phakmé Nyingtik, the Heart Essence of the Sublime Lady of Immortality.

A mandala is usually made up of the principal deity and their retinue. When a practice involves several deities, it is said to be a practice with many mudras. However, when all these deities are gathered into the main deity, it is a "single mudra practice". So the title, *Single Mudra,* signifies that this is the practice of the main deity and that she embodies all the deities in the mandala. When we practise elaborately, we meditate on the principal deity and the retinue, then recite the approach mantra of each deity. So for the Chimé Phakmé Nyingtik we focus on the main deity, the four Taras and the four gatekeepers. We can also do this practice by simply meditating on the main deity.

The traditional example of how this works is like inviting a king to visit you, although these days it would more likely be a high lama or an important statesman. When you extend an invitation to such a person, it is understood that the entourage of attendants, secretaries and so on are included. In the case of a king, whether you invite the entourage or not, they will accompany him as a matter of course. Similarly, when we meditate on the main deity, we automatically accomplish the retinue. The deities of the mandala don't just disappear because we're not thinking about them. Therefore, if we accomplish the main deity, we also accomplish all the deities in her retinue which is why it isn't necessary to think of each deity individually. So if we meditate on this *Single Mudra* daily practice, we don't have to worry about anything being incomplete. Everything will be accomplished because everything that's necessary is there.

> Homage to the Guru, sublime Tara!
> *This is the daily yoga practice of Chimé Phakmé Nyingtik as*
> *a single deity, the essence of the root sadhana called "Activities*
> *for Uncovering Primordial Wisdom", in three sections: the*
> *preliminary, the main practice and the conclusion.*

The title of the root sadhana of the Chimé Phakmé Nyingtik is "Activities for Uncovering Primordial Wisdom", and the daily practice that we're discussing today, the *Single Mudra*, is an essentialization of that root sadhana. *Single Mudra* has three sections: the preliminary, the main practice and the conclusion.

I. THE PRELIMINARY

> *Someone who has correctly received the empowerment for*
> *this practice, who keeps the samayas and vows well, who has*
> *trained their mind in absolute and relative bodhichitta and*
> *whose diligence is unwavering should retire to a secluded place*
> *and embark on the conduct conducive to meditation.*

There is not one Vajrayana deity that you can practise unless you have received the appropriate empowerment. You must therefore first receive the empowerment for this practice, and having received it you must keep the samayas and vows. Before you begin any Vajrayana practice, you must have trained your mind in both absolute and relative bodhichitta. Bodhichitta is the basis or support for Vajrayana practice, and relative bodhichitta is the generation of the mind of enlightenment both in aspiration and in action. Without holding both absolute and relative bodhichitta in your mind, you cannot practise the Vajrayana. Whether you practise in a Sutric or Tantric context, without a certain amount of diligence you won't accomplish anything. Therefore, cultivate diligence as much as you can and abandon laziness.

The text goes on to say that you "should retire to a secluded place" which means somewhere without sentient beings, no people during the day and no gods or demons at night. Sit on a soft cushion "and embark on the conduct conducive to meditation", meaning that you meditate on the deity, having stabilized your mind. To start with, avoid agitating the mind. Turn inwardly and look at your mind. Whatever thoughts arise, just relax in the vast expanse. Also allow your breath to settle so that you are at ease and relaxed. Relaxing and being at ease are what the text describes as the conduct conducive to meditation, but that's a little difficult. Thoughts like "now I'm going to meditate on the deity" and "I'm going to have a session of practice" should be avoided. Of course, if we didn't ever have that kind of thought, we wouldn't do any practice at all.

In the moments before you start to practise, this is what you should do. Basically, rest naturally on your cushion, avoid agitating your mind with ideas and whatever thoughts arise, leave them alone. Just look at the mind itself. In this way your thoughts will be naturally liberated by themselves. Similarly let the breath settle in its natural flow. To remain relaxed in this way is conducive to meditation.

> I imagine that the guru, the Wish-Fulfilling Wheel, in whom all sources of refuge are embodied appears in the sky before me. Before her, I and all sentient beings focus body, speech and mind on a single aim, take refuge and arouse bodhichitta.

From this state of ease imagine that the guru, the Wish-Fulfilling Wheel in whom all sources of refuge are embodied, appears in the sky before you. The Wish-Fulfilling Wheel is the deity we practise, and she is indivisible from the lama. Visualize yourself and all sentient beings standing before her as you pay homage with body, speech and mind. Show respect with your body by folding your hands in the anjali mudra, show respect with your speech by reciting the words of refuge and fill your mind with one-pointed devotion. Body, speech and mind are all focused on a single aim and coordinated to take refuge and arouse bodhichitta at the same time. As it says in the four-line refuge prayer, "We take refuge in Guru Wish-Fulfilling Wheel." We rely on her as our object of refuge and also as the witness to the arousal of bodhichitta in our minds. The refuge and bodhichitta prayers have been translated into English and the meaning is easy to understand so there is no need for explanation.

A. Taking Refuge

NAMO
Until we attain enlightenment, I and all sentient beings
Take refuge with unwavering devotion
In you, Guru Wish-Fulfilling Wheel, who are
The very essence of the Three Jewels!

B. Generating Bodhichitta

Ho
Sentient beings are as numerous as space is vast,
In order to free every one of them from the ocean of suffering
By attaining immortality through this yoga of Jetsun Phakma,
I arouse the enlightened mind of bodhichitta.

Throughout the refuge and bodhichitta prayers Guru Wish-Fulfilling Wheel has been in the sky before you, but now she instantaneously dissolves into you.

C. Expelling the Negative Forces

HUNG HUNG HUNG
The natural sound of this vajra mantra drives away all malevolent forces.

A mantra practitioner should continuously meditate on their yidam deity. If at this point you aren't, you should meditate on a deity like Hayagriva or Vajrakilaya—a wrathful deity. The deity appears instantly and from his heart emanates a large assembly of male and female wrathful deities who produce weapons and swirls of fire. As you say HUNG HUNG HUNG, the natural sound of this vajra mantra resonates and the weapons and swirls of fire drive all obstacles to the attainment of enlightenment and all malevolent forces far away. This is the visualization. For the mantra, HUNG HUNG HUNG is enough. The sound of HUNG is the self-radiance of primordial wisdom and indivisible from the mind of all the buddhas. Within the mind of the buddhas, there is not a single obstacle.

D. Protective Spheres

BENDZA JNANA RAKSHA AH HUNG
Visualize that with this, you have stabilized the protective spheres.

Once the malevolent forces have been driven far away say, "BENDZA JNANA RAKSHA AH HUNG" and meditate on the protection spheres. The usual visualization is of a fence of vajra prongs, blazing masses of wisdom fire and male and female wrathful deities. This is what you visualize. The visualization should be clear yet stable and like it's really there. How do you achieve that kind of visualization? By imagining it again and again.

E. Blessing the Offerings

If you have real offerings prepared, consecrate them with:
OM AH HUNG SARWA PUDZA MEGHA SAMAYE HUNG
and the Sky Treasury mudra.

If you have made material offerings, it's necessary to bless them. If not, then the blessing isn't necessary. Generally, there are two kinds of offering, the real and the imagined. Real offerings are either pure or impure, depending whether or not they are perceived with dualistic grasping and therefore need to be blessed. But we don't think that imagined offerings really exist, so we don't grasp at them, right? Therefore, they cannot be impure and don't need to be blessed.

Mantrayana practice requires four elements—deity, mantra, mudra and samadhi. It's important to accompany the blessing mantra with a mudra, so to bless the material offerings you have made, you should now do the Sky Treasury mudra.

The Sky Treasury mudra includes a wish-fulfilling jewel that you make with your hands. With the creation of the wish-fulfilling jewel, the material offerings become beautiful to look at, emit a pleasant sound, smell delicious, taste delectable and feel wonderful (the five sensory stimulants), and outer, inner, and secret offerings multiply to become inconceivable in number and inexhaustible—they will remain without diminishing for all time. The causes for making our offerings so inconceivably vast are the blessings of the buddhas, the force of the aspirations of the bodhisattvas, our own accomplishment of the two accumulations and the incredible power of deity, samadhi, mudra and mantra. This is what you must meditate on.

An elaborate practice to bless the offerings involves a great deal of recitation and ritual, but in short practices like this one there are just a few lines. Whether the practice is long or short, it must be complete. What makes a practice complete? If you recite mindlessly even when you recite a long prayer, the meaning behind the practice will not be complete. However, if you recite a short prayer like the prayer in this practice and think about every word you say and actualise it in your mind, the point of the practice will be accomplished. Of the three sections in this practice—the preliminary, the main practice and the conclusion—the preliminary is now finished.

II. THE MAIN PRACTICE

> *The second part, the main practice, is in two parts:*
> *A. The principal phase is to cultivate the practice of meditative equipoise by focusing your meditation on the deity and*
> *B. The subsidiary phase is to practise the concentration of the mantra recitation.*

There's a little to explain here. Why is the principal phase meditating on the deity? Because it is said, "The mandala of the deity matures the body." If you didn't have a body, how could you speak? And the three realms of samsara come into being based on body, speech and mind, don't they? So you must purify body, speech and mind. To do that, you practise the meditation yoga of the deity which also starts with the body. First focus on meditating on your body as the mandala of the deities which is the main focus here.

A. Meditation on the Deity

There are three steps to meditation on the deity:
1. Create a clear visualization of the samayasattva,
2. Invite and merge the jnanasattva indivisibly with the
samayasattva,
3. Keep the mind focused on the vivid presence and clear
appearance of the form of the deity which is samayasattva and
jnanasattva indivisible.

1. Visualization of the Samayasattva

Here, to generate the cause is to plant the structure of the three
samadhis . . .

It is completely wrong to try to meditate on deities without the three samadhis. This doesn't mean that there's no form of kyerim practice that can
be done without the three samadhis as there are many different kinds of
kyerim. But for the Mahayoga kyerim practice that we are doing here, the
three samadhis are necessary because they establish the framework. A framework in this context is the root of the practice upon which you accomplish
the result.

> *. . . and the result is the creation of the mandala of the palace*
> *and the deities, support and supported, which you do by*
> *bringing to mind the meaning of the words as you read them.*

Meditate on this. Here "meditate" means that you create the visualization of the mandala in your mind as you focus on the text that you recite.
You need to understand what you are doing as you go along. This is why it
is said in the teachings that, "Vajrayana is recitation and meditation."

So what is the point of recitation? What is the point of the chanting we accomplish by using our mouths and voices? The sound of our
voices directs our minds to what we must meditate on. "Recitation and
meditation" means that we recite or chant the words of the practice and
actualise the meaning of those words in our meditation. For example, the
word "house" immediately evokes in our minds the image of a building in

which people live. Similarly, the word "seat" evokes the kind of furniture people sit on. If I were to add ". . . and an old man with a long beard", you would immediately picture an old man sitting in the house. Visualization practice is like that except that we don't bring ordinary, worldly images to mind.

"House" ordinarily makes us think of the kind of house we live in, not the inconceivably vast and beautiful palace that is the home and support of the deities which isn't something we can imagine. A "person" implies an ordinary human being who is someone like us, living in a house and who is made of atoms, blood and flesh, not a wisdom deity whose nature is light that shines in all directions. A "seat" is something that a human being sits on like a chair which is all our minds are capable of picturing. We can't imagine the seats of lotus, sun and moon that the deities sit on. Since we are unable to picture in our mind's eye what these palaces, seats and deities look like, we do a sadhana practice that helps us visualize them clearly and eliminates mind's impure concepts that continuously relate back to samsara. So as we visualize, we eliminate ordinary, impure conceptions and actualise the pure mandala of the deities.

Recite the mantra,

OM MAHA SHUNYATA JNANA BENDZA SOBHAWA EMA KO HANG

As you recite the mantra, remember that all phenomena both of samsara and nirvana are empty. If it weren't for emptiness, nothing would be possible. It is because space is empty that it can be permeated by the world in the same way that when a house is empty a person can live in it. Only when a cup is empty can we pour something into it. If it's already full of something, we cannot add anything else.

However, emptiness isn't easy to talk about. First you establish the framework of the three samadhis. The first two lines talk about the samadhi of suchness,

> All things in samsara and nirvana are
> The primordial, luminous space of suchness, in which
>> arises . . .

This is easy to understand. "Samsara" refers to the six kinds of sentient being who go round and round in the three realms, "nirvana" refers to those whose minds have turned towards going beyond samsara and who hope to reach the level of buddhahood and so on. All phenomena in both samsara and nirvana are primordial clear light. In the words of the Buddha,

Mind is devoid of mind, the nature of mind is clear light.[28]

Buddha saw that all phenomena are clear light which is the natural radiance of primordial wisdom. Dzogchen practitioners call this clear light "the energy of rigpa" (*rigpa'i tsal*). Clear light is nothing other than suchness.

There is just one line for the samadhi of great compassion,

The power of all-illuminating compassion.

Within and united with this emptiness, this clarity is "great compassion". It's not a small compassion, it is hugely vast like the shining sun. When the sun shines all the obscurations of ignorance are completely eliminated and cannot manifest. So the compassion that is in union with emptiness is great, and the energy of great compassion is the samadhi of great compassion.

The next two lines refer to the third samadhi, the causal samadhi,

. . . their union
Is the causal samadhi, a white TAM,
Appearing like a rainbow from the sky and . . .

From the energy of the union of emptiness and compassion arises the causal samadhi. "Causal" means that the syllable is the cause of all samsara and nirvana, in the form of a white letter TAM which appears like a rainbow from the sky. This letter TAM is not visualized in Indian characters. The Sarmapas consider Indian characters to be extremely sacred and say that this is how we should visualize the syllables, but Khyentse Wangpo told Tibetans to imagine Tibetan letters.

These three samadhis are extremely important. Without the three samadhis kyerim practice is completely useless. So when you practise meditate as follows,

> All things in samsara and nirvana are
> The primordial, luminous space of suchness, in which
>   arises . . .

Rest, meditating on the meaning of emptiness. If your teacher has introduced you to your true nature through the pith instructions (*mengak*), rest in that. If not, rest in the form of meditation that you are familiar with.

Actually, everything unfolds within the samadhi of suchness so in fact there is no wavering from suchness. However, we do waver and move away from it which is when we accumulate the negative emotions and karma that lead us to spin around in samsara where we experience never-ending suffering. As we bring to mind all the deluded sentient beings in the three realms of samsara who exist in this way, we immediately embrace them with compassion. This is what is called the "power of all-illuminating compassion".

The causal samadhi arises from the energy of the union of suchness and compassion, and you meditate on a white syllable TAM which appears like a rainbow from the sky. The nature of TAM is light and the radiance of that light, and this corresponds to buddha nature which is the ground of all sentient beings. Buddha nature contains all the infinite qualities of the buddhas such as the thirty-two major marks and the eighty minor marks, which appear as light and the emanation and reabsorption of rays of light.

The three samadhis are explained in major texts like the *Secret Essence Tantra* or the *Lamrim Yeshe Nyingpo* which present in great detail all the key aspects of the practice, for example the purpose of purification and what we purify from the perspective of ground, path and fruition. These explanations are good to know.[29] If you don't know this information and try to practise using these verses on the three samadhis while ignoring what I've just explained, which is the bare minimum of information that you need, your practice will be completely incorrect. What comes next is easier.

The Palace

> Sending out light that purifies clinging to reality in the
>   world and amongst beings.

From the syllable TAM stream rays of light.

Within the expanse of the five elements, the consorts, . . .

The five elements are the nature of the five consorts and appear one on top of the other. "Within their expanse" means that above them, we visualize,

> . . . the celestial mansion of great liberation,
> Made of precious crystal,
> Complete with four sides, four doors and all its features.

What does the palace look like? It has four doors, four corners and all the features of a palace which according to the *Secret Essence Tantra* represent the thirty-seven elements leading to enlightenment.

The Seat

> In its centre on a four-petalled lotus are
> Skilful means and wisdom—sun and moon fused
> together— . . .

The Deity

> In the centre of which is the syllable TAM, as their union, . . .

This means that if we take rebirth in the three realms of existence, we must rely on the four modes of birth, one of which is to be born to a father and mother from the mother's womb. This is represented by the essence of your consciousness appearing between the sun and the moon in the form of a syllable TAM which purifies the habit of being born from a womb that samsaric sentient beings have formed.

At this point in the process of rebirth from a womb, there is a mind but there is no physical form. Over the course of nine months the human baby gradually takes shape, and to purify this habitual tendency the syllable TAM emanates and reabsorbs rays of light,

> Light emanates from TAM as an offering to the noble ones,
> Gathering and bringing back the quintessence of samsara
> and nirvana, . . .

After nine months and ten days in the womb, the human baby's body has been formed and is born. Then the TAM,

> Which transforms into the magical body of wisdom,
> Embodiment of the enlightened activity of the buddhas,
> 　　past, present and future,
> Wish-Fulfilling Wheel, bestower of immortality.
> Brilliant white, with one face and two hands,
> Her right hand in the mudra of supreme generosity,
> Her left grants refuge, symbolizing the Three Jewels,
> And holds an utpala flower on which rests the vase of
> 　　longevity.
> Peaceful, smiling, with seven eyes of wisdom,
> She is lovely. Adorned with silks and jewelled ornaments,
> Her two legs are crossed in vajra posture,
> She sits on her lotus and moon disc seat.

The form of the deity is now complete. Since we have a body when we are born, we already have a form. So the visualization of the form of the deity is to purify our habitual tendency of taking a form.

> As her natural radiance, the supreme skilful means, the
> 　　Lord of the Dance,
> Holds a lotus flower and long-life vase,
> And embraces her in union.

The deity Wish-Fulfilling Wheel appears in union with her male consort to symbolize the indivisibility of skilful means and wisdom. The Lord of the Dance is Avalokiteshvara.[30]

This concludes the section on the visualization of the support, the palace, and the supported mandala of the deity.

2. Inviting and Absorbing the Jnanasattva

Humans have body, speech and mind right? Similarly the deities must have enlightened body, speech and mind—the three vajras. We therefore now receive the blessings of the three vajras.

The crown of their heads, throats and hearts,
Are marked with the syllables of the three vajras,
From which rays of light stream out and
Invite the jnanasattvas.

This means you visualize yourself clearly as the samayasattva, and from your body rays of light shine out to invite the jnanasattva. Conceptually we tend to think of ourselves as being different from the deity. To purify this concept, you invite the jnanasattva, the wisdom deity, which dissolves into you in the form of the samayasattva. Recite the words of invitation,

HRIH
Long-life Goddess with supreme discerning wisdom,
Crowned by Amitabha, the Buddha of Limitless Light,
Lady who is the enlightened activity of the buddhas of
        past, present and future,
Approach! You who manifest as the Wish-Fulfilling Wheel
With the retinue of assembled families that you emanate,
Rupakayas that magically arise
From the dharmakaya beyond arising.
Your samaya of great compassion obliges you to
Confer the supreme siddhi on this practitioner.
Direct your wisdom mind into this mandala of the
        samayasattva,
And arouse in me indestructible vajra wisdom!
SAMAYA HO SAMAYA STAM E A RA LI HRING HRING DZA
        JNANA SATO AH

With this, the jnanasattvas are invited. And with,

BENDZA JNANA DZA HUNG BAM HO . . .
DZA invites the wisdom deities,
HUNG receives the wisdom deities as they arrive,
BAM pleases the wisdom deities and
HO makes the wisdom deities indivisible with the samayasattva.
        . . . SAMAYA TISHTALEN

This mantra requests the deities to remain. So,

> *. . . they are invited, dissolved, pleased and requested to remain steadfast and constant.*

Paying Homage

If you wish, you can briefly offer prostration, offerings and praise.

This means that if you don't want to do all that, it's fine; but if you want to prostrate, make offerings and express praise, you can.

AH LA LA HO is an expression of wonder.
AH TI PU HO represents prostrations to the deity—the person prostrating is the activity deity that you, as the samayasattva, emanate—and PRA TI TSA HO auspiciously concludes the prostration to the deity.

Offerings

Make outer, inner and secret offerings and the offering of suchness, with:
OM
Whether actually present or manifested by the mind,
All the offerings in infinite universes, inner, outer and
   secret . . .

All offering substances—outer (drinking water, washing water, flowers, fragrance, light, perfumed water, food, music and so on), inner (visual forms, sounds, odours, tastes and tactile sensations) and secret (amrita, rakta and torma)—are offered.

> I offer to you, noble Wish-Fulfilling Wheel;
> Accept them and grant me the siddhi of immortality!

These two lines are easy to understand. I'll explain the mantra briefly. It starts with OM, then ARYA TARA refers to Jetsun Drolma who is surrounded by the retinue of deities, so SAPARIWARA refers to all the deities. As you make the offerings:

—to represent drinking water, you say ARGHAM,

—washing water is PADAM,

—flowers are PUSHPE,

—fragrance is DHUPE,

—light is ALOKE,

—perfumed water is GENDE,

—food is NEWIDYA and

—music is SHAPTA.

The inner offerings are:

—all beautiful forms are RUPA,

—all sounds are SHAPTA,

—all fragrant smells are GENDE,

—all tasty things to eat are RASA and

—all good clothes are SPARSHE.

Finally, PRATITSA SOHA offers the outer and inner offerings.
For the secret offerings:

—SARWA PENTSA AMRITA is amrita,

—MAHA RAKTA is rakta and

—MAHA BALINGTA KHAHI is the torma.

SARWA DHARMADHATU means all phenomena have dissolved into dharmadhatu, emptiness. With SARWA EMA KO HANG you offer all phenomena. This mantra encompasses great depth of meaning and involves all the aspects of offering, union, liberation, suchness, emptiness and so on. So at the beginning of the offering section the text says,

> *Make outer, inner and secret offerings and the offering of suchness.*

This is what the offerings are. In terms of what you visualize, emanate an activity deity in front of you that is the same as yourself in the form of Jetsun Tara. From the lotus she is holding and from her forehead, throat and heart (the three main centres), she emanates an infinite number of offering goddesses. These goddesses present the offerings we've just spoken about to the mandala.

There are many traditions and methods for making offerings, but essentially you should offer as much of the best quality food, drink and so on as is possible and consider that the offerings are inexhaustible.

Praise

Offer praise with . . .

Imagine that Brahma, Vishnu, the four great kings, all the protectors of the world, all the buddhas of the ten directions and all the bodhisattvas offer praise in one voice.

> You were born from the tears of
> The Lord of the World and Master of Compassion.
> Mother of the buddhas of past, present and future,
> Wish-Fulfilling Wheel, to you I pay homage and offer praise!

At the end of this part of the practice, the deity making the offerings and offering praise dissolves into you.

3. Focusing the Mind on the Form of the Deity

Focus your mind exclusively on a clear image, both the overall outline and specific details, of the form of the deity, the great mudra, in which samayasattva and jnanasattva are inseparable.

"Great mudra" is also known as mahamudra. Generate an image in your mind of the Glorious Wish-Fulfilling Wheel with seven eyes in union with the Lord of the Dance. Focus your mind one-pointedly and visualize them so clearly that you can even see the white and black parts of their eyes and clearly differentiate the colour of their bodies. Clear visualization is important.

The great tantras say that when you meditate on deities, you should have a samaya support to look at that has been blessed. These days you can find many photos of this White Tara. Look at it without getting distracted. If you concentrate your mind one-pointedly as you look at the image, eventually you will be able to see it in your mind's eye. But remember that the mental image you create in your mind is different from the photograph. As you meditate you must train your mind so that the image can be bigger or smaller and that the deities actually move—which they don't in the photograph, do they?! You should also see that the bodies of the deities are made of light, be able to enlarge and reduce their size and increase the stability of your visualization.

The practical advice the masters give here is that you should practise often and in short sessions. Until you've meditated and trained yourself in this way for some time, kyerim will be difficult; but once you're used to meditating like this, there is no doubt that you will accomplish a clear visualization. Right now though you are not used to what the deity looks like. But this will become similar to when you think of your father for example, you don't have to remember each of his features, you just think of him and he appears in your mind's eye without much effort because you're familiar with what he looks like.

Feel the firm and stable confidence of vajra pride.

On the absolute level all sentient beings have buddha nature, sugatagarbha, and it is exactly the same buddha nature as that of the deities and buddhas. It is because we have buddha nature that enlightenment is possible. "Sugatagarbha" is the cause that ultimately results in enlightenment. In the same way there is no oil in sand and however hard you press the sand you'll never get any oil, anything that doesn't have sugatagarbha like stones and earth cannot reach enlightenment. On the other hand sesame seeds already contain oil, and you can extract it simply by pressing the seeds.

For all of us although buddha nature is our ground, that ground is temporarily obscured. Yet it is exactly the same as the ground of the buddhas. Because buddha nature brings with it all the qualities and wisdom of the buddhas, once our obscurations have been eliminated we become buddhas. This is how you should think, and you should feel the stable confidence or pride that you and the deity are one and the same.

Once an experience of clarity and stability has developed, remember the purity, ground and fruition, and in this way train your mind so that the kyerim practice matures you and brings you closer to attaining the supreme siddhi.

So you must cultivate a clear image of the deity in your meditation and also develop the stable confidence that you are the same as the deity. When you can hold a clear image of the deity in your mind, have a stable confidence that you are the deity. Then realise that both experiences are simply the display of the energy of emptiness on the absolute level; in the context of the ground they exist and in the context of fruition they are empty, yet they must be connected. Your meditation should be an experience of clear visualization and of stable vajra pride which you immediately know to be the emptiness of fruition, without taking any notice of the idea that you recognize that emptiness.

When meditating upon clear appearance, focus exclusively on the clear visualization of the deity. Make every effort to visualize as clearly and in as much detail as possible. At the same time even when the visualization is extremely clear, be aware that the deity isn't something new you've created. On the absolute level the deity is indivisible from you. Right now while you are on the path, your sugatagarbha is obscured, but it will become manifest as the real buddha at fruition. Bearing this in mind will give rise to stable vajra pride. Stable vajra pride is the confidence that you really are the buddha, and you arrive at that confidence once you've eliminated any idea that "Buddha is better" or "the deity is good, but I am inferior". Just think, "I am the deity!" This is the kind of confidence that should be generated here.

> Once an experience of clarity and stability has developed,
> remember the purity, ground and fruition, and in this way
> train your mind so that the kyerim practice matures you and
> brings you closer to attaining the supreme siddhi.

When you finally experience clear visualization and stable vajra pride, don't grasp at it. It's not appropriate to grasp at this experience, right? At this point the deity is an image, a representation that appears in your mind, and mind is empty, the energy of emptiness liberated within the state of rigpa. Whatever practice you are doing, this is where you remember the purity by calling to mind that the deity doesn't exist in itself, thus applying the seal of emptiness. This is the best way to meditate on the deity, and if you apply this method during kyerim you will move closer to the supreme accomplishment called the "great seal". How? As your habitual tendencies are progressively removed and the obscurations eliminated, the two accumulations are accomplished and there is not the slightest doubt that you'll attain the supreme siddhi of the great seal.

B. The Mantra Recitation

*Whenever you become weary of that kind of meditation, to
enhance your practice, train in the meditative absorption of the
mantra recitation.*

This means that if you practise creating the clear visualization of the deity and get tired of continually repeating this method of meditation, "In order to enhance your practice, train in the meditative absorption of the mantra recitation." The text goes on to say,

> I am sublime Tara: in my heart
> Is the jnanasattva Amitayus,
> Brilliant white and holding a long-life vase in the mudra of
>   meditation,
> Beautiful with his silk and jewelled ornaments,
> In vajra posture on a lotus and moon disc seat,
> Shining and resplendent amidst brilliant rays of light.

So visualize yourself as the samayasattva Sublime Tara, Wish-Fulfilling Wheel, as I've already explained. At her heart is the jnanasattva Amitayus, white in colour with one face, two hands and holding a long-life vase in the mudra of meditation. At his heart is a white lotus on top of which, at the centre of a locket made by a sun and a moon, is a white syllable TAM, the samadhisattva. These are the three nested sattvas, and this is what you visualize as you recite the first part of the prayer.

> In the centre of his heart is a lotus and sun and moon discs,
> In the middle of which is TAM, encircled by the mantra
>   mala.

The ten-syllable mantra—OM TARE TUTTARE TURE SOHA—encircles the syllable TAM. It is white and arranged clockwise and the OM stands in front of the TAM.

Concerning the visualization of the encircling mantra mala, in general we visualize mainly its arrangement for the approach, the mantra turning for the close approach, the palanquin (*doli*) during the accomplishment and the emanation and reabsorption during the great accomplishment. If we follow the Nyingma Kama tradition, the first example to illustrate the visualizations of the mantra is the "moon and the garland of stars" which refers to the phase of *approach*. When the moon is shining in the sky, it is surrounded by stars that are sharply defined and clearly distinguishable from one another. Similarly, at the centre of the sun and moon locket, the white syllable TAM is surrounded by the ten syllables OM TARE TUTTARE TURE SOHA arranged clockwise, distinct from one another and as vividly clear as the stars surrounding the moon. This is the visualization that you create just for the approach practice. What does "approach" mean? It's like meeting someone you don't know; when you approach that person for the first time and see what they look like, you know who they are. This is "approach". Therefore, reciting the mantra while focusing on the core seed syllable and mantra mala is the approach practice.

Then "the mantra turning for the close approach" means that the *close approach* meditation focuses on the slow rotation of the syllables of the mantra mala around the TAM. As the syllables are arranged clockwise, they must turn counterclockwise. "Close approach" is like getting closer to someone we already know, that's its purpose. So the mantra mala should slowly turn counterclockwise, emanating rays of light.

The visualization during *accomplishment* practice is called the "palanquin". As the stream of mantra malas revolve the TAM remains where it is. From OM, the first syllable of the mantra, the mantra syllables stream out through the mouth of the self-visualization, enter the mouth of the front visualization then leave through the navel to re-enter the self-visualization through its navel. One after another, the stream of mantra malas revolves in this way like "a whirling firebrand" which is a wooden stick ablaze at both ends that creates the illusion of a circle of fire if you twirl it quickly.

The stream of mantra malas can turn between the self-visualization and front visualization and so on or through the mouth of the female deity and into the mouth of the male deity, then out through his secret place and into hers. This palanquin visualization that resembles a whirling firebrand is the accomplishment practice. Once we have met the deity through approach practice, we become better acquainted through close approach practice, then accomplish indivisibility with the deity by means of the accomplishment practice. This is the task that we accomplish.

"The emanation and reabsorption during the *great accomplishment*" means that the circling stream of mantra malas emanate rays of light which make offerings to all the victorious ones and their heirs residing in the ten directions of infinite space. We then receive all the blessings and siddhis of body, speech and mind—body in the form of deities, mind in the form of ritual hand implements and speech in the form of seed syllables—which gather within us and in the seed syllable TAM. The commentary says,

> Yet it is enough to visualize its arrangement when
> practising essentially.

This means that when you practise more essentially, for example the daily practice rather than the more elaborate sadhana, it is enough to visualize the syllables of the mantra around the TAM. You don't have to visualize them moving. In most of the Mother Tantra cycles for female deities, which apply to this practice, the syllables are usually arranged counterclockwise. However, here it is explained that the mantra should be arranged in a clockwise direction as in all the sadhanas of the Sarma tantras. So here the syllables are placed clockwise. None of this is difficult.

Now the emanation and reabsorption of rays of light.

> In the centre of his heart is a lotus and sun and moon discs,
> In the middle of which is TAM encircled by the mantra
> mala.

As you slowly recite the mantra, you invoke Amitayus' wisdom mind,

> Reciting the mantra evokes his wisdom mind, causing
> A stream of boundless light to burst out

> From the top of the jewel on the ushnisha at the crown of
> his head, . . .

So visualize yourself as the samayasattva, the Sublime Lady of Immortality, Chimé Phakmé Nyingtik's main deity, and at her heart is the jnanasattva, white Amitayus. At Amitayus' heart is the samadhisattva, the syllable TAM, around which revolves the mantra mala. Rays of light stream from the top of Amitayus' head and out through his ushnisha.

> . . . from which appears the sublime Vijaya,
> The colour of crystal. Her right hand, . . .

"The colour of crystal" in this case is white.

> In the mudra of granting refuge, holds a hook;
> Her left, in the mudra of supreme giving, holds a long-life
> vase.
> She radiates light, as limitless forms of herself
> Stream out like specks of dust in sunbeams.

How should we visualize sublime Ushnisha Vijaya? The *Retreat Manual* says,

> Her right hand in the gesture of granting refuge is poised
> on her right knee and forms the threatening mudra . . .

This means that her hand forms this particular gesture.

> . . . as she holds a hook that gathers nectar. Her left hand at
> the level of her heart in the mudra of supreme giving holds
> a long-life vase, from which she pours a stream of nectar . . .

The nectar overflows and pours out of the vase. Jamgön Kongtrul continues,

> Her feet are loosely crossed in the sattvasana.

Generally, vajrasana[31] or vajra posture is the posture of the male deity, and the posture of the consort sitting in the male deity's lap is the sattvasana. That is how to meditate on Ushnisha Vijaya.

Rays of light emanating from the heart of Amitayus leave his body through his ushnisha and stream into you in the form of the Sublime Lady of Immortality, then leave your body through your ushnisha, to become innumerable Ushnisha Vijayas.

> She radiates light, as limitless forms of herself
> Stream out like specks of dust in sunbeams.
> They draw in all the subtle vital essence of samsara and
>   nirvana,
> The animate and inanimate universe,
> In the form of the quicksilver that accomplishes all,
> Marked with the symbols of great bliss.

"Samsara and nirvana" refers to everything in the animate and inanimate universe. From samsara, the vital essence is drawn from all the samsaric beings who enjoy long life, are free of illness and who are wealthy including the universal monarchs, the rishis, Indra, Vishnu, gods, nagas, humans and so on. And from nirvana, it is drawn from all those who have gone beyond samsara and are ascending the bhumis, the perfect buddhas and bodhisattvas.

So from all the beings of samsara and nirvana, the vital energy of the inanimate environment of this world (like earth, water, fire, wind and so on) and its inhabitants is gathered into a nectar that's marked with the symbols of great bliss. You are in the form of Chimé Phakmé Nyingtik and here the nectar dissolves into bindus of enlightened body, speech and mind at your forehead, throat and heart.

"They draw in all the subtle vital essence of samsara and nirvana—the animate and inanimate universe" needs some explanation. Once the vital energy is drawn in, the rays of light that are then reabsorbed into Chimé Phakmé Nyingtik consist of an alchemical substance of rejuvenation, *rasayana*, that resembles quicksilver. This nectar is pure white like an autumn moon and emanates rays of light like the sun, and even the rays of light are also completely white. As the nectar pours into you, it coils down clockwise and is marked with all kinds of auspicious patterns like svastikas, coils of joy, eight auspicious symbols and so on. The power of this nectar is tremendous. It can transmit to whatever it touches the strength of an elephant, it has the same life span as the sun and the moon[32] which do not seem to age and it has the seven qualities of a vajra: indestructibility, unbreakability, stability and so on. It has the ability to give old people in their sixties or seventies, for example, instantly the vigour of a sixteen year old. If it touches iron, the iron is transmuted into gold. If it's sprinkled over a dead and withered tree, the tree will immediately burst into life sprouting abundant leaves, fruit and flowers. This is the kind of nectar that pours down into you in the form of Chimé Phakmé Nyingtik.

> It dissolves into me and the ritual implements,
> Granting me the siddhi of immortal life,
> And intensifying the wisdom of great bliss.

As the nectar pours into you, imagine you are filled with great bliss and that you blaze with splendour. It intensifies the wisdom of great bliss. This is how you should meditate on the nectar.

> *While you recite these words and bring to mind their meaning,*
> *maintain an acute awareness of the practice.*

To "maintain an acute awareness of the practice" means that you concentrate one-pointedly on the practice and don't let your mind wander or be distracted.

The Mantras

OM TARE TUTTARE TURE SOHA
Spend most of your time reciting these ten vajra syllables
mantra. At the end of a session, recite the mantra that
combines approach, accomplishment and activity all in one:

OM TARE TUTTARE TURE HRIH DROOM BENDZA JNANA AYUKE
  SOHA
Recite this as much as is appropriate. Then if you wish
to continue, and you can, recite a few OM AMARANI
DZIWANTIYE SOHA and OM AMRITA AYURDADE SOHA.

The main mantra you recite is the ten-syllable mantra OM TARE TUTTARE TURE SOHA. Accumulate as many as you can. At the end of each session, whether or not you've been visualizing the mantra OM TARE TUTTARE TURE SOHA rotating in the heart of the jnanasattva, recite also the mantra OM TARE TUTTARE TURE HRIH DROOM BENDZA JNANA AYUKE SOHA. The rest of the visualization is the same, just the mantra changes. When you just recite OM TARE TUTTARE TURE SOHA, don't visualize the other mantra. But when you do the combined practice, you must visualize the second mantra HRIH DROOM BENDZA JNANA AYUKE SOHA following the first (OM TARE TUTTARE TURE) in the mantra mala. Then you must recite the mantras OM AMARANI DZIWANTIYE SOHA and OM AMRITA AYURDADE SOHA for a while. In Kongtrul Rinpoche's instructions on this practice, he writes that after the combined practice mantra we must recite and visualize these two mantras, one after the other.

Vowels and Consonants and Essence of Dependent Origination Mantras

Then,

> *Just before you finish the recitation session, recite the vowels and consonants and the essence of dependent origination to make up for any duplications and omissions and to stabilize the effects of the mantra practice.*

Offering and Praise

Make a brief offering and praise . . .

The Nyingma lamas of the past would recite the vowel and consonant mantras, the essence of dependent origination mantra and the offering and praise prayers for every thousand recitations of the mantra. But that's not done any more. These days it's acceptable just to do this form of recitation at the end of each session. You can recite the offering and praise prayers from the practice—they're short.

Confession

. . . and confess any error with the hundred-syllable mantra.

During the practice session you may have made mistakes in your recitations or missed syllables and your kyerim practice may have lacked clarity and so on, so you must confess all these faults as you recite the hundred-syllable mantra three times.

III. THE CONCLUSION
A. Dissolution & Rearising

Then the dissolution,

> Aн
> All the features of the samayasattvas, rigpa's natural display,
> Like faces and hands, dissolve into all-pervading space.

If you were born, you must also die, so we practise dissolution to purify all habitual tendencies associated with death. The words of the practice mean that all the deities you have been meditating on and have until now considered the display of your rigpa dissolve:

— the universe and all beings dissolve into the palace,
— the palace dissolves into the deity's retinue,
— the retinue dissolves into the main deity,
— the main deity dissolves into the jnanasattva at the heart of the main deity,
— the jnanasattva dissolves into the samadhisattva,
— and the letter TAM slowly dissolves from the bottom up, and we rest in the state of emptiness.

In this case there are no deities in the retinue, so the universe and beings dissolve into the palace, the palace into the main deity, the main deity into the jnanasattva at her heart, the jnanasattva into the samadhisattva and then the letter TAM slowly dissolves from the bottom up and you rest in the state free of reference.

Then you arise as the deity once again in order to purify the habitual tendencies of birth.

Once again, like a rainbow appearing from the sky,
I arise as deity and mantra, as the play of great wisdom.

Now the clear image of the deity—in this case Chimé Phakmé Nyingtik—arises once more. With this, dissolve the appearance of the deity into the expanse of clear light and re-emerge in the form of the deity in which appearance, emptiness and so on are one. Then the three syllables OM AH HUNG appear clearly on the visualized body of the Sublime Lady of Immortality to,

Seal body, speech and mind with the three vajras.

B. Concluding Prayers

Then,

Through the merit of this practice, may I swiftly
Accomplish the Sublime Lady of Immortality,
And may every single sentient being, without exception,
Be led to that state of perfection too!

That's easy!

*With this, recite prayers of dedication and aspiration, as well
as appropriate auspicious prayers for the conclusion of a session,
before you return to your daily activities.*

You must now recite prayers of auspiciousness. Any prayer of auspiciousness is fine, for example the one from the longer sadhana.

IV. *SINGLE MUDRA* COLOPHON

*Based on the principles of the path of flawless perfection,[33] I
have written this Single Mudra yoga as a practice for beginners*

or more generally as an easy daily practice. I wrote it at the command—the repeated command—of omniscient Vajradhara Lodrö Taye, whose coming was prophesied by the Buddha and for whom my faith is so profound that he constantly adorns the crown of my head.

Following the basic terma text exactly, the lake-born guru's favourite servant, Pema Osel Dongak Lingpa, composed this at the Yiga Chödzin temple, at Palpung Monastery, which so delights Tara.

May the merit of this serve as the cause for the glorious and holy gurus' lives to remain secure for hundreds of kalpas and for all limitless beings to accomplish the wisdom body of immortal Jetsun Tara. Mangalam!

V. RETREAT INSTRUCTIONS
Approach, Accomplishment and Activity in Chimé Phakmé Nyingtik

In order to practise the approach, accomplishment and activity of Chimé Phakmé Nyingtik elaborately, for the approach practice follow the explanation given above. For the accomplishment phase, practise the four Taras adding the recitation of their mantras. And for the activity phase, do the visualizations associated with the four Gatekeeper Taras who carry out the activities. This is how to practise approach, accomplishment and activity in the Chimé Phakmé Nyingtik.

When you practise the approach, you only need to prepare a small offering. When you practice the accomplishment, arrange the torma, the mandala and all the appropriate substances but augment the offerings you made in the approach by adding more. Then do the recitations associated with the four Taras. When you do the activity practice, do the activity visualizations.

If you only do the approach practice, you can accumulate as many mantras as you want to, as I've explained above. You should focus on accumulating the ten-syllable mantra OM TARE TUTTARE TURE SOHA, then at the end of each session recite OM TARE TUTTARE TURE HRIH DROOM BENDZA JNANA

AYUKE SOHA which is the approach mantra that combines the three deities of long life. After that at the end of the session, recite one hundred of each mantra as you do the visualizations of the jnanasattva and nirmanasattva.

Fire Puja

After practising approach, accomplishment and activity, to complete the practice, you must do the fire puja in the Chimé Phakmé Nyingtik.[34] It's good to do it after you have accumulated several hundred thousand mantras.

This is how you practise the Chimé Phakmé Nyingtik in retreat based on the *Single Mudra* daily practice text.

CHAPTER 5:

The Sweet Ambrosia of Immortality

Concise Instructions on Kyerim and Dzogrim based on Single Mudra, the Daily Practice of the Heart Essence of the Sublime Lady of Immortality

by Jamyang Khyentse Chökyi Lodrö

Namo Guru Arya Tarayai![35]
Noble Lady, the merest recollection of whom
Brings the accomplishment of perfect longevity,
Bhagavati, Wish-Fulfilling Wheel,
Inseparable from the guru, grant auspiciousness!

Your sadhana, oral instructions from the great master of Oddiyana,
Is a treasure that arose from the dark casket of the profound expanse
Of the wisdom mind of Ösal Trulpe Dorje.*
This heart essence of the Noble Lady, I shall now explain in stages.

Among the various kama and terma teachings on the immortal White Tara, Wish-Fulfilling Wheel, bestower of longevity, which originate with accomplished acharyas, here we are concerned with the essence of the wisdom mind of the master of Oddiyana, knower of the three times, a profound mind treasure of Pema Ösal Dongak Lingpa, the teaching of the Heart Essence of the Sublime Lady of Immortality, which is a profound and vast dharma cycle. Here I shall explain in stages the instructions on the unelaborate *Single Mudra*, the daily practice which is the essence and distillation of the sadhana, *Activities to Uncover Primordial Wisdom*. This will consist of preliminaries, main part and concluding stages.

---

* Jamyang Khyentse Wangpo.

I. THE PRELIMINARIES

This section includes: A. the preliminaries to the session and B. the preliminaries to the commentary.

A. The Preliminaries to the Session

Sit on a comfortable seat in the seven-point posture of Vairochana. The crucial point of speech is to allow the circulating wind-energies to settle in their natural place. Expel any stale wind-energy from the right and left nostrils in turn and then both at the same time, nine or three times. This will separate the pure and impure essence of the wind-energies. Then rest for a while. This preparation will make you a suitable vessel for meditative concentration.

In the space before you appears Buddha Amitabha, indivisible from your root guru. He is in nirmanakaya attire, and his two hands rest in the posture of meditative equipoise, holding an alms bowl filled with the ambrosia of immortality. He is seated upon a lotus and moon disc seat. With ardent devotion and fervent longing, recite the following prayers at least three times,

> Glorious root lama . . .[36]

And,

> Essence of the buddhas of past, present and future,
>   precious guru, to you I pray:
> Inspire me with your blessings;
> Grant your blessings, so the extraordinary realization of the
>   profound path is born in me;
> Grant your blessings, so that I may, in this life, attain the
>   immortal wisdom kaya!

At the end, imagine that your guru melts into light and dissolves into you. Leave your mind in a state free of grasping, clear yet empty. When a thought arises suddenly, do not indulge it, but apply the relevant visualizations as explained in this commentary. It is crucial that all the stages outlined below are preceded by what has been explained here.

B. The Preliminaries to the Commentary

This has two parts: 1. the common preliminaries and 2. the uncommon preliminaries.

1. The Common Preliminaries

The profound treasure text *Vajra Verses of Tara* says,

> In an isolated and pleasant place
> Inspire yourself with strong renunciation.[37]

At first, exert yourself only in the methods that inspire renunciation and the wish to be liberated from samsara. Contemplate the following: whether you are born in higher or lower realms, you will never escape the three kinds of suffering and not enjoy even so much as a hair's breadth of happiness. Furthermore, if you are reborn in any of the three lower realms, you will experience unbearable suffering. If you cannot endure even a single day of intense heat, cold or hunger right now, how will you possibly cope with the suffering of the lower realms?

If you take birth in one of the three higher realms and are unable to remove ignorance—the cause of samsara—you might for a while experience a tiny amount of defiled happiness. Yet that semblance of happiness is itself a cause for experiencing only suffering. When you realise how you will naturally sink lower and lower, you will be overcome with sadness. Throughout time without beginning until now, you have wandered in these realms. Yet still the actions of your body, speech and mind are mostly negative and unvirtuous. It is certain therefore that when you die, you will immediately go to the lower realms. The Thus-Gone One has said that whatever actions you have done will not go to waste and that you will never experience the karma of things you have not done. You are the sole recipient of the ripening of your actions which cannot be transferred to someone else. As there can be no washing away or avoiding what you have done, you must experience the intense ripening of karma for a long time. As a result of some slight virtuous action, you might be reborn in the higher realms; yet even as a human, you will still experience the suffering of birth, old age, sickness and death. If you are reborn as a god you will experience the suffering of death, transmigration and fall. In the upper realms you might remain in meditation for a long time, yet when that mind is exhausted you won't escape the fall to lower states, which means you must experience continual suffering. From now on therefore, adopt only virtuous actions and avoid what is unvirtuous.

You must immediately devote yourself to practice right now! Postponing it until tomorrow or the day after will be to no avail. Your life is as impermanent as bubbles on water, as susceptible to momentary change as a candle in the wind and as transient and unstable as clouds in the sky, liable to disappear at any moment. The outer world too is always changing with the arrival and passing of the four seasons. And beings within it, regardless of their status, lead uncertain lives. There is no escaping the fact that the time of death is uncertain, conditions that lead to death are uncertain and everyone is certain to die. When you experience the suffering of death, your strength, wealth, family, looks or possessions—however excellent they might be—will be of no help at all. You alone must experience this suffering.

The suffering of fear in the intermediate state is inconceivable, undirected you will have no control over where you might be reborn or where you might go. Even your cherished body must be left behind, and when you die and go on to the next world your only refuge and protection will be the sacred dharma. Not to practise but to procrastinate and fail to strive at this very moment to practise the divine, sacred dharma would be to deceive yourself foolishly as if a mighty demon had entered your heart. So do not cheat yourself but look after your own best interests through the sacred and divine sun of dharma.

The perfect support for practising the divine dharma is to have a body complete with the eighteen freedoms and advantages. If you possess such a support, it is because you have accumulated good deeds in the past. However, be sure not to lose this valuable asset for you will not find such an excellent support again even among the gods, much less anywhere else, and even the supposedly great loss of a few prized possessions would be nothing in comparison.

The support of this body makes it possible to secure lasting happiness. Just look at the life stories of the buddhas and bodhisattvas and the scholars and adepts of the past. It could also lead to ruin in this life and the next. Look at the stories of wrongdoers reborn in the hell realms. This marks a crossroads—the point at which you could go up or down—so do not lose sight of what will work out well or badly and do not fall prey to mistaken ideas or flawed advice.

Now that you have found the jewel of the freedoms and advantages, do not squander them, but strive with enormous effort physically, verbally and mentally in order to make the most of them. The focus of your energy should be the sacred dharma, the nectar that dispels all the various faults of existence and quiescence, the great medicine that cures the chronic illness of samsara. Yet this cannot be understood through your own ingenuity, you must rely on the condition of an authentic spiritual friend and serve him or her with the three means of gratification[38] and by carrying out every command. With the devotion of seeing everything the teacher does as authentic, preserve the life force of the path. Do not disregard what issues from the excellent vase of the teacher's mouth but with devoted application, continuous application and strong, insatiable diligence, practise until your mind turns towards the dharma, the dharma progresses on the path, the path pacifies confusion and deluded perceptions dawn as wisdom. Think, "O guru, grant me such ability. Three Jewels, care for me! Let me attain such ability! Inspire me with your blessings so that I become just so!" With thoughts such as these, generate strong renunciation like the flow of a river. When you arise from your session, dedicate the merit and carry out the activities of post-meditation while never losing your heartfelt renunciation. This also applies to everything that follows.

2. The Uncommon Preliminaries

This has five parts. There are instructions on a) taking refuge, b) generating the mind set upon supreme awakening, c) purifying the unfavourable circumstances of negative actions and obscurations, d) gathering the favourable circumstances of the accumulations and e) the blessings of guru yoga. The *Vajra Verses* say,

> Take refuge, strive to purify and increase,
> Meditate on the blessings of guru yoga,
> Receive the four empowerments, and blend mind and
>   wisdom.

a) Taking Refuge

Imagine that your surroundings are like the blissful realm adorned with infinite clouds of excellent offerings. In the space before you is a multi-coloured, hundred-thousand-petalled lotus. At the height of its anther is a moon disc seat upon which your root guru sits in the form of the Sublime Lady without consort. Consider that she is the embodiment of all sources of refuge. In front of her on a ground made of lapis lazuli, you and all sentient beings take refuge with body, speech and mind in unison. Consider with one-pointed faith and devotion that the guru's body is the sangha, speech the sacred dharma and mind the buddha, and recite the following from the Chimé Phakmé Nyingtik sadhana,

> NAMO
> Until we attain enlightenment, I and all sentient beings . . .

In each session recite this one hundred or one thousand times, whichever you can manage without letting your mind be distracted. At the end of the session rays of light stream from the objects of refuge, striking you and all other sentient beings, purifying your negative actions, obscurations and habitual tendencies and transporting everyone to a pure realm. The object of refuge, the Venerable Bhagavati, melts into light, in essence the ambrosia of immortality, and dissolves into you. Imagine that the blessings of her three secrets enter you. The nature of your mind has always been free from arising and ceasing, it is the primordially deathless, natural state. This is the true nature of the Sublime Lady's three secrets, and to maintain it is the absolute refuge of the way things abide.

b) Generating the Mind Set upon Supreme Awakening

Just as space is boundless in measure, there is no limit to the number of sentient beings. Each of these limitless beings moreover has been our own father and mother more times than could be measured even with the particles of the earth. Each time they were our father or mother, they helped us in infinite ways and protected us from incalculable harm. Although they showed us nothing but incredible kindness, their ignorance regarding the law of cause and effect means that their actions conflict with their deepest desires. Think to yourself, "I possess the necessary cause, a human body complete with the freedoms and advantages as well as the necessary condition of having met a spiritual friend. As this has nothing to do with my own proverbial 'masculine cunning' or 'feminine guile', there could be no greater shame than to fail to free these beings, my very own parents, from the cage of their suffering. Thus, I shall do all that I can within this lifetime to liberate myself and all other beings from the ocean of existence. To this end I shall exert myself in the stages of the path of the Great Vehicle and especially the Vajrayana which brings liberation in a single lifetime and is so rarely encountered throughout the past, present and future and specifically the quintessence of the infinite Mother Tantras of Unsurpassable Yoga, the practice of the Sublime Lady." With such a motivation, recite the following,

Ho! Sentient beings are as countless as space is vast . . .

Begin by meditating on your mother from this life and training your mind. The way to train the mind is to generate love and compassion time and again. Until you are able to take your mother's suffering upon yourself, it is vitally important that you continue to train your mind. Then gradually extend the meditation to include more and more sentient beings until finally you are able to meditate on all sentient beings who are as limitless as space. Furthermore, it is crucial that your vow of aspirational bodhichitta remains extremely stable and that you conduct yourself according to the six transcendent perfections, the precepts of bodhichitta in action. When generating the mind set upon awakening, imagine that you receive it from your guru—visualized as the object of refuge—who acts as witness.

Ordinarily you would not dissolve the objects of refuge right away, but first generate the mind set upon awakening and only then dissolve the field of refuge. Alternatively, you could visualize rays of light emanating from the body of your guru who is in the form of the Sublime Lady. If you are feeling dull, consider that these rays dissolve at the point between your eyebrows. If you are feeling agitated, consider that they dissolve at your navel. When your mind is balanced, consider that they dissolve into your heart. Then focus on the brilliant white essence in your head, at your navel or at your heart and practise calm abiding.

Within that state, consider how all thoughts that grasp outwardly or cling inwardly are insubstantial, do not leave any trace behind and are like an illusion or a dream. They lack true existence and transcend the extremes of singularity and plurality. To see them vividly as the great union of clarity and emptiness is to see reality itself. Settle for as long as you can in this meditative absorption of calm abiding and clear seeing. By meditating on intense clarity in short sessions many times over, the duration of your sessions will gradually increase. This will happen automatically as the practice becomes more familiar. This advice comes from the pith instructions of *The Profound Essence of Tara*.[39]

c) Purifying the Unfavourable Circumstances of Negative Actions and Obscurations

Although the visualization and recitation of Vajrasattva as a means of purifying negative actions and obscurations is not included here, it may still be added based on other sources.

Sentient beings are utterly pure by nature, but they do not recognize this and wander in samsara as a result. The principal obscurations that are brought about due to ignorance conceal reality but do not taint their basic nature and are only adventitious, which is why they may be purified. There are countless methods of purification, but the greatest form of activity among the skilful methods of Vajrayana is to practise the yoga of the guru as Vajrasattva. This constitutes the *power of support*. Feeling intense regret and remorse for negative actions committed in the past constitutes the *power of repentance*. Purification through the flow of ambrosia and recitation of mantra constitutes the *antidotal power*. Resolving never to succumb to negative actions again in the future even at the cost of one's life constitutes the *power of resolve*. When these four powers are complete, all natural and proscribed misdeeds and downfalls will be purified.

Here you may recite any appropriate text from a treasure revelation of similar type or use the root text of *The Heart of Blessings: A Practice of the Guru (Vima Ladrup)*,[40] which is a branch of this very practice. Visualize Vajrasattva about one handspan above your head. Consider that a stream of white ambrosia flows from the mantra garland at Guru Vajrasattva's heart

and enters your Brahma aperture. It washes away all disease which is expelled in the form of black blood, all demons which take the form of insects
and other creatures and all negative actions and obscurations which take the
form of black smoke. They emerge from your sense organs and all the pores
of your body which is left cleansed and clear like a sphere of crystal. The
flow of ambrosia fills you completely and makes you entirely white. Consider that through this, the blessings of Guru Vajrasattva's three secrets infuse
your being. Recite the hundred-syllable mantra as many times as you can.
At the end through your confessions and pledges, Guru Vajrasattva confirms
that all your negative actions and obscurations have been purified. He melts
into light and dissolves into you through which you sustain an experience
of natural awareness, clarity and emptiness free from grasping which is the
true face of the Vajrasattva of definitive meaning.

d) Gathering the Accumulations & e) Guru Yoga

Here we combine the practices of gathering the accumulations and guru yoga,
showing how they can be practised as a unity. For the outer practice of this
dharma cycle, it is crucially important that the practices of gathering the accumulations and the guru yoga recitation follow the *Secret Path to Immortality,
A Guru Yoga Based on the Three Deities of Longevity*[41] composed by the Omniscient Guru, Khyentse Wangpo himself, either in an elaborate or concise way.
Were I to explain this elaborately, I fear it would become too long-winded, so
I shall state only a few crucial points related to the guru yoga.

In general, the Tibetan word "lama" refers to what is unsurpassed. The
Sanskrit word "guru" which means heavy suggests being heavily laden with
qualities. In reality our guru, the glorious protector, is certainly none other
than the Buddha himself. The guru might display pure or impure appearances, but as is evident from the biographies of the accomplished adepts of
the past, the deeds of the buddhas and bodhisattvas cannot be judged based
on ordinary concepts of good or bad. Impure perception is similar to a bile
disorder which causes a white conch to appear yellow, it is our own impure
mind that is at fault. If our mind is impure, we will perceive even the likes
of Buddha Shakyamuni as flawed. Therefore, any perceived faults do not belong to the guru but only reflect our own shortcomings. We must consider

how the guru is equal to the buddhas in terms of qualities but greater than the Buddha in the matter of kindness. We must reflect again and again on this exceptional kindness. We cannot recall gifts and rewards that the guru lavished upon us or words of praise and encouragement, but it is most important to consider repeatedly the kindness of bestowing the highest benefit and happiness—both temporary and ultimate. This is a crucial point. How is this bestowed? By pointing out the co-emergent wisdom of naturally arisen awareness.

The guru who points this out is one's root guru. The deep connection that exists between you and this guru is based on the following. In general, we are connected because all sentient beings are one within the all-pervading space of reality, and there is therefore no one with whom we are unconnected. More specifically in the past when the precious guru was training in bodhisattva conduct on the path of learning, we took on a form such as that of a tiny insect and were touched by the guru's shadow or else we overheard a fragment of the guru's speech or were struck by a glimmering ray of the guru's wisdom intent. Whichever the case from the moment this connection was first forged—whether directly or indirectly, good or bad—the teacher became what is known as "a guru connected through past lifetimes". Moreover, just as all appearances are but our own perception, the guru too arises through the pure perception within our own mind. The guru does not exist outside us, ultimately it is our own awareness that is the true guru. The expressive power of the appearance quality of this awareness manifests externally according to one's mental capacity as the guru's form body (*rupakaya*). This also accounts for how the appearances of samsara arise to someone whose mind is disturbed by habitual tendencies and how the experience of nirvana arises due to the gradual purification of delusion and the appearance quality of the wisdom of great equalness in which the two truths are indivisible. The arising of one's own mind as the guru is thus an especially crucial point.

With this understanding, follow the points of meditation provided in the recitation text. Purify all phenomena into emptiness with the mantra and generate therefrom the pure realm of great bliss, in the centre of which in the sky before you your guru arises in naturally abiding form as the essence of the three deities of immortal life. As a concise method of gathering the accumulations, perform the visualization of the seven branches in the usual way. You could also gather the accumulations by offering the mandala a hundred thousand times. Perform the recitation of invoking the guru's sacred pledge and wisdom mind. Gather and dissolve the vital elixir of longevity and consider that the ambrosia of longevity gradually fills you beginning at the point between your eyebrows, thereby conferring the four empowerments. Repeat this visualization again and again. The guru melts into light and dissolves into you, and you sustain an experience of wisdom intent in which mind and wisdom blended as one.

II. THE MAIN PART: THE EXPLANATION OF THE DEITY

This has three parts: A. the explanation of enlightened body: the kyerim phase of the mudra, B. the explanation of enlightened speech: the mantra recitation which is an aspect of kyerim and C. the explanation of enlightened mind: concise instructions on the suchness of the dzogrim phase.

A. The Explanation of Enlightened Body: The Kyerim Phase of the Mudra

This has three parts: 1. expelling obstructive forces and visualizing the protective sphere, 2. blessing the offering substances and 3. the actual meditation on the deity.

1. Expelling Obstructive Forces and Visualizing the Protective Sphere

HUNG is the syllable of non-duality beyond grasping, the life force of the infinite bliss-gone ones—peaceful and wrathful—and the awareness of the mudra.[42] As you utter it, you transform into the deity of the genuine nature, Lotus Heruka (Hayagriva). His body is red and his two hands hold a lotus and a bell. His form is wrathful and fierce and he is adorned with the wrathful accoutrements. Imagine that HUNG syllables shoot out from his nostrils. They obliterate everything in the ten directions and emit sparks of fire which incinerate and destroy all obstructive forces. To subjugate thoughts associated with the three poisons and the demons and obstructive forces that they engender, melodiously recite three HUNGS, the natural expression of the three kayas. Obstructive forces are thereby expelled.

As the HUNG syllables return, visualize the vajra sphere of protection while reciting the mantra. Consider that the sphere's vajra foundation is formed of tiny vajras without any spaces between them sealed with molten metal. The vajra fence is formed of horizontal and vertical vajras, and within it is the vajra tent shaped like a helmet. At its single peak is the top of a half-vajra. Within the space of the fence and tent descends the vajra canopy. On the outside, the fence and tent are covered by a net of tiny interwoven vajras, in the middle it is bound together with a chain of vajras. A ring of fire resembling the burning coals of a smith blazes out limitlessly in all directions with such strength that it is impervious to water from within or apocalyptic gales from without. This exceedingly robust, formidable protection is utterly impenetrable to demons and obstructive forces alike. On an ultimate level, to settle into the vast expanse of naturally arisen awareness—which has never been tainted by the elaborations of self-centred thoughts and ideas—is the absolute protection sphere.

2. Blessing the Offering Substances

Arrange outer and inner offerings if you have them. If not—by understanding how all appearance and existence are the mudra of offering—imagine that everything is purified into emptiness with OM, multiplied with AH and transformed with HUNG into outer, inner and secret offering substances. Bless the offerings by reciting the mantra three times, together with the Sky Treasury mudra.

Taking refuge has as its objects of purification—your own and all other beings' adoption of false paths, your failure to secure the protection of the Three Jewels and your espousal of false views, throughout beginningless time. The means of purification is to take refuge authentically. The result of purification is to actualise enlightenment endowed with the three kayas. Generating the mind set upon enlightenment has as its objects of purification—the fact that you have entered the lesser vehicle, selfish concerns, anger towards others and so on. They are purified by this very means of purification (generating bodhichitta). The result of purification is uninterrupted enlightened activity based on great, non-referential compassion.

Expelling negative forces and visualizing the protection sphere have as their objects of purification all deluded thoughts that obscure the natural state, as well as the guardians of the directions and the male and female haughty spirits that they engender, who are gathered and overpowered. In particular, those who have not entered the Secret Mantra Vehicle and those who have entered it but have fallen into mistaken view and behaviour are eliminated here. The practice itself brings about the purification, and the result of such purification is the destruction of the maras when awakening is attained.

Blessing the offerings has as its objects of purification—the perception of the world and its inhabitants as ordinary and the impulsive consumption of sensory pleasures. Purification is achieved through the blessing of the offerings, and the result of such purification is to experience the infinite display of primordial wisdom upon attainment of awakening.

Generally speaking there are what are known as the four doors of Secret Mantra: 1) the door of words as a reminder of the ultimate meaning, 2) the door of secret mantra as an invocation of the wisdom mind, 3) the door of meditative concentration for single-pointed focus and 4) the door of the display of the mandala forms showing the symbols laden with meaning. As this suggests your meditation needs to follow the words of the text that you recite. This is crucially important at every stage above and below.

3. The Actual Meditation on the Deity

This has three parts: a) visualizing the samaya deity, b) inviting and dissolving the wisdom deity and c) focusing the mind on a clear appearance of the deity's form.

a) Visualizing the Samaya Deity

This has two parts: (i) establishing the framework through the three samadhis and (ii) generating the result, the palace and deities of the mandala.

(i) Establishing the Framework through the
Three Samadhis

Recite the mantra OM MAHA SHUNYATA . . . while settling in its meaning which is that all phenomena included within dualistic perception are completely purified into great nondual wisdom whose nature is indestructible.

The text to be recited may be explained as follows. The line that begins, "All things in samsara and nirvana . . ." refers to the samadhi of suchness. All these phenomena that are visible and audible to us and to others have always been utterly pure and naturally luminous. They are none other than the great emptiness of the indestructible, all-pervading space of suchness. Rest for a long time in that space-like experience devoid of appearance. This serves to cleanse and *purify* the bardo of death. By planting the seed of actualising the dharmakaya, you create the interdependent circumstances for the result to be *perfected*. This *ripens* you and lays the foundation for the luminosity of the higher path of the completion phase to arise in your mind. When it is said that purifying the bardo of death is the dharmakaya, this shows the connection between ground and fruition and how we should cultivate confidence in that relationship, which we should maintain throughout the following sections of the practice.

The second line refers to the samadhi of universal manifestation. As you rest in the samadhi of suchness, from that experience of great, all-pervading space beyond conceptual elaboration, you feel an illusion-like great compassion free of grasping towards the illusory objects, all beings who lack such realization and who appear while being devoid of true existence. Through the power of the pervasive unity of these two,* you develop the thought, "I shall lead them to the level of supreme awakening!" This purifies the intermediate state (*bardo*) and creates the interdependent circumstances for perfecting the result of the sambhogakaya. It lays the foundation for great compassion, the cause of arising out of clear light as a deity of union.

The third line refers to the causal samadhi. Awareness arises instantly in space as the cause, a white syllable TAM shining like a crystal. It emanates

---

* "Two" here could be understood as the two samadhis of suchness and universal manifestation, or as the subject, great compassion, and the object, illusory beings.

five-coloured light rays in every direction, without boundary or limit, as if
a rainbow had arisen in a pristine sky. They purify all grasping at the world
and its inhabitants as ordinary and create a vast, expansive sphere of protection like the one visualized earlier. This purifies all unfavourable conditions
and obstacles concerning the place of birth in the next life, creates the interdependent circumstances for overcoming the four maras at the time of
fruition and lays the foundation for eliminating any obstacles or potential
pitfalls in the practice of the channels, wind-energies and essences during
the completion phase.

(ii) Generating the Result, the Palace and Deities of the Mandala

Rays of light radiate from TAM, the cause of the protective sphere, and transform into the mandalas of space, wind, fire, water and earth, together with
Mount Meru, into their utterly pure essences in the vast expanses of Dhat-
vishvari, Samayatara, Pandaravasini, Mamaki and Buddhalochana. Upon
Mount Meru is an expansive ground, smooth and level, formed of vajra
dust. In its centre is a blossoming lotus flower made of jewels, multicoloured
and with a hundred thousand petals, at the heart of which is a sun mandala
as wide as the flower itself. In its centre is a twelve-pronged crossed vajra
with white prongs in the east, yellow ones in the south, red ones in the
west, green ones in the north and blue in the middle. Visualize the palace at
their centre. This purifies the foundation of the outer world formed on the
basis of the five elements and Mount Meru, for any location of birth as a
sentient being. It creates the interdependent circumstance for the result and
perfection within the dharmadhatu space of the five mothers, the realm in
which all buddhas awaken. It lays the foundation for the completion phase
when the five elements and Mount Meru, which are the five chakras and
the central channel, and the lotus, the sun and the crossed vajra, which are
the chakras of channels, the wind-energies and essences, are all made pliant
and workable.

At the hub of the crossed vajra is the palace of great liberation immeasurable in extent made of precious jewels and white crystal. It is square and
has four doors, one on each of its four sides. Each door has eight causal and
resultant toranas.[43] The eight-level resultant toranas consist of a basal frieze

with vajras upright, a frieze with a lotus-motif, a frieze with box-motif bev-
elling, white pearl pendant ornaments, a jewelled frieze, tassels and garlands,
sharbu ornaments and a roofed canopy. The eight-level causal toranas are
said to be in eight tiers on the outside of the doors much like a staircase.
The palace is further adorned with the terraces of sense pleasure, the gold-
en brick frieze, chains and hanging chains, *sharbu* ornaments, pagoda roof
and so on. In its centre the summit made of stacked elements is topped
with a vajra made of precious material. The palace radiates rays of light
everywhere and has no distinction between interior and exterior. Nothing
is obstructing. The sixteen offering goddesses dance on the red terraces of
sense pleasure and hold offering substances aloft. Immediately inside the
vajra fence, visualize that the perimeter of worldly deities, the guardians of
all that is good, such as the seventy-five glorious protectors, abide. This is
what the great lord guru who revealed this treasure himself said.[44] Visualize
in the centre of this perfectly constituted palace a white, four-petalled lotus
upon which a sun disc below and a moon disc above symbolize the red and
white essences.

The palace purifies all forms of residence in which beings might live or
move about. The lotus, sun and moon purify the semen and blood in the
mother's womb for womb and egg birth and the other two types of birth,
the birth from warmth and moisture and miraculous birth. They also purify
the habitual tendencies that cause attachment and clinging to environment
and body. This creates the interdependent circumstances for actualising the
great palace as a natural manifestation of primordial wisdom at the time
of the result. During completion phase practice the palace represents the
qualities of clarity, emptiness and bliss within a mind in which the channels,
essences and wind-energies have merged as one. The lotus seat represents the
chakra of channels at the crown of the head, the sun the chakra of channels
at the navel and red essence below, and the moon represents the chakra of
channels at the crown and white essence above. This lays the foundation for
the state of union of all aspects of the kayas and wisdoms of the supremely
immutable, great bliss in which the sixteen aspects of the four joys rise and
descend through the blazing and dripping of the blissful fire of tummo.

The generation of the supported, the deities, is as follows. In the space
between the united sun and moon is the causal syllable TAM. Moon, sun and

seed syllable conjoin, merging as one, within the essence of great bliss out of which rays of light shoot out and fill the sky, making offerings to the noble ones, waking the shravakas from cessation and bringing those on the path to the level of no more learning. The rays of light combine with the blessings of the victorious ones and their heirs throughout the ten directions, and the vital essence of samsara and nirvana and all the splendour of existence and peace gather together and dissolve into the mass of light rays which transforms instantly into the completely perfect form of the deity. This purifies the coming together of the white and red essences in the womb and the entrance of a consciousness from the intermediate state, as well as the combination of blood, semen and consciousness following the experience of transformation based on a potential father and mother's sexual intercourse. The radiation and reabsorption of light rays purify the gradual development of the body in the womb which comes about through the potential of the four primary elements and the ten winds which produce the aggregates, elements and sense sources. The full manifestation of the deity's form purifies the development of the foetus within the womb and its eventual birth. It also creates interdependent circumstances for the time of the result for buddhas to take on whatever forms are appropriate for beings to be trained and for displaying the deeds such as taking birth from a womb.

When practising dzogrim the significance of the union of the sun and moon is as mentioned before; or else, it signifies the union of bliss and warmth at the site of knots in the chakras within the central channel. The seed syllable represents wind-energy and mind entering the central channel and dissolving there. The radiation and reabsorption of light rays represents the bliss-emptiness that arises from melting bliss. The full manifestation of the deity's form lays the foundation for attaining the supreme wisdom kaya—the inseparable union of natural, co-emergent bliss and emptiness.

In essence Tara is the mother who gives birth to the four types of noble ones,[45] the Lady of the Transcendent Perfection of Wisdom (*prajnaparamita*), wisdom endowed with all qualities arising as an illusory, magical manifestation. She is the supreme mother who gives birth to all the victorious ones of the three times, the embodiment of enlightened activity and the sublime and noble lady, Wish-Fulfilling Wheel. Her body is white and luminous, the colour of the moon or crystal and immaculate. She has one face and two hands. Her hands are extremely supple, straight and soft like the *palasha* tree. Her right hand makes the gesture of supreme generosity. Her left hand, held at her left breast, is in the mudra of granting refuge and between her thumb and ring finger she holds the stem—supple, delicate and fresh—of a white utpala flower which blossoms at the level of her ear. The flower is mid-bloom and supports a long-life vase made of crystal and adorned with the fruits of a wish-fulfilling tree. To the right is a fruit-bearing flower, and to the left a flower that is closed.

She is peaceful and smiling and astonishingly beautiful. Her body is lithe and supple. Her waist is slender and her breasts prominent and attractive. Her secret lotus is not visible. Half of her hair is bound up in a topknot adorned with a jewel at its crest, the rest hangs loosely behind both ears. The hair is pitch black, the colour of a bee. Her eyes are wide and beautiful with high brows. Her nose and lips are unblemished and attractive. She is seated upright with a slender waist, and her legs crossed in vajra posture. She wears a silken lower garment of various colours which hangs like a warrior's bow, a blue-coloured sash, a lower garment of red silk, an upper garment of dark-blue silk, a crown featuring the crests of jewels, earrings studded with various gems, a choker, armlets, bracelets and anklets, a belt, a necklace that extends to her breasts and a necklace that extends to her navel. She has eyes on the soles of her feet and the palms of her hands, and her face has eyes to the right and left and in the centre—seven eyes which contribute to her dazzling beauty.

Her male consort, Lotus Lord of the Dance, is born of her own radiance. Since he is the appearing aspect of skilful means, his body is white with a tinge of red and he is filled with passion. He has a peaceful, smiling expression. His right hand holds a red lotus and his left hand a vase of longevity. He is beautifully adorned with silken garments and jewelled ornaments. Seated in cross-legged lotus posture he embraces the main deity. They are united in the great bliss and emptiness of the union of means and wisdom, and they abide in an expanse of boundless wisdom light.

At Tara's head upon a moon-disc seat, visualize a white syllable OM; at her throat upon a red eight-petalled lotus, a red syllable AH; and at her heart upon a sun-disc seat, a blue syllable HUNG. These syllables have the nature of Vairochana, Amitabha and Akshobhya respectively.

b) Inviting the Wisdom Mandala

Consider that rays of light like hooks and with all the brilliant radiance of a billion suns radiate from the three seed syllables at your three places and invite the mandala of wisdom deities. Invite them, draw them in, bind them and delight them with DZA HUNG BAM HO. In this way request the wisdom deities to remain steadfastly and joyfully.

You may also pay homage, make offerings and offer praise in the following concise manner: First, chant AH LA LA HO to express wonder and amazement at the qualities of the principal goddess' body, speech and mind. Then offer symbolic homage in the awareness that the deities—the indivisible union of samayasattvas and jnanasattvas—are the powerful radiance of the genuine nature of your own mind. Goddesses who emanate from your heart hold aloft the regular outer offerings and the inner offerings of the five sensory delights. They present the secret offerings: billowing clouds of amrita emanating further offering goddesses, rakta produced by the liberation of all malevolent beings throughout the three realms with red goddesses emerging from strings of bubbles on the surface, and the great torma made of samaya substances, the whole outer world which further emanates boundless sensory delights. Your undefiled sense faculties revel in delight, as the goddesses dissolve into the deities. Satisfied by the taste of wisdom in which subject and object are indivisible, you complete the great accumulations. Simply put, the offering of suchness refers to the fact that the offerings, those who offer them and their recipients are none other than the all-pervading space that has always been utterly pure. The vajra goddesses who emanate from you extol the qualities of the principal goddess, perform the dance of bliss and offer praise with sweet-sounding songs. At the end the goddesses dissolve into you.

c) Focusing the Mind on a Clear Appearance of the Deity's Form

Focus your mind on the general form of the deity—the great mudra—in which samayasattvas and jnanasattvas are indivisible. You are the principal goddess in union with her consort with their bodies, faces and arms all complete—empty in essence, blissful in nature, yet clearly apparent. The deities are the union of appearance and emptiness, appearing without obstruction in the form of light that has the essence of wisdom like the moon's reflection in clear water. Bring this vividly to mind.

If the appearance is unclear, direct your mental and visual focus single-pointedly to a painted image of the samaya deity. Consider that your own body instantly adopts such features. By meditating repeatedly in short sessions many times, your visualization will last longer and become progressively clearer. But your visualization should not be flat like a painted image or concrete like a statue. Train carefully and consistently in recognizing the inseparability of the deity as the essence of dharmakaya, form of sambhogakaya and expressive display of nirmanakaya and your own sense of identity. This unites kyerim and dzogrim.

Mental focus such as this is vitally important in and of itself. When you hear the name of someone you have met before for example, you can instantly recall the person's physique and facial appearance. We must recall the form of the deity in a similar way. One key is to meditate on occasions when the wind-energies and mind are clear such as at night. Then after visualizing the deity as a whole, focus on particular features such as her central eye or the tip of the jewel at her crown, down to her seats, the lotus and moon disc. Visualize her form without ornaments, then with them. Focus your mind on these individual aspects until each appears clearly. Then focus your mind with unwavering clarity on all aspects simultaneously.

No matter what your focus might be, direct your mind one-pointedly in a balanced way, neither too tightly nor too loosely. Allow your mind to relax completely. If you lose your hold on the clear appearance, alert yourself; if the visualization becomes unclear because of the thoughts raging in your mind, then relax. Should your thoughts become extremely disruptive, then stop and turn instead to reciting the mantra and so on. This is how you should eliminate the flaws of dullness and agitation as you visualize. On occasion consider how your body, speech and mind have never been ordinary and how you are in fact the Blessed Lady of the fruition with all faults exhausted and all qualities perfected. By intensifying the deity's clear appearance in this way and focusing your mind on the notion that this represents the deity in actuality, as your familiarity increases you will develop a continuous sense of actually being the deity.

Remembering the purity: the features of a deity's form are not like those of a coarse, ordinary body brought about through the force of karma and destructive emotions. Rather the qualities of the three secrets of the deities who have reached the ultimate fruition take on symbolic forms that hold significance in the perception of those to be tamed.

The natural state of the ground which has always been utterly pure by nature is indivisible from the resultant kayas and wisdoms. To maintain the life force of the practice by focusing on nothing other than the outward expression of this nature at the time of the path is the "purity of one's own awareness". Through the blessing of this, appearance and existence arise as the mandala of deities which is the "purity of phenomena as individual deities". To apply the seal of the view that is inexpressible and beyond arising, remaining and ceasing, and meditate on the union of appearance and emptiness is the "purity of the suchness nature of phenomena". Practise by combining these three forms of purity with clear appearance and remembering the pride of being the deity.

Since all phenomena are of one taste within suchness, Tara has a single face. Her two hands represent skilful means and wisdom, and her cross-legged vajra posture signifies the elimination of the extremes of existence and quiescence. The union of male and female deities represents appearance and emptiness. As a sign that she was born from the tears of the Lord of the World as part of the lotus family that is free of attachment and that she is overflowing with compassion, her body has the colour of the lustrous moon. As a signal of her love for beings, she smiles serenely and has an amorous demeanour. Her right hand is in the mudra of supreme generosity as a sign that she bestows the attainments of longevity and wisdom. To signify that she grants beings protection from fear and that the secret of her wisdom mind—profound, peaceful and beyond conceptual elaboration—is the Lady of the Transcendent Perfection of Wisdom, the mother of all the victorious ones, her left hand is in the mudra of granting refuge. To symbolize her unobstructed enlightened activity, she holds the stem of a white utpala at her heart. The flower which blossoms at the level of her ear supports a long-life vase to signify overcoming fear of untimely death.

As a sign of her perfection of virtuous qualities and care for others, some of her hair is bound in a topknot while the remainder hangs loose. To signify her freedom from the torment of negative emotions, she wears silken upper and lower garments. Her silk and jewel accessories signify the seven factors of enlightenment and how she has not abandoned sensory delights but enjoys them as adornments. She is embraced by the male consort, Lotus Lord of the Dance, who is her very own radiance and represents skilful means, supremely immutable great bliss and wisdom's aspect of appearance. The palace has the nature of the symbols, meaning and correspondence of the thirty-seven factors of enlightenment. The vajra fence is impervious to conceptual thought. The surrounding mass of flames signifies that habitual tendencies of conceptual thought have been overcome.

Thus, the recollection of such individual examples of purity serves to counteract any clinging to these features as ordinary. Training in this recollection of purity which connects ground and fruition serves as an immediate cause for the supreme accomplishment of kyerim. In this way you must visualize everything to its fullest extent with clarity, stability and purity in stages from the palace, vajra fence and mountains of flame on the outside through to the principal deity within.

Meditating on the phase of generating the deity in this manner purifies the following: at the ground stage being born as a child, growing up, being tormented by feelings of desire and seeking to fulfill them, taking a spouse, gradually developing one's physical, verbal and mental capacity and taking on the affairs of one's family. The result of purification is to be born as a nirmanakaya buddha, to renounce the world and practise asceticism in pursuit of awakening, to arrive at the seat of awakening (*bodhimanda*), tame Mara, develop meditative concentration and gain mastery of omniscient wisdom. In relation to the higher paths this lays the foundation for arising in the deity's form based on bliss, wind-energy and mind in order to accomplish the body of the wisdom deity of bliss and emptiness. It also lays the foundation for remaining inseparable from either a karma or wisdom mudra in order to attain the supreme accomplishment. It is thus the basis for gaining ever-greater familiarity with naturally arising wakefulness and thereby swiftly arriving at the supreme accomplishment. In this way the meditation serves as a means of ripening.

The blessing of the three places purifies your ordinary body, speech and mind. The means of purification are the three vajras. The result of purification is the attainment of the three secrets of all the buddhas.

The invitation of the wisdom deities and request that they remain have as their objects of purification the habitual tendencies of children to develop like the other beings of the category in which they are born and to acquire a similar level of intelligence. The means of purification is the absorption of the natural mandala of wisdom deities into the mandala of samayasattvas. The result of purification is to merge as one with the realization of all the Thus-Gone Ones.

The stages of activities such as paying homage have as their objects of purification the habitual tendencies of childish beings who indulge in sensory pleasures and pursue mundane concerns. The means of purification are to pay homage in recognition of the indivisibility of all-pervading space and wisdom, to make outer, inner and secret offerings and to offer praise while remembering the qualities of the three secrets. The result of such purification is to create the interdependent circumstances for the effortless arising of infinite offerings at the time of buddhahood and for becoming worthy of the reverence of all throughout samsara and nirvana.

This is in harmony with the following lines from the *Profound Essence of Tara,*

> Generate the mandala of support and supported.
> With clear appearance, stable pride
> And recollection of purity, cultivate a clear appearance.
> By reaching the limit of utmost clarity,
> Which has the ability to halt clinging to appearances as
>   ordinary, . . .[46]

B. The Explanation of Enlightened Speech: The Mantra Recitation

When you become tired of meditating in such a way, you need to train in meditative concentration on the mantra recitation in order to enhance your practice. As the section on the visualization for mantra recitation states,

> I am the sublime Tara: in my heart,
> Is the jnanasattva Amitayus.
> Brilliant white . . .

In the centre of Tara's heart is a white, four-petalled lotus. On its anther is a locket of the conjoined sun below and moon on top, in the centre of which is a white TAM, bright and radiant and surrounded by the ten-syllable mantra, the combined mantra, the mantra of the jnanasattva Amitayus and the mantra of the nirmanasattva Ushnisha Vijaya. They are all joined together and arranged in a clockwise direction. Focus your mind on them, and as you do so consider that limitless rays of light stream out from the life force at the deity's heart and the mantra garland. They emerge from the top of her crown and send out many forms of the Noble Lady Ushnisha Vijaya who is white and has one face and two hands. The right hand which is in the gesture of granting refuge and resting on her right knee forms the threatening mudra and holds an iron hook as a means of summoning; the left hand which is at the level of her heart and in the gesture of supreme generosity holds a long-life vase from which there flows a stream of ambrosia. She is seated in the cross-legged posture of a female bodhisattva. Her forms are as numerous as specks of dust in a sunbeam. They gather the wisdom of knowledge, love and power from the infinite victorious ones of the Three Roots, vajra dharma protectors and wealth deities as well as the vital essence of the inanimate world and animate beings throughout samsara and nirvana in the form of ambrosia, light rays and refined quicksilver. They dissolve into the subtle essences of one's own body, speech and mind, bringing the attainment of longevity and wisdom and the accomplishment of the vital force of vajra-like immortality. Consider all this as you recite the mantra.

The quicksilver that accomplishes all is the substance of alchemy and rejuvenation (*chulen*). It is white like the autumn moon and radiates rays of light like the sun. It swirls clockwise and forms various patterns of auspicious signs of accomplishment such as svastikas and coils of joy. Its power is such that whoever it touches gains the strength of an elephant, the longevity of the sun and moon and a vajra body. It has the power to grant the youthfulness and vigour of a sixteen-year-old. It can transform iron into gold at the merest touch. Scattering it over a dried-up tree will cause it to sprout new leaves, fruits and flowers instantaneously. Jamyang Khyentse Wangpo said that you should meditate on such forms blazing with the splendour of great bliss.

In general regarding the turning of the mantra garland, it is said that the approach phase emphasizes the arrangement, close approach emphasizes rotation, accomplishment emphasizes the palanquin and great accomplishment emphasizes the radiation and absorption of light rays. Ordinarily, however, it suffices to focus only on the arrangement. Then once you manage to visualize the arrangement clearly, you can begin to imagine its rotation. At that time consider that countless rays of light stream out in the manner explained above from the mantra garland which rotates rapidly clockwise[47] as it emits its own sound. For the recitation those who have not yet undertaken a retreat on the approach phase should emphasize the ten-syllable mantra, while those who have done so should focus mainly on the combined mantra. Recite a few mantras of the jnanasattva and the nirmanasattva as well.

This daily practice brings the three aspects of approach, accomplishment and activity together. On occasion therefore consider that rays of light stream out from the mantra garland ablaze with the splendour of the wisdom of great bliss, so that all that is animate and inanimate throughout the three realms is perfected as the mandala of the great illusory net—deities, mantra and wisdom. Or consider that the mantra garland arises uninterruptedly from the life-force syllable TAM and passes through the mouth of the wisdom deity and into the mouth of the principal goddess. It enters the mouth of the male consort, passes through his body and flows from his secret vajra into the female deity's secret space before dissolving into the life-force syllable. By turning like a whirling firebrand in this way, it engenders the wisdom of great bliss in the enlightened minds of the male and female deities. Consider that you attain the naturally arising, permanent and sacred accomplishment of supreme, unchanging deathlessness and recite the combined mantra. That is the visualization for accomplishment. Or as you recite the combined mantra consider that rays of light in colours that correspond to the four types of activity shoot out from her heart, fill the sky like messengers and carry out all forms of supreme enlightened action—pacifying, enriching, magnetising and subjugating—according to your wishes.

Do not interrupt the recitation with ordinary words or speech. You must recite the mantras with stable, single-pointed concentration. Should you grow tired of focusing on a single visualization, settle the mind for a time on the clear appearance of the deities' form. Or spend time generating compassion for those beings whose accumulated karma results in a short life. At times recite the mantra with a clear, stable perception of all sights and sounds as the venerable Tara. Most importantly it is by reciting the mantra while sustaining an experience of the view with faith and devotion devoid of doubt in the awareness of the inseparability of deity and mantra that you will swiftly accomplish the supreme and common attainments. No matter how much you might recite with a mind that is distracted, you will only succeed in slightly reducing your obscurations of speech and will not accomplish your desired aim. As the great guru of Oddiyana said,

> Recite with undistracted concentration.
> Otherwise, should you become distracted,
> Even reciting for an aeon will yield no result.

The counting mala should be authentic and consecrated. The *Magnificent Lightning Tantra* says,

> Neither too loud nor too soft,
> Neither too fast nor too slow,
> Neither too strong nor too weak,
> Not omitting any of the syllables,
> Not distracted nor while talking,
> Not interrupted by chatter or the like.

Avoid such faults as you recite the mantra. At times hold your breath and perform the silent recitation while remembering the mantra's form and sound, or practise the mental recitation in which you let go even of holding the breath and focus on the mantra's form or sound as you recite it in your mind.

The object of purification here is clinging to deluded language, the verbal utterances of names, words and syllables within the impure samsaric domain, together with associated habitual tendencies. The means of purification is verbal recitation performed repeatedly. Once such recitation has purified the verbal process and the sounds that are produced, the result of purification is to lay the foundation for acts that will benefit beings through vajra speech such as by turning the wheel of dharma, once you yourself have attained enlightenment. This also purifies general faults, especially those of the mind, and brings about the power of speech. As you call upon the wisdom deities repeatedly by name using mantras, it is inevitable that you will become close to them. Given that the deities take the form of these mantras, you should meditate on their seed syllables and perform the recitation with the confidence that they are mantras of wisdom awareness. As a result, they will definitely take the form of mantras, and the connection cannot but be established. In the shorter term you will accomplish the four types of activity—especially the increase of longevity, merit and wisdom—and ultimately this will serve as the uncommon, direct cause for obtaining vajra speech.

At the end of your session, make up for any additions or omissions and stabilize the effects of practice by reciting the vowels and consonants and the mantra of the essence of interdependent origination. Perform the offerings and praise in brief form and confess any mistakes with the hundred-syllable mantra. Consider that the appearances of the deities dissolve into the all-pervading space of luminosity like breath evaporating from the surface of a mirror. Or else imagine that rays of light shoot out from the heart of the principal deity and touch the whole world and its inhabitants, causing them to melt into light and dissolve into the palace. The palace then dissolves into the principal deities. The male consort dissolves into the female deity. She then gradually disappears beginning at her feet and head and dissolves into the TAM which disappears from the bottom upwards until all that remains is the *nada*—extremely subtle—on which you focus your mind. Then rest in the state of luminosity beyond reference.

Instantly arise once again in the body of union and recite the three syllables OM AH HUNG to seal your three doors as the three vajras. Remain inseparable from the "three carry-overs":[48] recognising yourself and all other appearances as the enlightened body of the Sublime Lady, all sound as her enlightened speech and all thought as her enlightened mind. Conclude by dedicating the merit and reciting whichever prayers of auspiciousness are appropriate. Then commence your daily activities.

The object of purification of the dissolution and re-arising as the deity is the death that reoccurs once youth is exhausted. The gradual dissolution of the supporting pure field and supported deities represents the phases of the outer and inner dissolution and dharmakaya luminosity at the time of death, while arising once more as the deity corresponds to the bardo of becoming. The means of purification are the stages of dissolution and re-emergence. As the result of purification since the appearance aspect of rupakaya—which is the activity of the dharmakaya—and dharmakaya wisdom are both by nature basic space, the rupakaya manifestations, which are absorbed into and emanate from this nature, will benefit beings uninterruptedly.

C. The Explanation of Enlightened Mind: Concise Instructions on the Suchness of Dzogrim

The dissolution of kyerim into luminosity and its re-emergence therefrom, as discussed above, eliminate the extremes of permanence and nihilism. This is when you practise the yoga of dzogrim without characteristics which may be briefly explained as follows. The *Profound Essence of Tara* says,

> Naturally arisen, momentary awareness
> Is brought within inconceivable basic space.
> From the illustrative wisdom of example
> The absolute co-emergent is made evident.
> And Vajra Tara, who possesses the three changeless
>   essences,
> Is accomplished in this life.[49]

As these vajra words suggest, the genuine nature of mind as such is not a real entity with concrete attributes and therefore not something permanent or autonomous. Nor is it non-existent since it provides an unceasing basis for the arising of the various experiences of samsara and nirvana. The fact that mere clarity and awareness does not cease means that it is not nothing whatsoever. It is also free from the extremes of both and neither, and thus transcends all forms of labelling, thought and expression. That is the *view*.

Taking the guru's pith instructions as a basis, do not think of anything and do not entertain any ideas. While experiencing the natural state, do not alter your mind with mental fabrication but simply leave it as it is. Do not be distracted from this space-like experience for even an instant.

Leave penetrating awareness in its natural condition and do not waver from an awareness that is without an object, naturally clear, vivid and distinct. That is the *meditation* that unites calm abiding (shamatha) and clear seeing (vipashyana).

Out of such a view and meditation, generate confidence during the post-meditation that all phenomena are illusory. Work for beings' welfare through the union of emptiness and compassion and let all your experience and activity serve as a support for the wisdom of co-emergent great bliss. That is the *conduct*.

Through becoming familiar with this training, you will actualise the natural state of the ground in which there is nothing to gain or lose and encounter the natural face of the ultimate venerable and noble lady, the transcendent perfection of wisdom. That is the *result*. First the illustrative wisdom arises during the paths of accumulation and joining. Then as this becomes increasingly familiar, you reach the path of seeing and realise the ultimate wisdom. Finally, you arrive at the level of no more learning.

You must strive to perfect this quartet of view, meditation, conduct and fruition.

As regards the definitive nature of kyerim and dzogrim, the later chapter of the *Guhyasamaja*[50] says,

> The dharma that the buddhas reveal
> Genuinely consists of two phases:
> There is the phase of kyerim
> And the phase of dzogrim.

As this says there is kyerim which purifies our grasping at the ordinary appearances of world and inhabitants, and dzogrim without characteristics which naturally and effortlessly binds wind-energy and mind within the indestructible essence, and brings about the kaya endowed with the supreme of all qualities. This concludes the explanation for now.

Among the countless profound ways of achieving immortality,
The one that stands as exalted as Meru is that of the Blessed One,
The Noble Lady Tara, known as Wish-Fulfilling Wheel,
A deity that vidyadharas in their millions have adored.

Her sadhana, which draws upon the experience and realization
Of three masters is the Noble Lady's Heart Essence,
Definitive and complete, the yoga of the single mudra,
Explained here in these stages of profound instruction.

My explanation draws on the omniscient guru's nectar-like words
And the teachings of scholars and adepts of the past.
Even though it is unspoilt by fabrications of my own,
If it is sullied by the stains of my own ignorance, forgive me!

Whatever stores of virtue might arise from this,
I dedicate entirely for the teachings and beings,
In keeping with Tara's aspirations and those of the lords of the three
families.
Through this, may I never experience the cause or result of untimely death!

Nourished by the food of practising the two phases,
May my body become as steadfast as a mighty vajra,
My speech blaze with the power of prophetic truth,
And all my thoughts arise as great luminosity!

May the lives of the glorious masters remain secure,
The dharma melody of their secret speech resound unceasingly,
And the mirrors of their wisdom minds of twofold knowledge remain
untainted,
And thus may they be of perfect service to the teachings and beings!

In all my lives, may I be guided by great spiritual friends
And may I receive the nectar of the dharma.
May I please my venerable gurus
And never tire of carrying out their enlightened activity!

May the teachings and holders of the teachings flourish and spread,
May patrons act according to the dharma and lead long, ever more
affluent lives.
And may I accomplish the three secrets of the Wish-Fulfilling Wheel,
She who is victorious over the enemy, the demon of the Lord of Death!

May the auspiciousness of an excellent stream of ambrosia
That bestows supreme immortality flow down into our crowns,
So that we obtain the splendour of immortal vajra life
And ascend to the kingdom of supreme accomplishment!

These instructions on the view of the Single Mudra, the daily practice from the Heart Essence of the Sublime Lady of Immortality were given by the lord and great treasure revealer, Lama Pema Ösal Dongak Lingpa, to our glorious master, the omniscient Situ Rinpoche, from whom I, Jamyang Lodrö Gyatso, received the transmission and explanation. I wrote this entirely on the third day of the twelfth month. May it be a cause for all beings to attain victory in the battle with the Lord of Death and for the lives of those supreme beings who are the holders of the teachings to remain firm and endure for hundreds of aeons! Mangalam!

CHAPTER 6:

A Drop of Moonlight Nectar,

Notes on How to Do the Approach and Accomplishment Practices of the Chimé Phakmé Nyingtik Mind Treasure

by Jamgön Kongtrul Lodrö Taye

Namo Guru Arya Taraya!
With unshakeable faith, I place Pema Ösel Dongak Lingpa,
Master of the seven transmissions,
One with the three immortal vidyadharas,
Upon the lotus at the centre of my heart.

INTRODUCTION

Jamyang Khyentse Wangpo, the great universal king of all learned and accomplished masters in the Land of Snow, received different treasures including mind treasures through all seven methods of transmission. The great Chimé Phakmé Nyingtik dharma cycle was one of his profound mind treasures. But he was only able to decipher and write down the root sadhana,[51] the sadhana cycle of the lama[52] and the practices of Amitayus and Ushnisha Vijaya. Here we are concerned with the root sadhana, *Uncovering Primordial Wisdom.*

Practitioners who wish to do the approach, accomplishment and activity of this practice need to have received the empowerment and reading transmissions and to abide by the samaya precepts. Then they should practise in the following way, following the three steps of practice:

I. The preliminaries: the stages of ritual preparation
II. The main part: approach, accomplishment and activity
III. The conclusion: receiving siddhis and so on

I. THE PRELIMINARIES: THE STAGES
OF RITUAL PREPARATION

On a good date—such as the eighth day of the waxing moon of the first month of a lunar trimester—in a practice place clean and pleasant, ornamented with decorations and with general supports of the Three Roots together with a statue or image of the principal deity of this practice, cover the shelf with a beautiful square of patched brocade.

On top place the general, peaceful eight-door-ledges (*torana*) mandala. Although in the mandala the sixteen offering goddesses are upon the red pleasure terraces surrounding the palace and the worldly protectors of positive inclination such as the seventy-five glorious protectors dwell within the vajra rim and surrounding the world system [in the space between the palace and vajra rim], when the mandala is drawn, only the environment is depicted, not the deities' implements. To gather all the conditions for a colour sand mandala is difficult so a correct drawing will suffice. Otherwise arrange a mandala plate, anoint it with scented water and arrange piles of white grain for each of the deities.

Place a tripod in the middle of the mandala. On the tripod arrange a good, three-part kapala[53] containing white pills made of the twelve different substances listed in the text[54] as the practice support, and cover it with a red cloth. In front or behind whatever is easier, place the white round offering torma (*chötor*) ornamented with white ornaments (*kargyen*) and arrange different offerings of food and drink around it. On its right and left, place amrita and rakta in their respective containers. Then place the two waters and the other offerings of sensory stimulants in front of or around the tormas, whichever is more convenient. Gather all the items you will need that are necessary to practise the sadhana text such as preliminary tormas—kator and gektor—extra shalze to enhance the offerings and many tepkyus, tsok offerings, cheto and Tenma tormas and so on.

II. THE MAIN PART: APPROACH, ACCOMPLISHMENT AND ACTIVITY

A. Approach
1. Preliminaries
a) The preliminaries to a retreat

Before the start of the approach, perform the usual practices to clear obstacles.[55]

b) Lineage prayers

Start during the afternoon session of the first day with the Seven Line Prayer and the relevant lineage prayers.

c) Kator

Then offer the white torma (*kator*) to the local deities as it is generally performed. Enjoin them to carry out activities for the complete accomplishment of the practice.

d) Refuge, bodhichitta and seven branches

Visualize the field of refuge in the space in front of you and take refuge, generate bodhichitta and offer the seven branches. Repeat each three times while you actualise the common visualization. Then dissolve the field of refuge into you.

e) Gektor

This is followed by the command to the obstacle makers. Recite the following as you actualise the visualization,

> I instantly become the magnificent Pema Heruka so
> wrathful he is difficult to behold.

As you hold the vajra pride of being the intervening deity,[56] sprinkle water on the gektor and purify with RAM YAM KHAM.

Say and actualise, "In the state of emptiness, the syllable DROOM arises and turns into vessels to suit each individual mind. These vessels contain the syllable KHAM, which transforms into the torma with the power to satisfy the five senses and appearing according to each one's individual experience."

Recite the Akaro mantra* together with its mudra three times to bless them.

Summon the obstacle-makers with the iron hook mudra, saying SARWA BHUTA AH KAR SHA YA DZA.

Recite the Sky Treasury mantra† together with its mudra three times to offer.

Issue the command with the verses of the text starting with, "HUNG Primordially, samsara and nirvana are inseparable . . ." Then say, "OM PEMA NATA KRITA HAYAGRIWA SARWA BIGHANEN HANA HANA HUNG PET" and the wrathful Sumbhani mantra,+ scatter blessed mustard seeds, scent with gugul and set the boundaries.

The gektor is only given during the first session and is not necessary afterwards. Then meditate on the protection spheres and the descent of blessings in order to bless the environment, the beings within it and the offering substances, reciting the mantra three times. This is how the preliminaries are accomplished.

2. The Main Part

The main part of the practice has two sections: the generation and the recitation.

a) Generation of the Samaya Mandala

The cause is the framework of the three samadhis which are like the three poles of a tepee. The result is the clear visualization of the support, the seats

---

* OM AKARO MUKHAM SARWA DHARMANAM ADYA NUTPANNA TOTA OM AH HUNG PET SOHA.

† SARWA BIGHANEN NAMA SARWA TATHAGATA BYO BISHA MUGEBE SARWA THAGAM UTGATE SAPARANA IMAM GAGANA KHAM GRIHANA DAM BALINGDE SOHA.

+ OM SUMBHANI SUMBHANI HUNG GRIHANA GRIHANA HUNG GRIHANAPAYA GRUHANAPAYA HUNG ANAYA HO BAGAWAN VIDYARADZA HUNG PET.

of the deities and the palace and the supported mandala of the deities as presented in the text of the practice.

As for the colour of the body of the male deity Garwang, the Lord of the Dance, the text says,

> As her natural radiance the supreme skilful means, the
> Lord of the Dance . . .

Accordingly, the appearing aspect of skilful means arises from her light. So fundamentally he is white. However, here the male and female deities are together in reversed union; and as it is explained that the desire of the male is greater than that of the female, he should therefore be visualized as red in colour because he is full of desire.

The four Taras, one at each of the four gates, are in a dancing posture with their right legs bent in the half-lotus dancing posture. Their right hands rest on their right knees in the gesture of bestowing refuge, and they brandish their respective hand implements (iron hook and so on) with the threatening mudra. Their left hands in the gesture of supreme generosity are at their hearts holding the stems of utpala flowers which blossom at the level of their left ears.

The jnanasattvas bless your three places, and you invite them. They arrive and dissolve into the samayasattva mandala. Pay respect with prostrations.

In the morning, the first offering of the two waters and the other five sensory stimulants should be done elaborately with each offering made individually. For each offering of the amrita, rakta and torma add KHA HI at the end of the text. However, during the later sessions of the day, simply do as indicated in the text of the sadhana without using these additions. Recite the absolute offering and sing praises with vajra songs.

b) Recitation
(i) Approach

The jnanasattva—white Amitayus—is in your heart while you clearly visualized yourself as Tara. At his heart on top of a white lotus and standing at the centre of a locket formed of conjoined sun and moon is the samadhisattva—a white syllable TAM—surrounded in a clockwise direction by the ten syllables of the mantra. Generally, we visualize the encircling mantra mala as follows: during the approach practice, we focus on visualizing the arrangement of the mantra mala; during the close approach practice, we visualize the mantra rotating; during the accomplishment stage, we visualize the palanquin; and during the great accomplishment stage, we visualize the emanation and reabsorption of rays of light. Yet it is enough to visualize its arrangement when practising essentially. In most of the Mother Tantra cycles and when you practise female deities like the Chimé Phakmé Nyingtik, the syllables are usually arranged counterclockwise. But in this sadhana the instruction is that the mantra should be arranged in a clockwise direction just like the sadhanas of the Sarma tantras. The root mantra, the combined mantra, the jnanasattva mantra and the nirmanasattva mantra are all arranged in a clockwise direction.[57]

First concentrate on this visualization until it is completely familiar. Then you can start visualizing the emanation and reabsorption while reciting the mantra. Once the visualization of the mantra arrangement is extremely clear, we can imagine it turning.

Visualize just the root mantra when reciting it. For the combined practice, visualize the root mantra with the rest of the combined mantra appended at the end. During the recitation of the jnanasattva mantra, the visualization is as follows: the core seed syllable TAM becomes HRIH encircled by its specific mantra. At the heart of the nirmanasattva, at the centre of the sun and moon locket, is a syllable DROOM surrounded by its mantra mala.

Then establish the ground of kyerim with clear visualization, remembering the purity and stable confidence. Focus single-pointedly on the visualization of the core seed syllable and the mantra mala and just recite the ten syllables with a mala blessed in the usual way.

When a clear visualization of it is attained, start visualizing Ushnisha Vijaya—the nirmanasattva—who emanates through the top of Chimé Phakmé Nyingtik's head. Her right hand in the gesture of granting refuge is poised on her right knee, forming the threatening mudra and holding the hook that gathers nectar. Her left hand in the mudra of supreme giving at the level of her heart holds a long-life vase from which she pours a stream of nectar.[58] Her feet are loosely crossed in the sattvasana.[59]

The quicksilver is obtained when she gathers the luminescent nectar of the animate and inanimate in samsara and nirvana. This nectar of quicksilver is the substance of alchemy and rejuvenation, white like an autumn moon shining bright as the sun, sparkling and gleaming with all kinds of auspicious patterns like svastikas and coils of joy and symbols turning to the right. Its power is such that whoever it touches can be transformed so they then possess the strength of an elephant, the life span of the sun and the moon and an indestructible body with the vigour of a sixteen year old. If it touches iron, the iron is transmuted into gold. If it is scattered on a dead, withered tree, the tree will immediately burst into life and grow leaves, flowers and fruits. So in your meditation, imagine these forms and images gathering as the blazing, brilliant splendour of great bliss.

At the end of the session [once you have recited the amount of mantras you planned to recite], you should also say a few of the combined mantra and the jnanasattva and the nirmanasattva mantras. Then recite each of the mantras of vowels and consonants, the hundred-syllable mantra and the mantra of interdependent origination three times to make up for omissions or additions.

The authentic tradition of the vidyadharas of the past was to recite the offering and praise after every thousand mantras. However, nowadays we only do it once at the end of a session. So make offerings by just reciting the offering mantra and say the first and the last stanzas of the praise prayer.

Confess with the lines in the sadhana that begin, "Ho In the mandala of the Sublime Lady…",[60] dissolve the mandala and rest in equanimity. Then arise again as the post-meditation deities, dedicate the practice and say the aspiration prayers and words of auspiciousness.

It is very good to offer a tsok during the first session. In that case practise as just explained, and when you have finished accumulating the mantra and "reciting offering and praise every thousand", after the final offering and praise, start by blessing the tsok. How you do that is laid out clearly in the sadhana text. Continue up to and including the remainder. You can also do the cheto, Tenma and horse dance. It is not necessary to do those three every day. After the mantra recitation, recite once more the brief prayers of offering and praise before reciting the confession. Then continue as before.

While practising the approach, it is also good to offer a tsok at the auspicious dates such as the 8th, 10th and 25th days of the lunar month. Each time you offer tsok, at the end of the afternoon session, add the practice of offering tormas to the protectors of the dharma and terma guardians as usual. Replenish the offerings during the evening session. Now you simply recite the text starting with refuge, bodhichitta, seven-branch offering and protection spheres prayers up until the offering of praise prayer. Conclude the session as before.

Next day, start the early morning session with the lineage prayers and do the elaborate version of the practice following the sadhana. Then practise in the morning, afternoon and evening. Divide your day into four sessions, and if you cannot do this then practise in three sessions—morning, afternoon and evening.

(ii) Accomplishment

After the approach, start the accomplishment stage. Practise the morning session with the short conclusion as before. Place a phumba made of precious materials containing the nectar of twenty-five substances[61] with a white cloth tied at the neck below the aperture ornament in the mandala to the right of the kapala, the main accomplishment substance. To the left put a stand made of precious substances that contains the edible long-life vase-shaped offering with tree leaves and flower ornaments. Since "edible offering" refers here to both food and alcohol, the food is made with alcohol in the shape of a long-life vase as are the pills which are arranged around the vase. Also add new amrita, rakta, torma and outer offerings.

In the afternoon session do the elaborate practice based on the sadhana starting with the lineage prayers. After the seven-branch accumulation, offer the gektor and issue the command. Practise as before, from the protection spheres prayer up to and including the offering and praise.

Then you need to "divide the house of the mantra" by reciting the mantra DROOM BISHO BISHUDHE TAM HRIH DROOM TAM DROOM HRIH HUNG DZAM HUNG BAM HO PET DZA. From the mandala of the self-visualization, a second mandala complete with both support (environment and palace) and supported (deities) separates into the space in front of you in the same way one butter lamp lights another. The fire surrounding the protection sphere framing the self-visualization almost touches the fire surrounding the protection sphere of the front visualization.

Briefly actualise the visualization of the approach phase at the start of accomplishment phase sessions. Then visualize according to the text beginning, "Again great cloud-like rays of light . . ." and for a while recite each of the three approach mantras and the mantra combining the three deities, focusing on each one individually.

When the visualization is clear, add the visualization of the emanation and reabsorption of rays of light from the heart of the main deity to invoke her retinue. First concentrate on accumulating Vajra Tara's mantra and recite the three others only briefly at the end of the session. Once you have completed the accumulation of Vajra Tara's mantra, you only need to recite it a few times before concentrating on accumulating Ratna Tara's mantra, which you do for most of your practice session. And so on.

The visualization is as follows. In the heart of each of the Taras of the four families is a lotus and a moon. On top of the moon within Vajra Tara is a dark-blue syllable TAM; in Ratna Tara, a yellow DROOM; in Padma Tara, a red HRIH; and Karma Tara, a black HUNG. Their respective mantra malas revolve around the syllable.

Conclude the session in the same way you concluded the approach stage except that here it is important to offer a tsok every day.

(iii) Activity

Once you have completed the appropriate number of accomplishment mantras, move onto the activity practice.

Divide the day into four sessions. The long sadhana should be recited in each one. Complete the accomplishment during the fourth session in the evening. The next day during the early morning session, recite up to its mantra as before briefly.

Then recite the activity section, beginning, "I am the samayasattva, the jnanasattva . . ." and clearly actualise the visualization. Say, "The four activity Taras with DZA HUNG BAM HO at their heart on lotus and moon discs" and visualize the four seed syllables in their respective colours surrounded by the mantra malas. Rays of light stream out from the five deities (the main deity and the four Taras in the retinue) to invoke Hook Tara. Hook Tara manifests many emanations, rays of light and infinite displays which accomplish the activity of pacifying all obstructing forces such as illness, negative spirits, negative actions, obscurations and so on. Accumulate only her mantra throughout the session. The conclusion is as before.

Then alternate as follows. During the morning session practise only Noose Tara's mantra and visualization, accomplishing the enriching activity. In the afternoon session practise only Iron Chain Tara's mantra and visualization and accomplish the magnetising activity. During the evening session practise only Bell Tara's mantra and visualization and accomplish the subjugating activity.

(iv) Measure of Each Phase of the Practice

The sadhana briefly mentions the three ways you can measure approach, accomplishment and activity practice: time, number of mantras or signs.

Time

Those of superior capacity should practise the approach for three weeks, accomplishment for one week and activity for one day which, including receiving the siddhis, makes one month. Those of medium capacity should multiply that by three, making a total of three months. The practitioner with lesser capacity should therefore practise for six months.

Numbers

In terms of numbers, we also distinguish practitioners of superior, medium and lesser capacities. Although it roughly takes the same amount of time, generally when you focus on the number of mantras you accumulate, the minimum should be:

—100,000 for each of the ten syllables of the main deity mantra, making 1,000,000

—700,000 of the nineteen-syllable approach mantra of the
combined practice
—400,000 of the jnanasattva and 400,000 of the nirmanasattva
mantras
—100,000 of each of the accomplishment mantras of the four Taras
—40,000 of each of the mantras of the four Gatekeeper Taras for
the activity.

This is the minimum number of mantras practitioners of medium capacity should recite and that should take three months to accomplish. So
the number of recitations for those of superior and lesser capacity are easy
to work out. For mere familiarization with the practice, you should recite:

—400,000 for the main deity's ten-syllable mantra
—100,000 for the combined practice
—40,000 for the jnanasattva and 40,000 for the nirmanasattva
mantras
—10,000 of each for the accomplishment mantras
—however much you can manage in one day for each of the
mantras of the four Gatekeeper Taras for activity.

These numbers are based on the speed of those with superior capacity.

Signs

The signs are clearly mentioned in the text. The best sign is realization, the
next best is experience and the least good is to repeatedly experience clarity
in dreams.

III. CONCLUDING PRACTICES
A. Receiving the Siddhis

It is very good if you can start the practice in the early morning session. The
morning session is also fine.

Place on your shrine a new offering torma (*chötor*) and long-life tormas
of the four activities as the siddhi substance, or more simply a "jewel-shaped

long-life torma" (*drangye norzukma*), surrounded by clean food and drink of all kinds such as the whites and the sweets, fruit, tea, alcohol, milk and yoghurt.

Do the elaborate practice following the sadhana text and recite a few of each of the mantras of approach, accomplishment and activity. Then do the offering and praise for a thousand recitations. From the hearts of the deities of the self- and front visualizations, rays of light shine out in the shape of iron hooks and pervade the whole of space. All the vital energy of the worlds and the inhabitants of samsara and nirvana are gathered into nectar appearing as rays of light that dissolve into the siddhi substances. Actualise this as you recite the mantra of the combined practice followed by KAYA WAKA TSITTA GUNA KARMA SARWA SIDDHI PALA HO one thousand times or more. Then you recite the *Inexpressible Ultimate Confession (Yeshe Kuchok)* followed by the descent of blessings that is in the sadhana text and the elaborate offering and praise prayers. Finally, recite the requesting siddhis prayer that starts with, "OM Sublime Lady . . ." which is in the sadhana. Actualising the usual visualizations, place the phumba on your head and take some of its water, place the nectar at your throat and drink some, place the long-life torma at your heart, eat some of the substances in the kapala and keep consuming what remains for a long time and so on as usual. Then offer a large tsok. Enjoy it. If you withheld the remainder earlier, offer it with the remainder torma. Request to fulfill their pledge. Do the cheto, Tenma and horse dance. After the confession and forgiveness, conclude with prayers of auspiciousness.

B. Amending Faults of Lack or Excess—Fire Puja

It is good to do a fire puja in order to make up for and correct mistakes, omissions and repetitions. If you choose to do this elaborately in relation to the mandala,[62] perform a fire ritual on the next day after you complete the four activities. If you do not relate the fire puja offering to the mandala, you can offer a fire puja either on the day you complete the practice and receive the siddhis, or the next day. When you offer the fire puja to complete the approach and accomplishment stages and make up for and correct mistakes, omissions and repetitions, you need to accumulate the fire offering mantra to the amount of ten percent of the total mantra accumulations. Also accumulate as much as you can the mantras to accomplish activities such as lengthening life and so on.

CONCLUSION

Even though this practice can be done more elaborately following the structure of a drupchen, here we only explained the difficult points of the practice and other instructions.

During a Chimé Phakmé Nyingtik drupchö for example, if it is an ordinary, simple drupchö, we may recite the main ten-syllable mantra one thousand times during each session. Accordingly, we should also recite three hundred mantras of the combined practice, the jnanasattva and the nirmanasattva, one hundred for each of the four Taras, and just twenty-one recitations for each of the four activities.

If you perform the practice mainly for long-life accomplishment, recite the ten-syllable mantra three hundred times and the mantra of the combined practice one thousand times since it is the mantra and clear visualization of the long-life accomplishment, while the other mantras are as before. The rest is the same as before.

When you practise the daily sadhana to "maintain the continuous flow of the practice", you can only recite the approach mantra and omit the accomplishment and activity mantras. As a main mantra of approach, the mantra of the combined practice is also very good. Having said that, to practise more elaborately by reciting and visualizing briefly the accomplishment and activity is not only *not* a fault but is very good, since approach is the foundation that comes at the beginning of approach, accomplishment and activity. So after the approach it is good each time to practise some accomplishment and also a little bit of the activity.

Glorious mother of the victorious ones of the three times
Indivisible from the lama, in all my lives take care of me,
So that I may perfect the conduct of a bodhisattva following the vajra path,
And quickly accomplish completely and perfectly the liberation of Tara.

Colophon

The supreme and omniscient great tertön lama* determined I was to be among the first recipients of these teachings. So he granted me the complete ripening empowerment and liberating instructions, and gave me permission to write down notes.[63] *Later at the request of many interested people, I, Pema Garwang Lodrö Taye, the mere reflection of a vidyadhara, as my body aged to eighty-seven, expounded this briefly at the strong insistence of Tana Lama Karma Jikdral, who said he had recited 100 million Vajra Guru mantras, in a solitary retreat place at Palpung called Tsadra Rinchen Drak in Kunzang Dechen Ösel Ling. Sang-Ngak Tenzin put it into writing. May virtue grow ever further!*

---

* Jamyang Khyentse Wangpo.

CHAPTER 7:

Chimé Phakmé Nyingtik:
Presentation of *A Drop of Moonlight Nectar*

by Tulku Orgyen Tobgyal

Dzongsar Khyentse Rinpoche has asked me to explain to you how to practise the Chimé Phakmé Nyingtik, which I'll do based on the instruction manual written by Jamgön Kongtrul called *A Drop of Moonlight Nectar: Notes on Chimé Phakmé Nyingtik Approach and Accomplishment.*[64] As the title states, this text explains how to practise the approach and accomplishment practices in the Chimé Phakmé Nyingtik revelation of Jamyang Khyentse Wangpo. The Chimé Phakmé Nyingtik begins with a homage to Arya Tara.

Namo Guru Arya Taraya!

"Namo" means homage. To whom are we paying homage? To Arya Tara who is inseparable from our own root teacher, the guru.

With unshakable faith, I place Pema Ösel Dongak Lingpa,
Master of the seven transmissions,
One with the three immortal vidyadharas,
Upon the lotus at the centre of my heart.

Jamgön Kongtrul pays homage with unwavering devotion as he imagines Pema Ösel Dongak Lingpa, Jamyang Khyentse Wangpo, sitting in the centre of his heart. Khyentse Wangpo mastered the teachings, which he received through the seven methods of transmission and therefore "owns" them. In essence he is inseparable from the three vidyadharas who accomplished immortality—Shri Singha, Vimalamitra and Guru Rinpoche.

INTRODUCTION

Jamyang Khyentse Wangpo, the great universal king of
all the learned and accomplished masters in the Land of
Snows, received many treasure teachings including mind
treasures through all seven methods of transmission. The
great Chimé Phakmé Nyingtik dharma cycle was one of his
profound mind treasures. But he was only able to decipher
and write down the root sadhana, the sadhana cycle of the
lama and the practices of Amitayus and Ushnisha Vijaya.
Here we are concerned with the root sadhana, *Uncovering
Primordial Wisdom*.

The Chimé Phakmé Nyingtik is a vast terma, but we only have a fraction
of it because the tertön was only able to write down the root sadhana, the
cycle of the lama (the *Vima Ladrup*) and the short Ushnisha Vijaya and
Amitayus practices. Even so, since we have the root sadhana, we are able to
practise the Chimé Phakmé Nyingtik. And it's this root sadhana that we will
be discussing today.

There are three stages to this practice: approach, accomplishment and
activity. To be able to practise all three stages, you must first receive the empowerment from a lama.[65] Having received the empowerment, the samaya
is to do the approach, accomplishment and activity practices, each of which
involves preliminaries, main part and conclusion.

I. PRELIMINARIES

Very simply, before you go into retreat, you must first do the preliminaries—
which means preparing everything you'll need, for example the mandala, the
tormas and so on. Having prepared properly, you then go into retreat and
practise the approach, accomplishment and activity, which is the main part.
Finally, having completed the main part, just before you come out of retreat,
you receive the siddhis or accomplishments—this is the conclusion. So that's
how you practise the preliminaries, the main part and the conclusion.

Before you go into retreat, you must decide which date to begin. The text recommends the eighth day of the waxing moon of the first month of a lunar trimester. But in your case you have already started your retreat, so it doesn't matter. Generally though, a retreat should start on an auspicious day.

A. Shrine Arrangement

The room in which you do your retreat should be clean and pleasant, and you should have already prepared the mandala, a thangka of Chimé Phakmé Nyingtik and the supports of the Three Roots—lama, yidam, dakini—specifically an image of Venerable Tara.

In the Nyingmapa tradition there are three ways of preparing a mandala. The best method is to use coloured sand, the middling method is to use a drawing or picture and the least you can do is offer for example heaps of rice, flowers and so on. In this retreat you can't really prepare the sand mandala, but you should at least have found an image of the mandala. I am sure you've done that. If you don't have a drawing, the simplest option is to pile heaps of white grain on a mandala plate, one pile for each of the deities in the mandala.

> Place a tripod in the middle of the mandala. On the tripod, arrange a good three-part kapala[66] containing white pills made of the twelve different substances listed in the text[67] as the practice support, and cover it with a red cloth.

Fold the red cloth neatly eight times.

You then add the torma. You can put it either in front of the kapala or behind it, wherever you prefer. But you need a torma. So if you can't make an elaborate torma of Chimé Phakmé Nyingtik, make a medium-style one or at the very least a simple one. The text says the torma should have all its ornaments and that you should arrange different offerings around it, for example food to eat and liquids to drink. To the right of the torma put the amrita and to the left the rakta, which must be made of specific substances. The offerings of the two waters—drinking water and washing water—flowers, incense, lamp, scented water and so on should be arranged clockwise around the torma.

B. Offerings Checklist

You will also need to make:

—A fresh kator (white torma) and a gektor (torma offered to
obstacle-makers) for the beginning of your retreat,
—A shalze (food offering torma), which is one of the eight offerings
that you must make every day,
—Cheto and Tenma tormas,
—Tsok offerings which are basically food and drink.

During a Chimé Phakmé Nyingtik approach retreat, you don't need to
offer a tsok every day. It's enough to do one at the beginning and another
at the end of the retreat, but it's also good to offer a tsok feast on auspicious
days like the eighth, tenth and twenty-fifth days of the lunar month. This
is the list of things you will need on retreat and that you must prepare be-
forehand.

To recap, briefly:

—Put a kapala on a tripod, fill it with pills made of the twelve
substances described in the text, then place a red cloth folded
eight times on top of it.
—Put the torma either in front of the kapala or behind it.
—Put the amrita to the torma's right and the rakta to its left, and
arrange the offerings around them.
—If you use a drawing of the mandala, make sure it's big enough.
If you don't have an image of the mandala, make a mandala with
piles of grains.

That is the preparation.

II. THE MAIN PART: APPROACH, ACCOMPLISHMENT AND ACTIVITY

A. Approach
1. Preliminaries
a) The Preliminaries to a Retreat

Now the main practice has three stages: approach, accomplishment and activity. It begins with approach (*nyenpa*).

> Before the start of the approach, perform the usual
> practices to clear obstacles.

Pray to the lama, make a smoke offering—a sang, such as *Riwo Sangchö* practice—offer tormas and so on. Do these practices as many times as you can, then begin the approach in the afternoon, not in the morning. Start all your sessions with the Seven Line Prayer and prayers to the lamas of the lineage, then recite the one-folio Chimé Phakmé Nyingtik lineage prayer.

Start during the afternoon session of the first day with the Seven Line Prayer and the relevant lineage prayers, and offer the white torma or kator to the local deities as it is generally performed. Enjoin them to carry out activities for the complete accomplishment of the practice.

On the first day of a retreat, it is customary to offer a white torma to the owners of the land. However, as you started this retreat some years ago, you don't need to offer it specifically for the Chimé Phakmé Nyingtik *nyenpa*,[68] but you can if you like. As you offer the white torma, entrust the owners of the land with various activities. For example, ask them to prevent obstacles to your practice of the Chimé Phakmé Nyingtik in this place and at such-and-such a time and to allow you to complete the practices of approach, accomplishment and activity.

b) Refuge, Bodhichitta and the Seven-Branch Offering

Visualize the source of refuge in the sky before you—which means all the deities of Chimé Phakmé Nyingtik inseparable from your lama—and take refuge, generate bodhichitta and offer the seven-branch offering as you direct the visualization in the usual way. There is no specific method for visualizing these practices in the Chimé Phakmé Nyingtik sadhana—or any other sadhana, for that matter. You always do it the same way, and that's what you do here.

Repeat each verse of refuge, bodhichitta and the seven-branch offering three times as you actualise the meaning of the words. Do it properly. Having done so, dissolve the field of accumulation into you.

c) Commanding the Obstacle Makers

We now give the gektor to the obstacle makers and issue our commands following the words of the text.

> I instantly become the magnificent Pema Heruka, so
> wrathful he is difficult to behold.

The sadhana is quite succinct. In an instant, you become Pema Heruka (Hayagriva) who is so wrathful and fierce that it's difficult to look at him. This is what you meditate on here. Hayagriva is an intervening deity, meaning he's not the actual deity you practise in this sadhana but the deity who accomplishes specific activities as you practise. So you now generate the pride of being the intervening deity.

Next the text says that you should sprinkle water on the gektor. Say RAM YAM KHAM to purify the torma, then recite the following and add three repetitions of the Akaro mantra to bless it.

> RAM YAM KHAM
> In the state of emptiness, the syllable DROOM arises and
> turns into a vessel to suit each individual mind. This
> vessel contains the syllable KHAM, which transforms into
> the torma with the power to satisfy the five senses and
> appearing according to each one's individual experience.
> OM AKARO MUKHAM SARWA DHARMANAM ADYA NUTPANNA
> TOTA OM AH HUNG PET SOHA[69]

Do the hook mudra and recite the mantra:

> SARWA BHUTA AH KAR SHA YA DZA

You are Hayagriva. From your heart you emanate wrathful male and female deities radiating hook-shaped rays of light to ensnare all the obstructing forces that create obstacles to the attainment of enlightenment. Since they are incapable of resisting, all the obstructing forces arrive instantly. Recite the Sky Treasury mantra,

> SARWA BIGHANEN NAMA SARWA TATHAGATA BYO BISHA
> MUGEBE SARWA THAGAM UTGATE SAPARANA IMAM GAGANA
> KHAM GRIHANA DAM BALINGDE SOHA

This mantra offers the obstructing forces sensory stimulants as inexhaustible as space which fulfill every one of their desires with beautiful forms, pleasant sounds, excellent fragrances, delicious tastes and soft, tactile sensations. Basically, they are given everything they want.

Then command the obstructing forces by reciting the gektor verses from the sadhana that begin, "HUNG Primordially, samsara and nirvana are inseparable . . ." The obstructing forces who hear your command and take it seriously obey and leave straight away. But others, the bad ones, remain. So you must expel them with "fierce meditation", by first reciting,

> OM PEMA NATA KRITA HAYAGRIWA SARWA BIGHANEN HANA
> HANA HUNG PET

This is followed by the wrathful Sumbhani mantra, the mantra of the four HUNGS,

> OM SUMBHANI SUMBHANI HUNG GRIHANA GRIHANA HUNG
> GRIHANAPAYA GRUHANAPAYA HUNG ANAYA HO BAGAWAN
> VIDYARADZA HUNG PET

This will frighten them. Scatter blessed mustard seeds, put gugul on the fire and throw the gektor outside. Once you've done that, all the obstacle makers will be driven to the other side of the ocean.

> The gektor is only given during the first session and is not necessary afterwards.

You only have to offer the gektor torma in the first session of the first day, you don't have to offer it in any of the other sessions.

d) Setting the Retreat Boundaries

As you have already started your retreat and put up your boundary shrines, you don't have to do it again. But you should actualise the visualization. Visualize yourself as Hayagriva, entrust the guardians of the four directions with activities and ask them to make sure no blessings leak out until your retreat has been successfully completed and that no obstacles are allowed in.

e) Protection Spheres

Then meditate on the protection spheres . . .

Visualize them as described in the text. Since you must continually meditate on the protection spheres throughout the entire retreat, you should visualize them again and again.

f) The Descent of Blessings

. . . and the descent of blessings in order to bless the environment, the beings within it . . .

The whole environment and the beings within it are blessed. Having received these blessings, the universe no longer appears ordinary and instead you see it as a pure land such as Sukhavati. Similarly, beings in this universe are no longer ordinary. They are now by nature male and female deities. This is how you bring down the blessings so that everything shines with the glory of the five wisdoms.

. . . and the offering substances, reciting the mantra three times.

To make the blessings descend, recite the mantra associated with each offering, for example the mantra that appears in the text.

This is how the preliminaries are accomplished. In other words, the preliminary sections of the sadhana are finished, and we now turn to the main part.

2. The Main Part

The main part of the practice has two sections: the
generation and the recitation.

The main practice involves the generation of the deity and the recitation of
the mantra.

a) Generation of the Samaya Mandala:
The Yoga of the Enlightened Body
(i) Visualization

The first step is kyerim meditation, the creation of the samaya mandala. This
means you must arise in the form of the samayasattva mandala.

The cause is the framework of the three samadhis which are
like the three poles of a tepee.

The three samadhis are the samadhi of suchness, the samadhi of universal manifestation and the causal samadhi. And it is with these three samadhis that you establish the foundation for the practice.

The result is the clear visualization of the support, the seats
of the deities and the palace, . . .

A specific feature in the Chimé Phakmé Nyingtik is that the palace walls
are made of crystal; the inside of the palace should also be white. Apart from
that, the Chimé Phakmé Nyingtik palace has all the usual characteristics
of a peaceful palace. A peaceful palace can have either four-level toranas or
eight-level toranas, and the Chimé Phakmé Nyingtik palace has eight.

Visualize the deities in the palace as described in the sadhana. The sadhana describes how to generate the deities, and you can look at how the deities
are depicted in a thangka. That is how you should meditate.

The visualization of the Chimé Phakmé Nyingtik looks like this: Inside
the eight-level torana palace made of crystal sits the main deity, Arya Tara,
white in colour, in union with the male deity. These two are the main deities
of the mandala. Above her head is Ushnisha Vijaya and at her heart, Amitayus. The three of them are known as the three deities of long life. In each

of the four directions stands one Tara, and a Gatekeeper Tara stands at each of the four gates, so nine deities form the mandala which you must visualize exactly as described in the sadhana.

Jamgön Kongtrul mentions a secret instruction about the colour of Tara's male consort, Garwang, the Lord of Dance. The sadhana text says,

> As her natural radiance the supreme skilful means, the
> Lord of the Dance . . .

As he is the natural radiance of Tara who is white, this line suggests that the Lord of the Dance is also white. However, Jamgön Kongtrul tells us that we should visualize him red tinged with white.

> As for the colour of the body of the male deity Garwang,
>   the Lord of the Dance, the text says,

> As her natural radiance the supreme skilful means, the
>   Lord of the Dance . . .

> Accordingly, the appearing aspect of skilful means arises
> from her light. So fundamentally he is white. However,
> here the male and female deities are together in reversed
> union; and as it is explained that the desire of the male
> is greater than that of the female, he should therefore be
> visualized as red in colour because he is full of desire.

The Lord of the Dance, the male deity—Avalokiteshvara or Amitayus, whatever you want to call him[70]—is described in the sadhana as Tara's natural radiance which suggests he is white. However, Jamgön Kongtrul's point is that he is red. As they are in union, he is full of desire, and since the desire of the male is greater than that of the female, he is red in colour. So you should visualize him as being red. This is how he appears in the thangka drawn by Jamyang Khyentse Wangpo which Jamgön Kongtrul used as his practice support. I now have that thangka.

> The four Taras,[71] one at each of the four gates, are in
> dancing posture with their right legs bent in the half-lotus

dancing position. Their right hands rest on their right
knees in the gesture of bestowing refuge . . .

This is also how they appear in the thangka. Their fingers form the threatening mudra while holding their respective hand implements: iron hook,
lasso, iron chain and bell, which correspond to the buddha family of their
direction. Each Tara holds her left hand at her heart in the gesture of supreme
generosity and clasps an utpala flower that blossoms next to her left ear.

You meditate on yourself as the deity as I just said, then bless your three
centres and invite the wisdom deity. This is how to meditate on the deities.

You must of course practise using all three key elements of kyerim—vajra pride, clarity of visualization and remembering the purity. Without these
three elements, there is no kyerim practice. If you practise one but not the
other two, or you practise two but not the last one, it won't work. To practise
kyerim, you need all three. Make sure you think about them again and again
in every practice session. Sometimes you can focus more on vajra pride,
sometimes on clear visualization and sometimes on remembering the purity.
Just having a clear visualization without the other two elements won't work,
it's not acceptable. But if you can meditate on a clear visualization as you
also remember the purity, you should then take hold of vajra pride. This is
how to practise all three. Most important of all, make sure you don't ever
forget them. Think about the instructions on clear visualization, vajra pride
and remembering the purity whenever you do kyerim, no matter which
sadhana you are practising.

(ii) Blessing the Three Centres and Inviting the Wisdom Deities

These deities—the main deity and the retinue—that we visualize make up
the samayasattvas, the samaya deities. Now we invite the jnanasattvas, or
wisdom deities, to appear in the sky before us who must then merge indivisibly with the samayasattvas that we've just been meditating on.

The jnanasattvas bless your three places . . .

Visualize a white OM at your forehead, a red AH at your throat and a blue
HUNG at your heart, or alternatively visualize Vairochana as the enlightened
body, Amitabha as the enlightened speech and Akshobhya as the enlight-

ened mind. Also meditate on the five syllables of the five buddha families (OM HUNG TRAM HRIH AH) on the crowns of the deities' heads. This is something you do in all sadhanas.

(iii) Prostration

> Pay respect with prostrations.

This means you do the prostration section of the sadhana. But don't stand up and physically prostrate, prostrate mentally.

(iv) Offering and Praise

Next comes the offering.

> In the morning, the first offering of the two waters and the
> other five sensory stimulants should be done elaborately
> with each offering made individually.

In the first session of the day, you offer drinking water, washing water, flowers, incense and so on as you recite the appropriate verse for each offering and perform its mudra. This is what is meant by "doing the practice elaborately". In fact, there's a separate practice text written by Jamgön Kongtrul that you must recite as you make the elaborate offerings in your first practice session each morning.[72] You should also offer amrita, rakta and torma as you follow the same offering text. But you don't have to do this practice as elaborately in the rest of the day's sessions,

> . . . simply do as indicated in the text of the sadhana . . .

After that, you must make the absolute offering and sing praises with vajra songs.

This completes the instruction on the visualization of the deity, the yoga of the enlightened body.

b) Recitation: The Yoga of Enlightened Speech
(i) Approach

A Drop of Moonlight Nectar is divided into two sections: the first is the generation and the second is the recitation. We have now come to the second part, the recitation.

Visualize yourself clearly in the form Arya Tara in union with her consort, who are the samayasattvas, as described in the text. At your heart is a white Amitayus who is the jnanasattva. In the thangka, he appears above the main deity because according to thangka painting tradition, the jnanasattva isn't drawn in the heart of the deity. In Amitayus' heart is a white lotus. Resting on the lotus is a locket formed of a sun and moon joined together, with a space in between; the red sun is below and the white moon above. At the centre of the locket is the samadhisattva in the form of a white syllable TAM. So you must visualize the three nested sattvas: yourself as the samayasattva; in your heart is the jnanasattva, white Amitayus; and in Amitayus' heart, the sun and moon locket that stands on a white lotus in the centre of which is the samadhisattva—a white syllable TAM. Clockwise around TAM visualize the ten syllables of the Tara mantra which are not rotating.

> Generally, we visualize the mantra mala as follows: during the approach practice, we focus on visualizing the arrangement of the mantra mala; during the close approach, we visualize the mantra rotating; during the accomplishment stage, we visualize the palanquin; and during the great accomplishment stage, we visualize the emanation and reabsorption of rays of light.

According to the most commonly practised Nyingma Kama tradition, the visualization in the approach phase is like the moon and garland of stars. At night, the individual moon and stars are seen in the sky and don't appear to be moving. Likewise, in the approach practice you visualize the TAM with the ten syllables of the mantra arranged around it like the moon and stars in a clear sky and they don't move. For the close approach, the syllables of the mantra rotate around the syllable TAM. For the accomplishment stage, the syllables circle between the self- and front visualization. And finally, in the great accomplishment stage, not only do the syllables circle between the self- and front visualization, they also radiate rays of light making offerings which satisfy all the buddhas and bodhisattvas. Then having gathered all their blessings and siddhis, the rays of light return to the heart of the deity. This is the emanation and reabsorption of rays of light.

> Yet it is enough to visualize its arrangement when
> practising essentially.

This means when you do a daily practice or a simple practice or when you're a beginner, it is better not to try to move the mantra syllables around the seed syllable in your visualization.

> In most of the Mother Tantra cycles and when you practise
> female deities like the Chimé Phakmé Nyingtik, the
> syllables are usually arranged counterclockwise. But in
> this sadhana the instruction is that the mantra should be
> arranged in a clockwise direction just like the sadhanas of
> the Sarma tantras.

Therefore, the syllables of all the mantras—the root mantra, the combined practice mantra (the longer mantra in the sadhana), the jnanasattva mantra and the nirmanasattva mantra—should be arranged clockwise, not counterclockwise.[73]

Having visualized the appropriate arrangement of syllables, start concentrating on your visualization of TAM surrounded by the syllables of the mantra OM TARE TUTARE TURE SOHA. Once you can see the syllables as clearly as if you were looking at them with your eyes,

> . . . then you can start visualizing the emanation and
> reabsorption of rays of light while reciting the mantra.
> Once the visualization of the mantra arrangement is
> extremely clear, we can imagine it turning.

If you can't clearly visualize the syllables when they're standing still, it'll be impossible for you to visualize them rotating. If a wheel isn't constructed properly, it won't be able to turn, right? At this point you're supposed to recite the root mantra OM TARE TUTTARE TURE SOHA, and as you do, concentrate exclusively on the arrangement of the syllables which remain still.

> Visualize just the root mantra when reciting it. For the
> combined practice, visualize the root mantra with the rest
> of the combined mantra appended at the end.

This means that to recite the combined practice mantra, visualize the root mantra OM TARE TUTTARE TURE SOHA and before the final syllable, add the rest of the combined mantra—HRIH DROOM BENDZA JNANA AYUKE. During the recitation of the mantra of the jnanasattva Amitayus OM AMARANI DZIWANTIYE SOHA, continue to visualize the locket of sun and moon but with HRIH instead of TAM, and the HRIH is surrounded by the mantra OM AMARANI DZIWANTIYE SOHA. Next, recite the mantra of Ushnisha Vijaya, the nirmanasattva, which is OM AMRITA AYURDADE SOHA. In the centre of the sun and moon locket at your heart, visualize the syllable DROOM around which stand the syllables of the mantra.

> Then establish the ground of the kyerim with clear
> visualization, remembering the purity and stable
> confidence.

You must have a ground or a foundation for your practice: clear visualization, remembering the purity and stable confidence are the ground.

Once you have laid the foundation with the three samadhis,

> Focus single-pointedly on the visualization of the core seed
> syllable and the mantra mala . . .

During the approach phase, the core seed syllable is TAM and the mantra mala is OM TARE TUTTARE TURE SOHA. Then you recite the combined practice mantra, adding HRIH DROOM BENDZA JNANA AYUKE to the Tara mantra in the visualization. Then for the jnanasattva Amitayus, the seed syllable at the centre of the sun and moon locket becomes HRIH surrounded by the syllables of the Amitayus mantra, OM AMARANI DZIWANTIYE SOHA. Finally, when you practise the nirmanasattva Ushnisha Vijaya, you visualize the seed syllable DROOM as indicated in the text encircled by OM

AMRITA AYURDADE SOHA. Basically, you visualize the relevant seed syllable and the mantra.

The syllables emanate and reabsorb rays of light whether you can make them move or not, and the rays of light reach all the buddhas and bodhisattvas, the deities of the Chimé Phakmé Nyingtik, Noble Tara and so on, making offerings to them. The light then brings all the wisdom and blessings of their enlightened body, speech and mind and all accomplishments back to be reabsorbed into you. This is what you must visualize.

> . . . with a mala blessed in the usual way.

The mala you use to count mantras should have been blessed in the customary way, and you should never use a mala that hasn't been blessed properly. A crystal mala is the best kind to use for the Chimé Phakmé Nyingtik practice. As you count your recitations with your blessed mala, first,

> . . . just recite the ten-syllable mantra . . .

Start by focusing on OM TARE TUTTARE TURE SOHA. Then,

> When a clear visualization of it is attained . . .

Once you're used to this visualization and can hold it in your mind—at least to some extent—actualise the visualization of Chimé Phakmé Nyingtik.

The nirmanasattva is Ushnisha Vijaya, and now from out of the top of White Tara's head, fly Ushnisha Vijayas in inconceivable numbers. This isn't found in any other sadhana. She should look like this:

> Her right hand in the gesture of granting refuge is poised
> on her right knee, forming the threatening mudra and
> holding the hook that gathers nectar. Her left hand in the
> mudra of supreme giving at the level of her heart holds a
> long-life vase from which she pours a stream of nectar. Her
> feet are loosely crossed in the sattvasana.

We visualize as many Ushnisha Vijayas as there are motes of dust in a beam of light. Her hooks grab and draw into the vase all the vitality of samsara and nirvana, the essence of the four elements (earth, wind, fire, water), the potency of all medicines, the longevity of the gods and rishis and so on. Millions of Ushnisha Vijayas are sent to collect these essences and the rest into their vases, they then bring them back to dissolve into you and grant the empowerment. According to the sadhana, the vase contains,

> All the subtle vital essence of samsara and nirvana,
> The animate and inanimate universe [. . .]
> A stream of boundless light bursts out
> From the top of the jewel on the ushnisha at the crown of
>   my head,
> From which appears the sublime Vijaya,
> The colour of crystal. Her right hand,
> In the mudra of granting refuge, holds a hook;
> Her left, in the mudra of supreme giving, holds a long-life
>   vase.
> She radiates light and rays of light, and
> Limitless forms of herself stream out like specks of dust in
>   sunbeams.
> They draw in all the wisdom, love and power of
> All the deities of the mandala,
> All the buddhas and bodhisattvas of the ten directions,
> All the yidams, dakas and dakinis, and
> All the protectors of the Vajrayana teachings.
> They also draw in all the subtle vital essence of samsara and
>   nirvana, the animate and inanimate universe,
> In the form of the quicksilver that accomplishes all.

The meaning of "all the buddhas and bodhisattvas" and "all the yidams, dakas and dakinis" and the following lines is quite straightforward. So this verse is clear, apart from the line, ". . . the subtle vital essence of samsara and nirvana, in the form of the quicksilver that accomplishes all." This is why Jamgön Kongtrul describes how we should meditate on the quicksilver. He writes in the commentary,

> The quicksilver is obtained when she gathers the
> luminescent nectar of the animate and inanimate in

samsara and nirvana. This nectar of quicksilver is the substance of alchemy and rejuvenation (*chulen*), white like an autumn moon shining bright as the sun, sparkling and gleaming with all kinds of auspicious patterns like svastikas and coils of joy and symbols turning to the right.

". . . all kinds of auspicious patterns . . ." refers to the eight auspicious symbols. Then he describes the power of the quicksilver nectar,

Its power is such that whoever it touches can be transformed so that they then possess the strength of an elephant, the life span of the sun and the moon and an indestructible body with the vigour of a sixteen year old. If it touches iron, the iron is transmuted into gold. If it is scattered on a dead, withered tree, the tree will immediately burst into life and grow leaves, flowers and fruit.

This is how the nectar should appear in your meditation, and it is one of the more complex points. So imagine these forms and images gathering as the blazing, brilliant splendour of great bliss. At this point all the Ushnisha Vijayas dissolve back into us and we blaze with the splendour of great bliss.

To recap:

—Visualize yourself in the form Arya Tara in union with her consort as described in the text.
—At her heart sits the jnanasattva, white Amitayus.
—At his heart stands the samadhisattva, the syllable TAM, on a white lotus at the centre of a sun and moon locket.
—Around the TAM, stands the syllables of the mantra OM TARE TUTTARE TURE SOHA.

Jamgön Kongtrul says to direct the practice as you recite the mantra, first visualize the syllables standing still.

—Once your visualization is clear and stable, you can start to visualize the mantra rotating around the seed syllable.
—Having mastered that, visualize rays of white light shining from

the rotating mantra and up through the deity's ushnisha which is the protuberance on the top of Noble Tara's head.
—As the rays of light leave Tara's body, they transform into enormous numbers of Ushnisha Vijayas holding hooks in their right hands and vases in their left.
—They fill the whole of space and hook all the subtle vital essences of samsara and nirvana, the animate and the inanimate universe into the vase.
—The nectar in their vases dissolves into you, and you receive all the blessings and siddhis as already mentioned.

This is the main visualization which you actualise as you recite the mantra.

Usually, when you practise most sadhanas elaborately, rays of light are emanated from which offering goddesses appear to make offerings and so on. If you practise a little less elaborately, the light becomes symbols. And the simplest method is just to send out rays of light. The special feature of the Chimé Phakmé Nyingtik is that we emanate Ushnisha Vijayas, but the meaning is the same.

> At the end of the session [once you have recited the amount of mantras you planned to recite], you should also say a few of the combined mantra, the jnanasattva mantra and the nirmanasattva Ushnisha Vijaya mantra. Then recite each of the mantras of the vowels and consonants, the hundred-syllable mantra and the mantra of interdependent origination three times to make up for omissions or additions.
>
> The authentic tradition of the vidyadharas of the past was to recite the offering and praise after every thousand mantras. However, nowadays we only do it once at the end of a session. So make offerings by reciting just the offering mantra (OM BENDZA ARGHAM PADAM and so on) followed by the first and last stanzas of the praise prayer.
>
> Confess with the lines in the sadhana that begin "Ho In the mandala of the Sublime Lady...",[74] dissolve the

mandala and rest in equanimity. Then arise again as the post-meditation deities, dedicate the practice and say the aspiration prayers and words of auspiciousness.

This is how you conclude one session of practice.

It is very good to offer a tsok during the first session.

This means the first session on the first day.

In which case, practise as just explained, and when you have finished accumulating the mantra and "reciting the offering and praise every thousand", after the final offering and praise, start by blessing the tsok. How you do that is laid out clearly in the text. Continue up until and including the remainder. You can also do the cheto, Tenma and horse dance.

However, if you offer a tsok daily,

It is not necessary to do those three every day. After the mantra recitation, recite once more the brief prayers of offering and praise before reciting the confession. Then continue as before.

While practising the approach, it is also good to offer a tsok on auspicious days such as the 8th, 10th and 25th days of the lunar month. Each time you offer tsok, at the end of the afternoon session, add the practice of offering tormas to the protectors of the dharma (Tseringma and so on) and the terma guardians as usual. Replenish the offerings during the evening session. Now you simply recite the text starting with refuge, bodhichitta, the seven-branch offering and the protection spheres prayers up until the offering of praise prayer. Conclude the session as before.

"Simply recite the text" means that you do these prayers exactly as they are written in the sadhana text. You don't need to add any extra prayers like the detailed offering prayer.

On the first day, you practise two sessions: an afternoon session and an evening session. That's it. That's what needs to be done on the first day.

> Next day, start the early morning session with the lineage
> prayers and do the elaborate version of the practice
> following the sadhana text. Then practise in the morning,
> afternoon and evening. Divide your day into four sessions,
> and if you cannot do this then practise in three sessions—
> morning, afternoon and evening.

This concludes the instruction for the approach practice.

Having made the effort to enter into a retreat, don't waste the opportunity! Make sure you cultivate and establish a clear visualization. To do that, you need the right instructions, otherwise you will have nothing to meditate on. If you don't follow the stages of meditation that are laid out in the text, if you don't recite the mantra and don't visualize, all you'll end up doing is locking yourself in a room and torturing yourself. Therefore, the first step is to learn what you have to do. This means you first translate the commentary, then study it thoroughly. The commentary was taught by Jamyang Khyentse Wangpo, so if you know this text it's enough, it's all you need. Jamyang Khyentse Wangpo gave all these instructions to Jamgön Kongtrul who faithfully wrote everything down; it is a very special oral linage instruction.

When you go into a solitary retreat, you must first receive the empowerment and instructions on the practice you intend to do. But you shouldn't think about receiving any other teachings or empowerments at that time. Make sure you study this text on the Chimé Phakmé Nyingtik very thoroughly and put the teaching into practice exactly as instructed. Don't get distracted by a desire to receive many other teachings and transmissions. When you're practising approach, accomplishment and activity in retreat, thinking about wanting to study, imagining you need to receive many more teachings or that you should be working are all obstacles to your retreat. Similarly, when you're studying if you start thinking that study isn't helping and that you should go somewhere solitary to practise, that is also an obstacle. Basically, when you practise, practise one hundred percent; when you study, study one hundred percent. Whatever you set out to do at any given time, make sure you focus exclusively on accomplishing just that and don't get side-tracked.

When you practise the Chimé Phakmé Nyingtik, concentrate on doing only that. Focus your mind constantly on the Chimé Phakmé Nyingtik. After you have finished a session, make sure you constantly bring to mind the appearance of the deity and recite the root mantra even though it won't count towards your accumulations. Recite the mantra while you're walking around for example. Even in your dreams, keep thinking of the deity. If you do, you are focusing one-pointedly on practice. If you don't, you aren't.

(ii) Accomplishment

> After the approach, start the accomplishment stage.
> Practise the morning session with the short conclusion as
> before.

This means that you practise during your morning session in the same way as you did for the approach stage, including the short conclusion and the dissolution from which you arise again as the deity and so on.

> Place a phumba . . .

You included it as a practice support at the beginning of the retreat.

> . . . made of precious materials containing the nectar of
> twenty-five substances . . .

Include water with the twenty-five substances.[75]

> . . . with a white cloth tied at the neck below the aperture
> ornament in the mandala to the right of the kapala, the main
> accomplishment substance. To the left, put a stand made of
> precious substances that contains the edible long-life vase-
> shaped offering with tree leaves and flower ornaments.

This makes it look like a long-life vase. "Edible offerings" refers to anything you can eat. So this sentence means that you should make a long-life vase from dough and put it to the left of the kapala.

Since "edible offerings" refers here to both food and
alcohol, the food is made with alcohol in the shape of a
long-life vase, as are the pills which are arranged around
the vase. Also add new amrita, rakta, torma and outer
offerings.

"Food" means tsampa dough. So prepare a long life-vase with dough
made of tsampa and alcohol, surrounded by long-life pills made from the
same dough. You should also make fresh offerings of amrita, rakta, torma
and so on.

In the afternoon session do the elaborate practice based on
the sadhana starting with the lineage prayers.

Here "elaborate" means that we make elaborate offerings and that each
of the general offerings is accompanied by its appropriate four-line stanza.
Also offer the amrita, rakta and torma as described earlier. This is the only
difference between the elaborate and the simpler practice.

After the seven-branch accumulation, offer the gektor and
issue the command.

Offer the gektor again.

Practise as before, from the protection spheres prayer up to
and including offering of praise prayer.

This means you practise as you did during the approach. After you've
offered praise,

Then you need to "divide the house of the mantra" . . .

To practise the accomplishment phase, you must create both self- and
front visualizations—you need both. But for the approach practice, you
only need to create a self-visualization. That's the difference. Therefore, here
you need to divide the house of the mantra,

. . . by reciting the mantra DROOM BISHO BISHUDHE TAM
HRIH DROOM TAM DROOM HRIH HUNG DZAM HUNG BAM
HO PET DZA.

> From the mandala of the self-visualization, a second
> mandala complete with both support (environment and
> palace) and supported (deities) separates into the space in
> front of you in the same way one butter lamp lights another.
> The fire surrounding the protection sphere framing the
> self-visualization almost touches the fire surrounding the
> protection sphere of the front visualization.

The mandalas are the same as the mandala you have been visualizing until now, the only difference is that instead of one, you now visualize two.

> Briefly actualise the visualization of the approach phase at
> the start of accomplishment phase sessions. Then visualize
> according to the text beginning, "Again, great cloud-like
> rays of light . . ." and for a while recite each of the three
> approach mantras and the mantra combining the three
> deities, focusing on each one individually.

Do the approach practice briefly as you recite just a few mantras. Then recite the combined practice mantra followed by the Amitayus mantra OM AMARANI DZIVANTIYE SOHA as you visualize the deities as before. And lastly, recite the Ushnisha Vijaya mantra OM AMRITA AYURDADE SOHA. With each mantra make sure you create their respective visualizations, as already mentioned, by briefly focusing on each one individually as you recite the appropriate mantra. If your visualization is clear,

> . . . add the visualization of the emanation and
> reabsorption of rays of light from the heart of the main
> deity to invoke her retinue.

Visualize according to the text from, "Again, great cloud-like rays of light emanate and reabsorb" to ". . . become the wheel of the net of magical manifestation."

As you actualise the text,

> First concentrate on accumulating Vajra Tara's mantra (OM
> TARE TAM SOHA) and recite the three others only briefly at
> the end of the session.

From the main deity Arya Tara's heart, rays of light shoot out and touch Vajra Tara's heart, urging her to fulfill her pledges. Then rays of light shine from Vajra Tara's heart as you recite the Vajra Tara mantra OM TARE TAM SOHA.

Jamgön Kongtrul's commentary says that when you do the recitation of the four Taras, spend most of your time on Vajra Tara and, at the end of the session, briefly recite each of the other three mantras: OM TARE DROOM SOHA, OM TARE HRIH SOHA and OM TARE HUNG SOHA.

> Once you have completed the accumulation of Vajra Tara's mantra, you only need to recite it a few times before concentrating on accumulating the Ratna Tara's mantra which you do for most of your practice session. And so on.

After Ratna Tara, focus on Padma Tara and similarly only recite a few Vajra Tara and Ratna Tara mantras before focusing on the main accumulation of Padma Tara. Then conclude with a few Karma Tara mantras. Jamgön Kongtrul Rinpoche says this is how to practise each of the four Taras.

The visualization for all four Taras is as follows,

> In the heart of each of the Taras of the four families is a lotus and a moon.

Visualize in the hearts of each of the four Taras a lotus and a moon disc seat. As you practise each Tara,

—For Vajra Tara, visualize a dark blue TAM standing on it
—For Ratna Tara, visualize a yellow DROOM
—For Padma Tara, visualize a red HRIH
—For Karma Tara, visualize a black HUNG.

Around each Tara's syllable, visualize her mantra. In this way, focus on each of the four Taras individually as you recite her mantra which emanates and reabsorbs rays of light. When you practise Vajra Tara, your main focus is Vajra Tara; when you practise Ratna Tara, your main focus is Ratna Tara and so on.

> Conclude the session in the same way you concluded the approach stage, except that here it is important to offer a tsok every day.

For the accomplishment phase, it is better to offer a tsok every day.

(iii) Activity

Once you have completed the appropriate number of
accomplishment mantras, move onto the activity practice.

Once you've completed the accomplishment phase, practise the activity
phase. Practise in four sessions every day and do the entire sadhana once
each session. You should complete the accomplishment phase during the
last session of the day. You can choose to practise the accomplishment phase
for seven days or for thirty, but whichever you do you should finish the
practice in the fourth session which is the evening session. The next morning during the first session, follow the sadhana until the accomplishment
mantra as before, then just recite a few mantras.

Then recite the activity section beginning, "I am the
samayasattva, the jnanasattva . . ." and clearly actualise
the visualization. Say, "The four activity Taras with DZA
HUNG BAM HO at their heart on lotus and moon discs" and
visualize the four seed syllables . . .

Visualize the four activity Taras with lotus and moon disc seats at their
hearts to support their seed syllables, DZA, HUNG, BAM and HO.

. . . in their respective colours . . .

These are white, yellow, red and green.

. . . surrounded by the mantra malas.

The mantras are:

OM TARE TAM DZA SHANTING KURU SOHA

OM TARE DROOM HUNG PUSHTING KURU OM

OM TARE HRIH BAM WASHAM KURU HO

OM TARE HUNG HO MARAYA PET

Now what is the visualization?

Rays of light stream out from the five deities (the main
deity and the four Taras in the retinue) to invoke Hook
Tara. Hook Tara manifests many emanations, rays
of light and infinite miracles which accomplish the
activity of pacifying all obstructing forces such as illness,
negative spirits, negative actions, obscurations and so on.
Accumulate only her mantra throughout the session.

This means you concentrate on Hook Tara's mantra OM TARE TAM DZA
SHANTING KURU SOHA for one session.

The conclusion is as before.

Next, practise only Noose Tara's mantra and visualization and accomplish the enriching activity. Actualise the visualization for Noose Tara. As
the pacifying activities have been accomplished, imagine rays of light shining from Noose Tara's heart to accomplish all the enriching activities that
increase longevity, merit, magnetism and wealth.

In the afternoon session, practise only Iron Chain Tara's
mantra and visualization.

Again, from the heart of the five main deities (Tara Wish-Fulfilling Wheel
and the four Taras), rays of light invoke Iron Chain Tara, and many rays of red
light emanate from her heart to accomplish the magnetising activities.

During the evening session, practise Bell Tara who accomplishes the subjugating activities. The visualization is the same as Hook Tara's for all four activity
Taras. From the five deities, rays of light invoke Bell Tara from whose body rays
of light shine out and accomplish the subjugating activities. Actualise these
four visualizations, focusing on one in each of the four sessions of a day.

At the hearts of the standing activity Taras, on lotus and moon disc seats,
are their seed syllables: white DZA, yellow HUNG, red BAM and green HO.

(iv) Measure of Each Phase of the Practice

The sadhana briefly mentions the three ways you can
measure approach, accomplishment and activity practice:
time, number of mantras or signs.

We quantify approach, accomplishment and activity practice in three ways: by the amount of time we spend practising, the number of mantras we accumulate or by the signs of accomplishment we achieve.

> Those of superior capacity should practise approach for three weeks, accomplishment for one week and activity for one day which, including receiving the siddhis, makes one month. Those of medium capacity should multiply that by three, making a total of three months.

So practitioners of medium capacity practise approach for nine weeks, accomplishment for twenty-one days and activity for three days.

> The practitioner with lesser capacity should therefore practise for six months.

This is how you measure your practice in time.

> In terms of numbers, we also distinguish between practitioners of superior, medium and lesser capacities, which roughly takes about the same amount of time.

Basically, Jamgön Kongtrul says you accumulate as many mantras as you can in the time you've given yourself to practise. That's all. There are no special instructions, just do as many as you can. Generally though, when you focus on the number of mantras you accumulate, the minimum should be:

—100,00 for each of the ten syllables of the main deity mantra, making 1,000,000
—700,000 of the nineteen-syllable approach mantra of the combined practice
—400,000 of the jnanasattva and 400,000 of the nirmanasattva mantras
—100,000 of each of the accomplishment mantras of the four Taras
—40,000 of each of the mantras of the four Gatekeeper Taras for activity.

This is the minimum number of mantras you should recite. For a medium-length practice, it should take three or four months to accomplish which is a good length of time. For mere familiarization with the practice, you should recite:

—400,000 for the main deity's ten-syllable mantra
—100,000 of the combined practice
—40,000 of the jnanasattva and 40,000 of the nirmanasattva mantras
—10,000 of each for the accomplishment mantras
—however many you can manage in one day for each of the mantras of the four Gatekeeper Taras for activity.

These numbers are based on the speed for those of superior capacity.

> The signs are clearly mentioned in the text. The best sign is realization, the next best is experience and the least good is to repeatedly experience clarity in dreams.

The best signs are meeting the deity face-to-face, for the amrita in the skull cup to start to boil or for a butter lamp to light itself. The medium sign is to have meditative experiences and stabilize them; the least good is to repeatedly experience clarity in dreams.

III. CONCLUDING PRACTICES
A. Receiving the Siddhis

Whether you practise the longest, medium-length or shorter option, you will eventually finish the activity phase. It is good to receive the siddhis the following morning when you should practise especially early. If you can't practise early, the usual morning session is also fine.

Before you start the session, make a new offering torma (*chötor*). The siddhi substance should be the four activity long-life tormas which are each a different colour—pacifying white, enriching yellow, magnetising red and subjugating green. If you can't, one "jewel-shaped long-life torma" (*drangye norzukma*) is fine. Around the torma, arrange a variety of washed food and drinks of all kinds, for example white offerings like milk and curd, red offerings like fruit, tea, alcohol and so on.

> Do the elaborate practice following the sadhana text
> and recite a few of each of the mantras of approach,
> accomplishment and activity.

Then recite the offering and praise prayer.

> From the hearts of the deities of the self- and front
> visualizations, rays of light shine out in the shape of iron
> hooks and pervade the whole of space. All the vital energy
> of the worlds and the inhabitants of samsara and nirvana
>
> . . .

This means all sentient beings and perfectly enlightened buddhas.

> . . . are gathered into nectar appearing as rays of light that
> dissolve into the siddhi substances.

These are the substances that you have arranged on the shrine.

> Actualise this as you recite the mantra of the combined
> practice OM TARE TUTTARE TURE HRIH DROOM BENDZA
> JNANA AYUKE SOHA followed by KAYA WAKA TSITTA GUNA
> KARMA SARWA SIDDHI PALA HO one thousand times or
> more.

> Then you recite the *Inexpressible Ultimate Confession* (*Yeshe
> Kuchok*) followed by the descent of blessings that is in the
> sadhana text and the elaborate offering and praise prayers.
> Finally, recite the requesting siddhis prayer that starts with,
> "OM Sublime Lady . . ." which is in the sadhana.

> Actualising the usual visualizations, place the phumba on
> your head and drink some of its water, place the nectar at
> your throat and drink some, place the long-life torma at
> your heart, eat some of the substances in the kapala and keep
> consuming what remains for a long time and so on as usual.

Keep the remaining siddhi substances and eat a little of them regularly.

> Then offer a large tsok and enjoy it. If you withheld the
> remainder earlier, offer it with the remainder torma.

In retreat you don't take the remainder offerings out, you keep them with you throughout your retreat. But at this point at the end of the retreat, you take all your remainder offerings out.

Invoke the wisdom mind of the protectors to whom you offer the remainder and request that they fulfill their pledges. Then do the cheto, the Tenma and the horse dance. Make your confession and ask for forgiveness, then read the text until the prayer of auspiciousness which is the end.

B. Amending Faults of Lack or Excess—Fire Puja

> It is good to do a fire puja in order to make up for and
> correct mistakes, omissions and repetitions. If you choose
> to do this elaborately in relation to the mandala, perform
> a fire ritual on the next day— after you complete the four
> activities.

If you want to, you can practise the fire puja elaborately while the mandala is still set up. This Chimé Phakmé Nyingtik practice includes a recitation for the four activities involving Iron Hook Tara, Lasso Tara, Iron Chain Tara and Bell Tara. Offer the fire puja after the recitation for Bell Tara but before the retreat is over. This means you offer the fire puja before you receive the siddhis.

> If you do not relate the fire puja offering to the mandala . . .

This is permissible.

> . . . you can either offer a fire puja on the day you complete
> the practice and receive the siddhis, or the next day.

Also, to complete the approach and accomplishment stages, recite another ten percent of the total mantra accumulation during your recitation and do ten thousand fire puja accumulations at the end, plus whatever is necessary to accomplish the activities such as lengthening life. There is a mantra within the fire puja that lengthens life and so on, so do as many of these mantras as you can.

CONCLUSION

> Even though this practice can be done more elaborately
> following the structure of a drupchen, here we only
> explained the difficult points of the practice and other
> instructions.

Drupchen actually involves even more elaborate and detailed practices. However, it would take too long to explain it all so Jamgön Kongtrul says he hasn't mentioned it in this text.

If you do the daily practice to "maintain the continuous flow of the practice", you can just recite the approach mantras (Tara, combined practice, Amitayus and Ushnisha Vijaya mantras). You don't have to do the accomplishment mantras of the four Taras and the activity mantras of the four activity Taras, but you can recite them if you want to.

This commentary was written by Jamgön Kongtrul Rinpoche when he was eighty-seven years old.

CHAPTER 8:

Explanation of *Activities for Uncovering Primordial Wisdom*, the Root Sadhana of the Chimé Phakmé Nyingtik

by Tulku Orgyen Tobgyal

INTRODUCTION
Why I am Talking to You Today

First, let me tell you why I am talking to you today. It all started with Prashant, who has asked me again and again to talk here at Deer Park; then Khyentse Rinpoche repeatedly backed him up. From my point of view, to flout Khyentse Rinpoche's command would be highly inappropriate, and so that is why I came here today to talk to you. Turning to the dharma teaching I have been asked to talk about, it is a terma that was revealed by Jamyang Khyentse Wangpo. Of all the different termas this great master revealed, the Chimé Phakmé Nyingtik is one of those that focuses on practice. Specifically, it is a sadhana or a "means of accomplishment" and to say a little about it might serve those who relate to such explanations—basically practitioners—and that's another reason I agreed to talk about it today.

The Chimé Phakmé Nyingtik is part of the vast body of teachings Jamyang Khyentse Wangpo received through the seven authoritative transmissions. I practise the Chimé Phakmé Nyingtik and am somewhat familiar with it. Although I haven't attained any kind of accomplishment through my practice, I believe sharing my experience of practice and what I have learned as a result of it could be helpful. These are my reasons for talking about the Chimé Phakmé Nyingtik on this occasion.

Let's turn now to the dharma teaching at hand. To begin with, it is important to know that the range of dharma teachings is extremely vast. According to the Nyingma tradition, there are two great categories of teachings—the teachings of the causal Vehicle of Characteristics and the Vajrayana teachings. The Chimé Phakmé Nyingtik belongs to the second category, the Vajrayana vehicle that uses fruition as the path. Its teachings are divided into categories, and the Chimé Phakmé Nyingtik belongs to the teachings of the Mahayoga that emphasize the generation phase (kyerim). How do we practise these teachings? By following a sadhana that brings the practitioner to realization.

Ground

Before we enter into the Chimé Phakmé Nyingtik itself, it might be good first to talk generally about the view, but I won't go into great detail. The Buddha taught that the ground is the buddha nature present in all sentient beings. Even though all schools of Tibetan Buddhism accept that all sentient beings have buddha nature, each has its own way of proving it. The Chimé Phakmé Nyingtik follows the approach of the Nyingma school. According to the Nyingmapas, there are two types of teaching—the kama and the terma. Chimé Phakmé Nyingtik is a terma teaching. Of the many termas that have been revealed, the Chimé Phakmé Nyingtik was brought out during the time of the three Jamgöns—Chokgyur Dechen Lingpa, Jamyang Khyentse Wangpo and Jamgön Kongtrul. I will therefore show that buddha nature is present in all sentient beings by following *Lamrim Yeshe Nyingpo* which in many ways is the root tantra of all the profound termas revealed by the three Jamgöns and will repeat the explanation exactly as Guru Rinpoche presented it in that text.

The proof that buddha nature exists in all sentient beings also appears in other teachings. For example, the *Sublime Continuum* offers teachings on buddha nature from the Sutrayana perspective, and the Tantrayana perspective is explained in the *Secret Essence Tantra*. But since *Lamrim Yeshe Nyingpo* brings together very essentially the pith instructions of both approaches and is a direct instruction of Guru Rinpoche, I will use it as the basis for a very clear and simple presentation about how all sentient beings have buddha nature. If this is not enough for you, refer to the teachings Dzongsar Khyentse Rinpoche began in 2011 in Canada on *Lamrim Yeshe Nyingpo*. You could also consult the commentaries on this text that go into great detail based on quotations from the sacred texts and using logical reasoning.[76]

I will now present this teaching very simply without using extensive quotations or going into the different logical arguments, but rather will wholly rely on the original text. Buddha nature is the essence or nature of the buddhas. So "all sentient beings have the ground of buddha nature" means that all sentient beings have the nature of a buddha. This can be understood to mean that we are buddhas or, as some think, that there are two different things—the buddhas and our buddha nature. There are those who take "sentient beings" to mean all human beings and forget about other kinds of sentient beings. This is a misunderstanding. Here "sentient beings" means all human and non-human beings who are able to perceive and feel things, who are "sentient". If we allow ourselves to contemplate this sentence for a moment, what can we make of it?

Basically, the buddha is our mind. As it says in the termas, "Apart from mind there is no buddha." All sentient beings have a mind—there is not one sentient being without a mind. Therefore, we all have this buddha nature which is the cause for enlightenment. Hearing this, many people are often taken aback. We tend to think of the Buddha as the most extraordinary of beings with qualities beyond our imaginations. So when we hear that our minds are buddha too, it dumbfounds us. It's true, it's not easy to accommodate such ideas, but to be able to practise the Secret Mantra Vajrayana, you need to accept that it is possible. If you can't, you will not be able to practise the path of the Mahayoga that emphasizes kyerim.

Don't look outwardly too much. If you do, you will get lost in the arguments and quotations that explain why all sentient beings have buddha nature. Don't get drawn into that kind of thinking and conceptualization. Instead, look inwardly. You have now been told that all sentient beings have this extraordinary buddha nature, and your master has told you that buddha nature is your mind. So investigate and probe the idea to test whether or not it is true. When you eventually see that it is true, just rest with that certainty. Think, "All sentient beings have the ground of buddha nature and so I too have buddha nature." Verify this statement for yourself and meditate on it. If you have buddha nature, you must also have all the incredible enlightened qualities described in the sutras and tantras because as a buddha, it would be impossible not to have them. So check whether it's true or not. Think about it very carefully. If you have all those qualities, you have the ground of buddha nature. If you don't have buddha nature, to repeat the words that your mind is buddha and has all the incredible qualities of enlightenment would be sheer invention.

Other vehicles or paths teach that the enlightened qualities of buddha nature are not present in us at this very moment, but rather that they exist as a seed. Once the seed of our buddha nature has fully matured, all its qualities will manifest and this is what happens when we reach enlightenment. However, if you want to practise the Chimé Phakmé Nyingtik, you must think, "I already have all the enlightened qualities. They are already in me and not something new that I have to acquire." Actually, this is true for practitioners of all the practices of the Mahayoga that emphasize kyerim, not just those who practise the Chimé Phakmé Nyingtik. Whatever practice you do, you must consider that you already have all the enlightened qualities. To imagine you don't and by doing this practice you will acquire them is a mistake. In short, the mind that practises the sadhana is actually the Buddha. All his enlightened qualities which are even greater than their extensive descriptions in the sutras and tantras and beyond imagining are complete within your mind. So you need to make a clear and confident decision that this is how it is.

As I am presenting these teachings so essentially, you may not understand what I'm trying to say. Or rather, you might be able to hear what I'm saying and even understand most of the words I use but find you don't trust that what I say is true. If this is the case, then maybe you should spend some time studying the teachings of the sutras and especially the tantras, since they offer a vast array of authoritative references from the sacred texts and logical arguments that support this truth, which you should examine and reflect upon. Having studied in this way, if you are still not confident that the mind is the Buddha and that all his enlightened qualities are present within your mind and if you still harbour a "maybe they are, maybe they aren't" kind of attitude, you will need to accumulate a lot more merit and purify your obscurations. If even this approach does not work, it probably means that you lack the good fortune to be a recipient of teachings of the path of the Mahayoga, the higher path of Anuyoga or the path of Dzogchen.

Delusion

As it is said,

> All sentient beings have the ground of the buddha nature,
> mind is the Buddha.

This doesn't mean that all these people are the Buddha—just to have the ground of buddha nature, doesn't make you a buddha. Sentient beings have that ground, but it is temporarily hidden by both cognitive and habitual obscurations, and these two kinds of obscuration are explained at length in the sutras and tantras, so I won't go into them here in any detail. At the most basic level though, obscurations are our thoughts, and at this very moment, it is our thoughts that obscure our buddha nature. This is what we call ignorance or "not knowing" which is a more literal translation of the Tibetan term. What is it that we do not know? That buddha is our nature. And we are deluded because we do not recognize the buddha that is our nature. It is said, "Know, and you are a buddha; ignore, and you are a sentient being." At the moment we are ignorant, and that very ignorance is concealing our buddha nature.

Now we must identify what delusion really is. Many people think delusion is any one of the destructive emotions (like desire, aversion, jealousy or pride), the ten negative actions and so on, and that positive thoughts and emotions like faith, devotion and so on are not delusions, but it's not like that. All our thoughts involve grasping at subject-object duality, and based on all those dualistic thoughts we accumulate karma, then repeat the process endlessly. This is what we call delusion.

Path

Once you understand the nature of delusion clearly, you realise that although mind is the ground of your buddha nature, it is deluded and impure. To remove those impurities, you must follow a path that eliminates all contaminations and reveals your inherent purity. This is why we practise sadhanas, even though a sadhana is itself a delusion and so are the deities. But the Buddha tells us just as we must rely on a material that is as strong as iron in order to cut through iron, we must rely on the delusion of deity, samadhi, mantra and so on to cut through and remove our fundamental delusions. So even though all aspects of the path of kyerim fall into the category of delusion, it is through such practices as kyerim that we are able to realise the nature of our mind, the primordial ground.

Atiyoga or Dzogchen teaches that mind is the Buddha, and Atiyoga practitioners meditate by simply looking directly at mind itself. It is a path that does not involve the elaborations of visualizing deities, performing mudras, reciting mantras, resting in samadhi and so on and is suited only to those of superior capacity. Others, those of middling capacity for example, won't benefit from the Atiyoga approach and should rely instead on Mahayoga practices that are taught as pith instructions and involve deity, mantra, mudra and samadhi. Through such practices, their intrinsic nature which is the primordial ground will be liberated.

There are infinite deities of all kinds to correlate with the many dispositions of sentient beings. Each aspect of each deity—the face, expression, number of arms, whether they are peaceful or wrathful and so on—manifests based on the corresponding propensities of the sentient beings they help. We always say that there are infinite deities corresponding to the infinite dispositions of beings, but if you imagine this means you can do whatever you like, your practice is not likely to be very beneficial. Great practitioners like Guru Rinpoche or Vimalamitra are able to see all phenomena as the deity, and if Guru Rinpoche says, "The stone in front of me is the deity", it works because for such great masters, there are no deities with characteristics to be held onto. The ultimate point of kyerim is that all that appears and exists is infinite purity. But to count or make lists of all the different deities and their aspects would take all your time, and you'd never get to the infinite purity of all that appears and exists. So when those who have yet to realise that infinite purity first set out on the path, they take as the support of their practice a specific deity and mantra which they then accomplish. In this case, we will rely on the Chimé Phakmé Nyingtik, the main deity of which is Tara in union with Amitayus in a mandala of three main deities with a retinue of eight. This will be explained as we go through the text.

Fruition

It is important to recognize that the reason we follow the path of the deity is to eliminate delusion and that the fruition of this path is liberation within the primordial ground. Mind is the deity, there is no deity other than mind. Once you realise this, you will have accomplished the deity. If you don't, to have dreams about the deity or even meet the deity face-to-face won't help you much. Having said that, dreaming about or meeting the deity are signs you are getting closer to realising that your mind is the deity and the deity is your mind.

From the perspective of the ground, all sentient beings are buddhas— the minds of sentient beings are buddhas. As sentient beings do not recognize mind is buddha, they are said to be deluded or obscured, and the path through which practitioners free their minds from delusion is the practice of meditating on the deity. Once we have freed our minds from delusion, the fruition is fully manifest.

Conclusion

If you don't know at least this much about ground, path and fruition, you will have nothing to practise, so first you must understand this much. Dilgo Khyentse Rinpoche said that buddha nature is present in all sentient beings and all sentient beings are buddhas. It is because we have this ground of buddha nature that by following the path, we can become enlightened. The example he often used was of a sesame seed. By pressing a tiny sesame seed, as the seed itself is destroyed, the oil will be extracted, but even if you pressed a stone for thousands of years using all manner of contraptions, you would never be able to extract oil, because stone does not have the same nature as sesame seeds. It is because sentient beings have buddha nature that we can attain enlightenment. If we sentient beings did not have buddha nature, we would not be able to attain enlightenment. That's one example, but giving too many examples isn't always helpful.

Let's look again at delusion. To think, "I am deluded. I need to remove all my delusion", then to apply various different methods for eliminating delusion will of course have some impact. But the most helpful kind of thought is, "I am deluded, but my ground is buddha nature, and if I realise the nature of my mind directly within the primordial ground, all my delusions will vanish."

For example, to meditate on the pointing-out instructions your master teaches makes it easier for you to remove delusion. In other words, once you are aware you are deluded, you find there are innumerable ways for eliminating that delusion like offering your own head or limbs to others. To apply these many different methods is of course helpful, but not that fruitful. However, to know you are deluded and to liberate the knower directly within the primordial ground will result in immediate liberation. The example used is of a house that has been kept in absolute darkness for thousands of years, yet the moment a light is switched on all the darkness completely disappears. There is not one dark patch left. Where there is no light, it is correct to say, "It is dark", but once you switch on the light, the darkness has gone. Similarly, if we follow a path that removes the darkness of delusion, there will be no darkness. This is where the practice of kyerim will help.

If you can understand this much, you will have the necessary basis from which to embark not just on dharma practice, but on the practice of the Vajrayana path. Problems will arise though if you have not established such an understanding. If for example you imagine the deity and you are separate and different, there will be nothing for you to accomplish. As you practise the Chimé Phakmé Nyingtik, if you imagine that the deity is extraordinary but you are ordinary, it won't work. This is the attitude adopted by the practitioners of Kriyayoga. Many people these days try to accomplish different deities in the same way that they make friends with people they think will eventually be useful to them. They accomplish a deity for a specific purpose, then move on to accomplish another deity for a different purpose and so on. This is an extremely limited approach and won't get you very far. If you really do manage to accomplish a deity, you also accomplish all the infinite number of mandalas. Beings are deluded by all manner of thoughts, and therefore many different deities manifest. But once all the delusions created by conceptual thought are eliminated, since the deity is the mind there will no longer be a deity—there is no buddha other than mind.

Therefore, our view should be the highest possible. If we adopt a high view, we must also be realistic about how we then conduct ourselves and practise the path. Practice will involve deity, mantra, samadhi and mudra as they occur in the sadhana text. Essentially, as we visualize the deity using the methods of kyerim, we should also embrace dzogrim practice that dissolves our visualization into emptiness as we unite both kyerim and dzogrim. But I'll explain that more fully later when it comes up in the text. If we fail to do so and instead continue to grasp as we practise, our efforts will be useless.

Don't practise with the idea that the result is a long way away or that the fruition of your practice is something extra you need to acquire. Once our obscurations have been dispelled, the fruition of practice—our true nature—will manifest. For now, it is obscured or covered up, but it is definitely there. So we must develop the certainty that the result of our practice is already with us and by eliminating our obscurations, that result will manifest.

In this brief presentation of the ground, path and fruition of the Vajrayana, I have tried to set out the crucial understanding you need to arrive at in order to practise. People who are not familiar with the teachings may think, "Yes, maybe that is true. It sort of makes sense." People with more experience of the buddhadharma, but with little exposure to the Vajrayana teachings, might get a bit overexcited. Whichever the case, it is important you check thoroughly each point you get excited about and reflect on its meaning as presented in the great sutras and tantras. If you do, the conclusion you reach will be what I have just explained. There is no other conclusion possible. This is certainly true of practice, but also of empowerments which are the foundation of the Vajrayana path. Unless you understand at least this much about ground, path and fruition, you will not be able truly to receive the empowerments.

I. BEFORE YOU START TO PRACTISE

If you wish to practise the Chimé Phakmé Nyingtik and truly actualise its meaning, you must:

    A. Learn about the history of the teachings so you gain confidence in them.

    B. Receive the empowerment, which will mature you, so you can do the practice.

C. Hear the instructions that liberate and receive the
     related pith instructions.

To that end, I will start by telling the story of the teaching so you develop confidence in it.

A. The History of the Chimé Phakmé
Nyingtik Teachings

I will now outline briefly the general background of this teaching. There
have been many great practitioners of the Vajrayana both in India and Tibet.
The Indian practitioners included for example Garab Dorje, the great nirmanakaya teacher of Dzogchen who went to Akanishtha, received teachings
directly from Vajrasattva and managed to hear, practise and realise them
in one session. He was a practitioner with superior capacities. Many other
great masters followed who were at the same level as Garab Dorje. They
realised the teachings as they heard them but displayed a different approach
to practice by following a progressive path, for example the great vidyadharas Guru Rinpoche, Vimalamitra and Shri Singha. They practised and
perfected each of the three yogas of the Mahayoga that emphasizes kyerim,
Anuyoga and finally Atiyoga or Dzogchen, and demonstrated how individuals could follow the path in stages.

Each of them practised a specific yidam deity and went through the
process of progressing through the four vidyadhara levels by accomplishing
their yidam. This is the kind of master we are going to discuss now, and we
will base our discussion on the Nyingma approach.

Let's now turn to the origins of the Chimé Phakmé Nyingtik. Ushnisha Vijaya (*tsuktor namgyalma* in Tibetan) was so named after she emerged
from the protuberance on top of the Buddha's head (*ushnisha*) and because
she was fully victorious (*vijaya*) over the four maras. Ushnisha Vijaya sutras
can be found in the causal vehicle, while the Vajrayana offers Ushnisha Vijaya tantras and sadhanas. The great vidyadhara Shri Singha took Ushnisha Vijaya as his yidam, then practised and fully accomplished her, while
the great master Vimalamitra practised and accomplished Chimé Phakma.
Chimé Phakma, the Sublime Lady of Immortality, is White Tara known
as Yishin Khorlo, the Wish-Fulfilling Wheel. She came into being when

noble Avalokiteshvara helped sentient beings. He generated the enlightened mind and shed two tears of compassion, one tear became White Tara and the other Green Tara. The great Pandita Vimalamitra took white Tara as his yidam and gained mastery over birth and death, the state beyond decrease and increase. Guru Rinpoche accomplished the four levels of a vidyadhara. He practised Amitayus in the Maratika Cave to accomplish the level of a vidyadhara with power over life, and Amitayus in union appeared and bestowed the long-life empowerment on him, through which Guru Rinpoche became immortal and is able to remain in samsara to help sentient beings until eventually it is emptied.

These three great masters—Guru Rinpoche, Vimalamitra and Shri Singha—who had accomplished these long-life deities appeared to Jamyang Khyentse Wangpo, made prophecies and blessed him. As a result, Khyentse Wangpo revealed the mind terma of Chimé Phakmé Nyingtik combining all three long-life deities—Amitayus, White Tara and Ushnisha Vijaya.

The key points to understand here are that the three deities of long life are yidam deities. Guru Rinpoche, Shri Singha and Vimalamitra are the three great vidyadharas who practised and accomplished these yidams, becoming indivisible with them. All three great masters—with a single, indivisible wisdom mind—appeared to and blessed Jamyang Khyentse Wangpo. The play of these three great masters' indivisible wisdom mind is the mind terma. When Jamyang Khyentse Wangpo's mind became indivisible from the wisdom mind of Guru Rinpoche, Shri Singha and Vimalamitra, the wisdom mind of all these masters was one and the same. The play of this wisdom manifests in the form of the practice that accomplishes the three deities of longevity, and each vidyadhara accomplished one deity's sadhana. This unprecedented approach resulted in the Chimé Phakmé Nyingtik. Both the Sakya and Nyingma traditions have practices that accomplish each of the three deities individually, but the Chimé Phakmé Nyingtik accomplishes all three deities together and as such is a practice that had never before dawned upon this earth.

Jamyang Khyentse Wangpo may have looked like an ordinary person, but his mind was far beyond anything ordinary people could even conceive. Why? Because he was able to remember what had happened to him in a vast number of his past lives, for example when he was Vimalamitra. He could remember very clearly and vividly what happened at that time as if it were yesterday. For example, he sometimes imagined he still had certain brocades or other belongings but then realised they had been his when he was Vimalamitra or the accomplished yogi Vajraghantapada or Pratiharanandamati. He'd forget which lifetime he was in, wondering where specific objects that appeared in his mind that he'd owned when he was Vimalamitra now were. An infinite, limitless, unfathomable number of mind termas manifested in Jamyang Khyentse Wangpo's wisdom mind. He would have known all the different termas revealed by the one hundred and eight major tertöns and all the future tertöns and their termas. And it was within the wisdom mind of this great master that the Chimé Phakmé Nyingtik manifested as a terma.

He received teachings through all seven authoritative transmissions, which include the six types of termas. Mention is also made of eighteen categories of terma. But of all the different kinds that exist, the most profound is the mind terma. Why? A mind terma is revealed when the wisdom mind of the tertön and the wisdom mind of the yidam deity in the sadhana and of Guru Rinpoche have become indivisible. Until that happens, it cannot be revealed. For mind termas, there's no need to translate or decipher anything, the terma just appears in the mind of the master directly. Jamyang Khyentse Wangpo revealed this teaching, transmitted it to his main disciple Jamgön Kongtrul Lodrö Taye and since then it has been transmitted from teacher to student down to the present day.

This terma is very concise, it has very few words, yet its meaning is extremely profound. Anyone who practises this sadhana will eliminate all obstacles and obscurations and accumulate vast stores of merit. It has the power to cause an ocean of profound wisdom to swell and all five clear perceptions to manifest. The result of just seven days of practice is so powerful that the practitioner will be protected from untimely death. Noble Jetsun Tara will take the practitioner into her care, and he or she will ultimately be able to accomplish all the paths and bhumis in a single lifetime. Guru Rinpoche said that those who come across the Chimé Phakmé Nyingtik and have the opportunity to receive this cycle of teachings or simply to hear them must realise what extremely fortunate karma they have.

This concludes the first point which is learning about the teachings as a way of gaining confidence in them, because to hear how the teachings came about helps us develop that confidence. It is important, isn't it?

B. Receive the Empowerment

The second point is that practitioners must be matured by receiving the empowerment. Unless you receive the empowerment, not only can you not practise these teachings but you will not even be allowed to listen to them. That is the approach of the tantras.

C. The Instructions that Liberate

In terms of the liberating instructions, the way to do a *nyenpa*[77] practice of the Chimé Phakmé Nyingtik has already been explained by Jamgön Kongtrul Lodrö Taye. The text has been translated into English, and you can therefore consult it. I have nothing to add to Jamgön Kongtrul's *Retreat Manual*.[78] At the beginning of the Chimé Phakmé Nyingtik cycle is a tantra called the *Quintessential Blessings of Lama Practice*,[79] the commentary of which teaches the hidden meaning of the symbolic expressions that appear in the tantra and so on. But I'm not going to talk about the tantra today. What we are concerned with here is the sadhana which is the means for accomplishing this path. It is called *Activities to Uncover Primordial Wisdom, from the Heart Essence of the Sublime Lady of Immortality*.

In the Mantrayana, generally speaking, it is said that those of superior capacity merely have to read the title of a teaching to understand it. For those of middling capacity, it is necessary just to explain the meaning; while those of lesser capacity require each word to be explained. Those of superior capacity are able to understand the entire contents of a teaching just by being shown its title. Longchen Rabjam explained that this is like holding the tip of an arrow, the *raison d'être* of the weapon—if we understand the teaching just by hearing the title, its purpose is fulfilled. For those of middling capacity, the main points of the teaching must be explained which is like holding the spear in the middle of its shaft—its waist—to accomplish its purpose. For those of lesser capacity, every word of the text must be explained which is like holding the grip of a sword that is at the bottom end of the weapon.

1. The Title

So for those of you of superior capacity, I will present the title, *Activities to Uncover Primordial Wisdom from the Heart Essence of the Sublime Lady of Immortality*. Who is the deity of immortality? Externally, the essence of the yidam deity is the Buddha; internally, it is the mind. Mind doesn't die, it has never experienced death and this deathless mind is what manifests in the form of Jetsun Phakma for the sake of sentient beings to be tamed. The Tibetan word *phakma* means "most supreme" and here indicates that Jetsun Tara, the Sublime Lady, has risen above everything in samsara and nirvana. "Most supreme" Tara is the embodiment of the enlightened activities of all the sugatas of the ten directions and four times; Vajrakilaya is the male deity who embodies the enlightened activities of all the buddhas.

The buddhas are characterized by their inexhaustible wheels of enlightened body, enlightened speech, enlightened mind and enlightened qualities. Yet the ultimate expression, purpose or fruition of these four enlightened aspects is enlightened activity. Buddhas manifest through three kayas, dharmakaya, sambhogakaya and nirmanakaya. Ultimately, a buddha is dharmakaya and from a dharmakaya buddha's point of view does not manifest a physical body. To be able to guide sentient beings though, buddhas display bodies and these are the nirmanakaya manifestations that have the thirty-two major and eighty minor marks and even more enlightened qualities beyond our imaginations. They all make an impact on sentient beings, and it is said we accumulate incredible merit just by looking at the form of a buddha.

Although the enlightened form of a buddha is incredibly beneficial, enlightened speech is said to be even more important. The physical body of a buddha can only benefit sentient beings for a limited time, whereas the enlightened speech of a buddha reveals the three or nine yanas and so on—enlightened speech turns the wheel of the dharma of an infinite number of yanas. So enlightened speech benefits far more sentient beings than the body of a buddha. The enlightened mind abides in the samadhi of great equanimity in the fourth time beyond past, present and future, and therefore manifests for sentient beings outside the limitations of the three times. It is said to benefit sentient beings on an immense scale through the emanation and reconvergence of blessings borne on rays of light that spring from a pure and infinite array of mandalas.

Enlightened qualities are the root or source of the enlightened body, speech and mind that benefit sentient beings, and the fruit or power of these enlightened qualities are the enlightened activities of the buddhas. This is Jetsun Drolma or Tara; she is the embodiment of the enlightened activities of all the buddhas and was given the name Phakma, Sublime Lady, because her enlightened activities exceed those of any other buddha. She vowed to continue to manifest in the form of a woman for the sake of sentient beings until there is no one to be helped out of samsara. This amazed all the other buddhas because such a vow took such great compassion to make. She is also called Nyurma Phakmo, Swift Lady of Courage, and is extremely quick to respond.

"Nyingtik" means heart essence and in this case is the essence (*tik*) of the heart (*nying*) of Phakma, the Sublime Lady. The "essence of the heart" refers to the purest, most essential, innermost aspect with infinite qualities, one of which is activity. "Activity" here basically means sadhana. Anyone practising this sadhana will see the primordial wisdom being uncovered and all obscuring ignorance will disappear.

That was the title. If you are at the level where you can understand the text just by hearing the title, this is all you need! If not, there is still a little that can be understood from this title. This text is the heart essence of the Sublime Lady of Immortality, Chimé Phakma, in the form of a sadhana which—if applied—makes it possible for the light of wisdom to become the path, while the deluded ignorance of worldly beings and so on will be eliminated.

2. Symbolic Script

A number of symbolic scripts appear throughout the text and they are not unimportant. The *Lamrim Yeshe Nyingpo* mentions seven different purposes of symbolic scripts.[80] Basically, it indicates that this text is not the creation of the mind as a result of reflection, deep or otherwise, but a terma of Guru Rinpoche who mastered the dakinis' secret symbolic language. Even the most eminent linguist, someone who speaks all the languages of the world, cannot understand the language of terma—it would be like giving grass to a dog! But for an owner of the teaching with the right karma whose mind is indivisible from the wisdom mind of Guru Rinpoche, the entire meaning will appear within the expanse of his wisdom mind when he reads the secret dakini script. And he will also be able to write it down.

When the Indian or American governments produce a document, it always appears under the governments' own seal, which these days comes in the form of a letterhead for example. And the secret script of the dakinis indicates that the text is a profound terma of Guru Rinpoche. So whenever you see symbolic script, you immediately know you are in the presence of a terma.

Termas are not trivial, although these days revealing them seems to have become so easy that complete ignoramuses are doing it! But if you really think about it, you will realise that to reveal a terma is in fact extremely difficult. Were you to ask these modern-day tertöns to explain the meaning of what they write, they wouldn't be able to. Why? Because what they've done is gather bits and pieces from other termas, strung them together and announced, "Here is my new terma." They're like parrots, they can repeat what other people say but have no idea what their words mean! Such modern revelations have nothing in common with the termas uncovered by Jamyang Khyentse Wangpo through the seven transmissions. This concludes the explanation of the title.

3. The Explanation of the Text

Now, to the explanation of the text. Rather than go through the *Retreat Manual*, I will go through the words of the main sadhana itself and will simply explain the main points of the practice without spelling out the meaning of each word. In other words, I will use the teaching method for beings of medium capacity.

You should also know that I am not teaching this text because I want to share fascinating pieces of information. I am talking to those who will put this teaching into practise as their daily practice or even if they just want to do a one-week retreat. This teaching is given with the sole intention of helping such people.

There's no point in explaining this text in too much detail, we don't need to do that. Why not? Because if you explain in great detail and don't point out the actual meaning, most people are unable to retain all the information. Having received the teaching, when asked, "What did he say?", most of you will reply, "Ah, it was a very elaborate teaching, he gave a lot of detail!" But when you find yourself sitting on a cushion, you will be unable to put those details together meaningfully. As you then read your practice text, all manner of thoughts about those details will pop into your mind; but because you can't make sense of any of them, they will just clutter it up. Mind is quite limited and cannot embrace all these details. Instead, it just gets confused.

II. THE MAIN PART: THE SADHANA OF CHIMÉ PHAKMÉ NYINGTIK

The text begins,

> *O Immortal Wish-Fulfilling Wheel*
> *In devotion, I pay homage to you, body, speech and mind.*

The recipient of the homage is the Wish-Fulfilling Wheel of Immortality (Chimé Yishin Khorlo).

The author of the homage is Guru Rinpoche. The purpose of Guru Rinpoche's prostration to the Wish-Fulfilling Wheel of Immortality is that it will stave off any obstacle that might hinder the compilation of this sadhana and prevent it from being of benefit to sentient beings in the future.

> *I shall now elucidate the profound yoga of uniting one with*
> *   your nature,*
> *So practitioners may accomplish the two siddhis.*

This "profound yoga" is the Chimé Phakmé Nyingtik. What does profound mean here? We usually consider all dharma teachings to be profound, the Vajrayana teachings to be particularly profound, and the three inner yogas of the Vajrayana teachings to be incredibly profound, perhaps the most profound of all. Why? They are rich in methods involving very little hardship that aim at leading an individual to the enlightened state of indivisible unity—the level of Vajradhara—in a single lifetime.

To practise the path of this profound sadhana, it is necessary first to receive the ripening empowerment. Then when you practise the sadhana, it will be genuine practice if it includes two aspects—kyerim and dzogrim.

This practice isn't something you can just do for one session, one day or one month. It's not a "one-off" kind of practice, but a yoga which literally means "unite with the essence" or "nature". And a yogi is one who trains himself continuously to recognize all appearances, sounds and awareness as the play of the dharmakaya. What is the benefit of practising this profound yoga of uniting with the essence? Through it, we attain the two kinds of accomplishment or siddhi, the supreme accomplishment or the great seal of mahamudra and the ordinary accomplishments which are the eight great accomplishments. That is why Guru Rinpoche states that he has explained this profound yoga for "accomplishing the two siddhis".

Samaya!

This is to seal the text with samaya. What does that mean? The samaya associated with this text is that it should become known to those who need it, while those who cannot appreciate it should not see it. Also, when you have been granted the empowerment and have received the liberating instructions, you are ready to practise the sadhana; but if you haven't received the empowerment, you are breaking the samaya. This is what the "Samaya!" in the text indicates. If you own a jewel of great value but never take advantage of it, it is just a useless rock. Similarly, this path can lead you to the two accomplishments, but if you don't put it into practise, you will remain destitute of accomplishment. This is another aspect that "Samaya!" points to.

The root of all samayas in the Secret Mantra Vajrayana is the necessity for secrecy. Actually, nowadays lamas are more worried about not enough people turning up to receive their empowerments or teachings than they are about maintaining samaya. Indeed, they expend a great deal of energy making advertisements on video or in newspapers, declaring, "I am giving an empowerment, please come" or "I am teaching, you are welcome." The result of giving empowerments without showing any respect for the secrecy samaya is that very few people accomplish signs of actual realization.

Termas mention "samaya gya gya" specifically and repeatedly at the end of each section throughout the text as a way of sealing (*gya*) each element of the practice with samaya.

A. Preparing to Practise
1. Where Should You Practise?

In a supreme place, solitary and pleasant, . . .

The instructions given in the tantras about doing a practice to accomplish a deity like this one are that you should first gather the five perfections. If the five perfections are not complete, there is no ground to support the practice. This is especially true of great accomplishment practice or drupchen. In this case, the five perfections are an absolute requisite.

Clearly, if you don't have somewhere to practise, you can't practise, and masters have described the ideal practice environment at great length—the front should be lower, the back higher, the sun rising early and so on. There is no shortage of details, and even the direction in which the water should flow or the wind blow is described! However, these days it isn't essential to know all these details.

The most essential point is, "A place of solitude blessed by the great beings of old . . ."[81] The great beings of old are the practitioners of the past like the Buddha, and a place he visited or blessed is ideal. If it's not possible to go to such a place, choose somewhere pregnant with Guru Rinpoche's blessings or with those of any of the Indian and Tibetan siddhas. Basically, you should find somewhere the great masters of the past have set foot or where they attained accomplishment; these are the supreme places of practice. The Secret Mantra Vajrayana approach generally talks about twenty-four sacred places, thirty-two hallowed lands and eight great charnel grounds. There are also equivalent secondary sacred places that can substitute for the primary ones since they retain the same power. When you stay in such places, experiences, realization, wisdom and qualities flourish naturally, while destructive emotions and your host of thoughts subside equally naturally. This is how the qualities of sacred places are described.

To be more specific, what are the qualities we should look for in the place we choose to practise the Chimé Phakmé Nyingtik? As it is predominantly a long-life practice, the best places are on a mountain where the snow never melts, a place adorned by a turquoise lake of longevity, lush forests where trees are laden with fruit and places with bountiful harvests and perfect fruit. A barren desert like those in Australia is not good. The pith instructions particularly mention that where the sun rises very early in the morning and sets late at night will naturally gather all the qualities necessary for long-life practice and for attaining the siddhi of immortality. The suggestion that you practise in snow mountains doesn't imply you have to practise in the snow.

There are people who hear instructions like this and imagine they have to move to Canada. The teachings speak of mountains with everlasting snow, so a couple of snowy days would be worthless! "Turquoise lakes" suggest to such people that they should practise by the ocean, but in this case the teachings refer to a lake that never dries up. When they performed longevity practices, the great siddhas of the past used the mountains with everlasting snow as their long-life tormas and long-life pills, and turquoise lakes as their long-life alcohol for example. Such mountains and lakes retain their blessings which is why mountains with everlasting snow and turquoise lakes of longevity are recommended to us today as places to do long-life practices.

The above are the outer considerations to bear in mind when choosing a place to do long-life practices.

From a more personal perspective—the inner point of view—you should practise somewhere pleasant, somewhere your mind feels well. This point is clarified in the teachings. At first, you may feel good in a place, but after a few days or a week or two you don't want to stay there any longer. This is a sign that this particular place is not so good for practice. On the other hand, you may feel agitated when you first arrive somewhere, but find your mind slowly settles down and you feel increasingly happy. This is the sign the place is very good for practice. Wherever you practise, if experiences and realization happen easily and you like your environment—whether you are on a mountain, in a cave or in a house—that place will be good for your practice. So if you feel good in a house, it's fine to practise in a house. It is even said that providing the place you stay has all the genuine qualities, you can even practise in a town or a city.

The secret level concerns the mind. Wherever you practise, your mind should be joyful and enthusiastic. It is said that if the practitioner is not happy, their practice will not be beneficial. For a genuine dharma practitioner, the more virtue and merit that is accumulated, the happier he or she will feel.

In any case, it is said that the outer, inner and secret aspects of the place you practise are important. Why are they so important? In the past, the great masters left their blessings at the places they practised because that was where they accomplished the deity, mudra, mantra and samadhi. At present, these places appear impurely to us, yet the great masters blessed all these impure appearances—the earth, rocks, stones, trees and so on—as the pure mandala of primordial wisdom with the nature of the five feminine buddhas like Buddhalochana and Mamaki. This is because the nature of the five elements is the five feminine buddhas, and the power of mantra and samadhi is unfathomable.

As it is said, "As long as space endures, the accomplishments of mantras will not be lost." Since the accomplishments attained through mantra recitation will not be lost, the power of all mantra recitation will continue to bless those who stay in the sacred places, even beginners. Blessings are like fire. When you are cold, sitting next to a fire will warm you, won't it? But getting warm by a fire has nothing to do with you, it happens because of the quality of fire. You receive the blessings of a sacred place in the same way—as soon as you get to such a place, you feel well.

2. The Practitioner

The practitioner of mantra who has received the empowerment
and keeps the samayas, . . .

Such a place is a good platform for practice for the right kind of practitioners, in this case ourselves. We are the right kind because, obviously, we have obtained a precious human body without which it is impossible to practise Secret Mantra Vajrayana. There is a lot to say about this. You cannot practise Secret Mantra Vajrayana if you are born in the body of an animal for example. But there's not much point in talking about it right now.

You have obtained a human body, and it's not just any human body but the body in which you have met a lama. You can see that the lama who gives you empowerments is the lord of all the mandalas and therefore has the power to "pour and disperse". Through the empowerment, the lama is able to pour all the blessings into students, while dispersing all thoughts that grasp at the reality of phenomena.[82] The practitioner is someone who—having received such an empowerment—keeps the samayas.

The text indicates that you must keep the samayas. Sometimes, it is said that there are a hundred thousand samayas to be kept or that there are twenty-five samayas and so on. Guru Rinpoche said, in essence, the root of all samayas is the lama. The samaya of the lama relates to his enlightened body, speech and mind—and there is quite an important point to notice here. When you take ordination as a monk, according to the Vinaya you must consider the abbot from whom you receive the vows as your father and yourself as his son. When practising the Mahayana, practitioners consider the teacher to be a doctor and themselves as his sick patient. The master is a skilled doctor and unless you do exactly as he says, you will die. Once you have received a Vajrayana empowerment, it is said that you must consider your teacher indivisible from the lord of the mandala. All the Sarma and Nyingma schools agree on this point.

When it comes to empowerment, there are many categories we could talk about, but they boil down to the four empowerments:

—The vase empowerment enables the practitioner to visualize the deity.
—The secret empowerment authorizes the recitation of mantra.
—The wisdom empowerment makes it possible for the recipient to experience samadhi with bliss, clarity and no thought and to practise the emanation and reabsorption of rays of light.
—The word empowerment authorizes the practise of dzogrim.

We must receive the four empowerments fully—ideally, so our perception changes—before we can do these practices. People who practise the Mantrayana without having received empowerments will not achieve the fruition of the practice, besides that they will go to the hell realms when they die as a result of the samayas they have broken.

Those who have been empowered and practise deity, mantra, mudra and samadhi are called *ngakpas* in Tibetan. They are Vajrayana practitioners or "practitioners of mantra", as it says in the text. There are instructions in the teachings about the dress code for ngakpas including the ornaments they should wear, their long hair style, wearing a white lower garment and so on. But these are side issues, the main point is the practice.

3. Setting up the Mandala

. . . should set up a general mandala.

A practitioner of mantra first needs a mandala as the basis for the practice. The explanation of the mandala has probably been influenced by Hindu culture. "*Khyil khor*" is the Tibetan word for mandala: "*khyil*" means middle, the central unit, and "*khor*" refers to what surrounds it. There are elaborate discussions in the *Secret Essence Tantra* about how these two aspects relate to the masculine and the feminine, wisdom and skilful means, kyerim and dzogrim, male and female deities, main deity and retinue and so on. However, it is all contained in the palace, the support, and the deities supported by the palace. So when the palace and the deities come together you have a *khyil khor*, a mandala.

The mandala used in this practice is a general mandala. In the Mahayoga tantra tradition, the mandala palace is square with four doors, eight-level toranas, walls, jewelled murals, looping and hanging chains and so on—nothing you'd understand right now. It also has four pillars, eight beams, thirteen rings and so on. To be brief, the different features of the palace correspond to the thirty-two major marks of a buddha, but you won't get a handle on this concept straightaway. The text indicates that the mandala of the Chimé Phakmé Nyingtik is a general mandala. Practices like Vajrakilaya, Yamantaka or Kagye and mandalas of magnetising deities and so on generate their own specific mandalas. There is a lot to say about mandalas. There are different kinds of mandalas, for example the outer substantial mandala with characteristics, the inner mandala of aggregates as deities and the mandala of absolute definitive wisdom.

Without going into it too much, the tantras of the Nyingma tradition say the outer mandala can be a multi-coloured sand mandala, but if that's not possible use a drawing of the mandala. If you can't get hold of a drawing, even heaps of grain to represent each deity placed on a flat surface will work.

The Accomplishment Substances

Onto this general mandala are placed the accomplishment substances. They are crucial because their power is incredible and is similar to the extraordinary power latent in atoms that scientists today have made us aware of. Actually, we need many, many substances when we practise, for example representations of the enlightened body, speech, mind, qualities and activities, a bell and a vajra which are kept in front of the practitioner, a mala to count recitations and so on. But this text mentions only the most important ones. So what does the text say? Because this is a long-life practice, the most important substance is for alchemy and longevity, called "*chulen*" in Tibetan. Before introducing the substances required to prepare the *chulen*, the text describes the vessel that will contain it,

> *In the centre, place a bandha with three sections . . .*

This is a kapala divided into three by lines on its surface. There are several kinds of kapalas since there can be anything from one to nine such divisions, and each kind is classified according to quality—best, ordinary and low. There are detailed explanations about each one, but we will move on.

> *Filled with calcite, bitumen, the three fruits,*
> *Indra's hand, the "weeping ceaselessly" flower,*
> *And the five roots, all mixed together . . .*

The text mentions the twelve medicinal substances that should be gathered and placed in the kapala. Even if you were told the English translation of their names, I doubt you would be able to recognize what they are, so there's not much point in talking about them. The first is a calcite called "*chong shyi*" in Tibetan. It is the essence of stones chipped from white stone that was formed over hundreds of thousands of years. There are three types—male, female and neuter. All three are required here. Bitumen (*drak shum* in Tibetan) is a kind of black sweat, or nectar to use a more flattering term, that oozes from rocks that have been exposed to the sun for millions of years. The three fruits are arura, barura and kyurura. The next substance is called "Indra's hand". Indra had his hand cut off and of course he bled, and wherever his blood touched the ground, a small flower sprang up that looked like a hand which has since been used as a medicinal plant. The "weeping ceaselessly" flower is a kind of grass on which small flowers blossom that grows in holy places like the Wutai Shan mountains in China. There are three kinds—Manjushri's "weeping ceaselessly" flower, Avalokiteshvara's "weeping ceaselessly" flower and Vajrapani's "weeping ceaselessly" flower. The names given refer to the great bodhisattva who blessed each type. You also need five specific roots, which you can dig up or buy,

> *. . . and rolled into pills the size of peas.*

The benefit of consecrating such pills of longevity is explained later in the text.

> *Cover them with red silk, and set out offerings and tormas.*

Then cover the pills in the kapala with red silk. A kapala filled with long-life pills is the main support of the practice in the mandala. Set the offerings and tormas around it. The offerings are the outer, inner and secret offerings and the offering of suchness. Arrange the outer, inner and secret offerings on the shrine. The outer offerings are drinking water, water for cleansing, flowers, incense, light, scented water, food and music offerings. These offerings support the practice which means making water offerings is not enough. In this case you should offer flowers, incense and so on. Jamyang Khyentse Wangpo wrote an instruction describing how to prepare these offerings. The inner offerings are pleasant forms, sounds, smells, tastes and textures. The secret offerings are of amrita, torma and rakta. Amrita is made of eight root and one thousand minor ingredients. It is said, "We offer amrita nectar of eight major and a thousand minor ingredients." Merely to pour some whisky or wine into a container doesn't really do for amrita.

Rakta is made of thirty-five substances. The *Treasury of Precious Termas* contains a ten-page sadhana by Jamyang Khyentse Wangpo for consecrating rakta. If you gather the thirty-five substances, you will be able to obtain rakta. However, were I to explain the ingredients of amrita and rakta, you might be a little shocked—so much so that instead of encouraging you to practise, it might unnerve you and put doubts into your mind about having set out on the Vajrayana path in the first place! I say this for those who have limited powers of discernment.

In the absence of the minimum of three substances—amrita, torma and rakta—I think it would be very difficult to accomplish sadhana practices. You can, for example, practise without putting physical outer offerings on your shrine and instead just imagine that all the water in the world is offering water for drinking and cleansing, all the flowers in the world are flower offerings, all the great smells in the world are incense offerings, the radiance of sun and the moon and all illuminations are light offerings, all the wonderful smells form the scented water offerings, all nourishment is the food offering and all pleasant and unpleasant sounds are music offerings. If you can do this, it is acceptable to practise without gathering the physical offerings. The same goes for the inner offerings of form, sound, smell, taste and touch. But it is not possible to offer amrita, torma and rakta in this way because they are an unsurpassable, secret, crucial point of these teachings. If you don't have at least a little of each, you cannot do the practice.

Truly great, accomplished practitioners are probably able to practise without the physical substances. But look at Longchenpa, he was quite realised, wasn't he? In the Nyingma tradition, he is held up as the epitome of a realised master. Once when he was giving an empowerment, the peacock feathers on the phumba were missing. When the protectress of the Mantra teachings—Ekazati—appeared to him and told him about his lack of peacock feathers, Longchenpa said, "I meditate that they are there", to which Ekazati swiftly replied that he could not visualize symbolic items and substances.

Another very great practitioner was so realised that he could even fly in the sky. Once as he practised in his hermitage, he had nothing to eat for himself and so he certainly didn't have anything to offer, so he created the offerings in his mind. But when he offered tsok on the tenth and twenty-fifth days, the dakas and dakinis who would usually come from all the sacred places did not gather. He thought about it a lot and, having seriously investigated the matter, came to the conclusion that it was probably because he hadn't provided any offering substances. Then he remembered a small piece of sugar he had hidden away and on the next tsok day, he dipped it very briefly in a small bowl of water, because if he had left it too long the whole piece would have melted. He then offered the small bowl as a practice substance and did the tsok, and all the dakas and dakinis gathered for his tsok. This shows how extremely important offering substances really are.

Tormas

The text adds that we should arrange tormas, and there is a specific kind of torma for the Chimé Phakmé Nyingtik based on a pure vision that came to Jamyang Khyentse.[83] The Tibetan term "torma" is formed of two syllables, *tor* and *ma*. All phenomena included in the worlds of appearance and existence are the manifestation of dualistic clinging at subject and object. When they are all destroyed (*tor*), the ground, like a mother (*ma*), gives birth to all phenomena of samsara and nirvana as rigpa's primordial awareness. This is the meaning of "torma". Again, there is a lot more that can be said about what torma means, but essentially, there are four main ways to relate to tormas.

—Consider the accomplishment torma to be the deity. Meditate on the torma as the deity as you accomplish the practice. It is said, "Consider the vessel as the palace", so the vessel in which the torma is placed is seen as the palace while the torma is seen as the deity.

—Consider the offering torma to be an offering of sensory stimulants by imagining that the nature of the torma is an inexhaustible offering of everything it's possible to desire.

—Consider the siddhi torma to be amrita, something you eat when you receive the siddhis.

—The fourth is the kind of torma that is like a weapon for scattering, dispersing and eliminating the negativity when expelling the negative forces.

The best way to ". . . set the tormas . . ." as instructed by the text is to arrange the various kinds of tormas on your shrine—the offering tormas, fulfillment tormas, permanent tormas and support tormas. If you can't manage to make or find all these tormas, just make one that gathers all the qualities of the others. Interestingly for us Tibetans, the tormas are the easiest part of the practice because we always have tsampa and butter. But when westerners want to practise, making tormas always seems to be the difficult bit; and wherever they live in the world, they have to import torma makers from India! In any case, in retreat you need all three substances—amrita, torma and rakta.

Mala

To do a *nyenpa,* it is important to have a perfect mala. Again, there is so much to say about malas! There are many different kinds, but for the Chimé Phakmé Nyingtik the best would be one made of real crystal. What should you use if you can't get a crystal mala? These days, they are easy to find in India, but in Tibet in the old days that wasn't the case, so practitioners would make malas from dried fruit. But the mala must have one-hundred-and-eight beads.

Before the approach and accomplishment retreat, you must wash your mala with clean water, eliminate impurities with fire and bless it in the appropriate way.

Many instructions have been given about the kinds of string you should use to thread your mala, but the most important point is that it won't break easily because so many superstitions will clutter your mind if your mala breaks. For example, some say that if a mala breaks in the middle of a retreat, it means samayas have been broken, others that the practitioner will be unable to accomplish the deities and so on. Once Dzongsar Khyentse Rinpoche's mala broke when he was on retreat in Canada practising Chimé Phakmé Nyingtik, and he called me in the middle of the night about it! This is why I say you need a string that won't break. Obviously, there's no such thing as an unbreakable string, it simply doesn't exist. What I mean is a string that will at least not break during your retreat.

I am often asked, "And what can I do if I am not able to bless my mala?" The answer is to ask a lama who knows how to do it. For the lama just to blow on your mala is not that useful. Actually, there's a whole practice for blessing malas which the lama should perform if he is to consecrate a mala properly.

The mala you use for your *nyenpa* should not be displayed, and you shouldn't show it to anyone at all—keep it to yourself. It is said that your mala should never be separate from your body heat, and no one should see it even when you are using it.

Advice on Practicalities

There are many other instructions about practical aspects of the practice. For example, you shouldn't cut your hair or wash during a retreat and so on. Dzongsar Khyentse Rinpoche did a Hevajra retreat in Sikkim for six months and didn't wash the whole time, as instructed by Khenpo Kunga Wangchuk. Later, Khyentse Rinpoche said that not washing was the most difficult part of the retreat. There are also many dietary restrictions. The best way of putting these instructions into practice is to do your best to apply the ones you can and simply leave out those you can't.

What is the minimum number of substances you should have?

—The instruction says, ". . . a correct drawing of the body" which is a representation of the yidam's physical appearance that is used as the samaya support. This means you need an accurately made statue or thangka of the deity which has been consecrated.
—You also need the sadhana text, don't you? Make sure you get one without any errors. It is the support of the enlightened speech of the deity.
—As a representation of the enlightened mind, you need a vajra and a bell.
—As the representation of the enlightened qualities, the kapala filled with long-life pills we have just described.
—And, of course, a mala.

If you have this much, you can do the practice.

Arrange a Comfortable Seat

The text says,

On a comfortable seat, rest in equanimity, . . .

Having gathered everything you need to do the practice, you now need a comfortable seat. Although the text mentions the need for a comfortable seat, it does not say it should be high, yet nowadays the tradition seems to be for practitioners' seats to be as high as possible. Kyabje Trulshik Rinpoche used to say that his attendants didn't listen to him at all and even though he told them to arrange a low seat for him, they always seemed to make it higher than before, creating great difficulties for him because he had to climb up and down again each session. He also said, "The tantras mention a comfortable seat, not a high seat, and for me, high seats are so uncomfortable." Longchen Rabjam—in *The Treasury of Pith Instructions*—adds that the seat should be a little higher at the back than at the front because then it is more comfortable.

What is the point of having a comfortable seat? If you sit comfortably, your body will be at ease. When the body is at ease, the *lung*—the inner air in your body—will also flow easily. When your inner air is at ease, your mind is at ease. When mind is at ease, kyerim and dzogrim or whatever practice you do will unfold easily. But when the mind is tense and agitated, dharma practice is very difficult.

In one of his pith instructions about retreat, omniscient Longchenpa said that you should draw a svastika in white chalk under your seat, put some kusha grass on it, then some durwa grass with the roots facing forward in the direction you will be facing and the tips pointing to your back and then place your seat on top.

The reasons for taking care about what you sit on during your retreat are explained at length in the teachings—so you will be comfortable enough to sit easily for a long time for example, particularly so that auspicious interdependent connections for experiences and realization will arise naturally and easily and for the long life of the practitioner and so on. You should sit facing a specific direction, the instructions for which appear in each practice. As the Chimé Phakmé Nyingtik is an enriching practice, you should face south. The mandala arranged on the shrine should face the practitioner so that the samayasattva, the practitioner and the jnanasattvas face each other.

Expelling the Foul Air

Again, the text says,

On a comfortable seat, rest in equanimity, . . .

First, as a preliminary to the main practice, expel the foul air nine times—from the right nostril three times, from the left three times, then three times from both, which makes nine. By breathing out strongly through the left nostril, we expel all the poisons created by a host of thoughts rooted in desire. Breathing out through the right nostril expels all thoughts rooted in hate, and breathing out through both nostrils expels all thoughts rooted in ignorance. In this way, all thoughts and concepts associated with the three poisons are eliminated from the body. As you do this practice, it is important that you expel all the air from your lungs, without retaining the tiniest bit.

What is the point of doing this before you begin the main practice? Before you cook, you should wash the ingredients thoroughly and use clean cooking utensils. Similarly, as you are about to see your body as having the nature of the deity, first you eliminate all its impurities.

Before you breathe air out of your lungs, you must first inhale some, so you should draw the air in quite slowly. Once you have filled your lungs right down to your belly, think about all the destructive emotions—desire, aversion, ignorance and so on—that you will eliminate as you breathe out. This will probably take a while, and it is said you should retain the air in your belly for as long as it takes. Once you have thought long and hard about all the destructive emotions you are about to expel, breathe out strongly with the force of a shot arrow. Experienced practitioners can expel the air from the three main channels and the four chakras. As you expel the air if you visualize the body empty like an unfilled bottle with the central channel, the kyangma and roma channels inside and the chakras connecting them, the practice is even more powerful.

If you do not know how to do these *tsalung* practices, just practise as I explained earlier. Inhale slowly, then as you exhale consider that you expel all impure aspects whose nature are the three poisons—desire, aversion and ignorance—and that manifest as sickness, harmful spirits, misfortune and so on. Be confident that you really have expelled all the negativity from your body and that it is now completely clean and pure. It is now a pure vessel.

Having exhaled, now inhale a light stream of air that doesn't fill your whole body—and do it slowly. Then rest for a little while "at ease". At this point, avoid focusing outwardly where you will be distracted by what's going on outside. Instead, look inwardly. Look at your mind and its nature. What is my mind? What kinds of thoughts arise? Here, more experienced practitioners will recognize the primordial ground that is beyond the observer and the object to be observed.

You might not be a practitioner of superior capacity and therefore unable to see the nature of mind right now. But even practitioners with less capacity can see that the continuity of thoughts has been interrupted and the gross concepts are not there anymore. At this point when the antidote, which is the observer, presents itself, the object observed is seen as empty.

If you can rest in that state of recognition, sit with it. When you cannot, as thoughts arise in your mind, visualize in the space in front of you the main deity—here, white Tara Wish-Fulfilling Wheel—indivisible from your glorious root lama and surrounded by the masters of the lineage. As you actualise this visualization, recite the lineage prayers to invoke their blessings.

B. Preliminary Practices
1. The Seven Line Prayer

In the Nyingma tradition, we always begin with the Seven Line Prayer. Rest free from thoughts in the state of recognition of the nature of mind. A thought will inevitably arise and as it does, immediately recognize and transform it into the following visualization. Rays of light with hooked tips emanate from your heart and stream to the Copper-Coloured Mountain of Glory where they touch the heart of Guru Rinpoche, the ocean of panditas and rishis in his retinue and the dakas and dakinis surrounding them. As soon as they are touched by the light, they gather in gigantic clouds in the sky before you and bless your mind. Recite the Seven Line Prayer as you actualise this visualization. In the Nyingma tradition, the Seven Line Prayer is the number one practice! We do it before we begin any other practice, and it is the essence of all the termas of the hundred and eight tertöns. So this is the prayer you should recite at that point. In a terma on the Seven Line Prayer, Guru Rinpoche himself said,

> If you call out to me by singing the Seven Line Prayer,
> I, the Lotus-Born,
> Will come from the Rakshasa Island to the southwest,
> Riding the king of the sky.
> Instantaneously, I am in front of you,
> Have no doubt about this.

When you invoke Guru Rinpoche, the Lotus Born, and call out to him by chanting the Seven Line Prayer, he will come from the Rakshasa Island in the southwest to bless you in an instant. "The king of the sky" is the garuda who is able to cover long distances in a very short time, so Guru Rinpoche is saying that he will come that very instant to bless whoever prays to him. The prayer in Tibetan ends with the word *naraken*, which means "I swear, I promise, I'll be there for sure".

So with that we have established the power of the Seven Line Prayer through the sacred texts. It's also possible to prove through reasoning. Guru Rinpoche has obtained the wisdom kaya, so he can fit an aeon into an instant. He doesn't need to make an effort like ordinary beings and can manifest whatever he wishes.

Another important point here is that as Jamyang Khyentse Wangpo explained, tertöns can actually meet Guru Rinpoche, receive empowerments and blessings directly from him and make vows in his presence which means they can then consider him to be their root teacher. Although Guru Rinpoche is definitely present for ordinary people, we do not receive the empowerments from him or make vows in his presence. Instead, we receive such things from our root teacher which is why it is better for us to meditate on the lama in the physical form of our root teacher whose essence is Guru Rinpoche. Tertöns can visualize Guru Rinpoche directly, but for ordinary people it is better to visualize Guru Rinpoche in essence appearing in the form of their root teacher.

The Nyingma terma texts and most of the Nyingmapa teachers are held in Guru Rinpoche's care which is why their collections of texts are replete with prayers to him and other such writings. As Guru Rinpoche is omnipresent throughout the terma tradition, the ingrained habit of practitioners is to focus almost exclusively on him at the expense of their root teacher. If you have a personal relationship with Guru Rinpoche, that's fantastic! But those who don't must rely on a teacher while remembering that the lama is but the play of Guru Rinpoche's dynamic expression, his emanation. Bearing this in mind, consider your root teacher and Guru Rinpoche to be indivisible and pray to him. Since they are indivisible, you will receive Guru Rinpoche's blessings as a matter of course. This is said to be the most beneficial approach.

Each of the yidam deities you practise is the play of the lama's blessings. So by practising a sadhana you are also accomplishing the lama, which is what we call "guru yoga" or "uniting with the nature of the lama". Basically, you pray to and invoke the wisdom mind of the master. This is why at the beginning of every practice session you accomplish this crucial point of praying to the teacher which the teachings say again and again is extremely important. It's not something I came up with on my own, it is said repeatedly in the texts and has also been handed down through the oral tradition. Earlier I said that we practise once we have received the empowerment from the lama who is indivisible from the main deity of the mandala. If you imagine there is a difference between the lama and the deity or that for example the deity is somehow greater than the lama who may even lack some of the qualities of the deity, you are mistaken. Having invoked the lama in this way for some time, direct the practice towards receiving the four empowerments through the rays of white, red and dark-blue light that emanate from the lama. Even if you don't, at the end of the practice—having prayed and invoked the lama strongly—a delighted master will melt into light which dissolves into you. At this point, if you know the key point of practice, rest in that—rest in equanimity. This is what is meant in the text when it says,

> . . . *rest in equanimity,*
> *Then practise the preliminaries, the main part and the*
> *conclusion.*

There are three parts to the practice: the preliminaries, the main part which is from when you visualize yourself as the deity to offering praise and mantra recitation, and the conclusion which starts with a tsok offering and finishes with the prayers of auspiciousness. This is what we must put into practice. Again the text says,

Samaya!

This has the same meaning as before.

2. Refuge

The preliminary section is divided into two, and the first part is what has been explained so far and corresponds to the lines in the sadhana text that start, "In a sublime place . . ." up until ". . . on a comfortable seat." This deals with the different aspects we have been discussing like the right place to practice, the kind of empowerment practitioners need, how to set up the mandala, the necessary tormas and so on. These are all the preparations that must be completed before you enter into the main part of the practice. The second part is the actual preliminary practices.

> *The first preliminary practice is to take refuge.*
> *Visualize the objects of refuge in the sky in front of you.*

Visualize the field of merit instantaneously following the approach which is the complete visualization the moment the practitioner thinks of it. In an instant, the main yidam deity—Sublime Lady Wish-Fulfilling Wheel—appears before you, surrounded by the deities of the Three Roots, the Three Jewels and all the objects of refuge. If you want to visualize elaborately, there is a refuge tree for Chimé Phakmé Nyingtik that you should look at. Visualize the deities as a market crowd, a crowd of people gathered in one place in no particular order. If you can't, use the all-embodied jewel method. In the same way all wealth is gathered into a precious jewel, Sublime Lady Wish-Fulfilling Wheel is indivisible from the lama since all the deities of the Three Roots and the infinite retinue deities of the mandala are the manifestations of the main deity.

"To visualize" means to meditate which is not that simple. To visualize someone is like seeing them as clearly as you see your own reflection in a mirror. This is what qualifies as "visualization". If you can't do that kind of visualization, at least try to think about it.

Those who take refuge are yourself and all sentient beings. We take refuge from now until complete enlightenment. We take refuge as we prostrate with hands folded in a physical expression of homage with our body; with our speech, we say the words of the refuge verse; and with our mind, we think with devotion, "Sublime Lady Wish-Fulfilling Wheel, you know us! Care for us! Grant us refuge and protect us from the ocean of suffering that is samsara." The words you say are the four-line refuge prayer in the text,

> NAMO
> Until we attain enlightenment, I and all sentient beings
> Take refuge with unwavering devotion
> In you, Guru Wish-Fulfilling Wheel, who are
> The very essence of the Three Jewels!

There is a translation to help you understand the meaning of the words, and if you don't understand that, I am not going to explain each word for you. The explanation of refuge can be found in *The Words of My Perfect Teacher* and is dealt with in five or six pages. The meaning is encapsulated in various prayers, like the four-line verse given here which points towards relative refuge.

For absolute refuge, realise that in essence all aspects of the refuge—the field of refuge, the person taking refuge, the reason for taking refuge and so on—come from mind. The empty essence of mind is the dharmakaya, its cognizant nature is the sambhogakaya and its unimpeded compassionate energy is the nirmanakaya. Having recognized that this is reality, ultimate refuge is to rest in a state of direct recognition.

At the beginning of the teaching before we began discussing the Mantrayana, we learned that buddha nature—the ground—is present in all sentient beings. Buddha nature is mind, and mind is the Buddha. We also learned that all the practices we engage in as we follow the path are geared towards liberating us directly into the natural state of the ground. This is the context in which we should understand refuge.

Relative refuge is presented here in the words of the prayer. It is something the mind must think about, so think about the four lines from, "Until enlightenment, I and all sentient beings . . ." to ". . . the nature of the Three Jewels."

I have said already that all grasping thoughts that arise in our minds, both positive and negative, are just delusions. That's the relative aspect. Ultimately, all thoughts are just mind. The essence of mind is empty and is the dharmakaya. The natural manifestation arising out of the expanse of this empty essence is clarity or cognition, which is the sambhogakaya. All individual aspects that arise are the nirmanakaya. It is said that the dharmakaya of the Buddha gives rise to the sambhogakaya, out of which manifests the nirmanakaya. Therefore, "ultimate refuge" is to maintain, as we take refuge, the clear recognition that dharmakaya, sambhogakaya and nirmanakaya abide as empty essence, cognisant nature and infinite compassionate energy within our mind.

The Chimé Phakmé Nyingtik is strongly connected with the Dzogchen teachings, and the leading figures who clarified and established the Dzogchen teachings—Shri Singha and Vimalamitra—were teachers of Guru Rinpoche. Guru Rinpoche is the root source of all the Dzogchen teachings. Not only are Shri Singha, Vimalamitra and Guru Rinpoche great Dzogchen masters, but the moment they received the empowerment into the dynamic energy of rigpa (*rigpa'i tsal wang*), which is the heart of the Dzogchen path, they immediately accomplished its fruition and attained immortality. They are therefore still present in the form of the rainbow body of great transference to be of benefit to sentient beings until samsara is empty. What is the rainbow body of great transference? It means that having attained rainbow body, which is the final result of Dzogchen practice, the elements of their bodies are now beyond decay and degeneration. All three masters have achieved the rainbow body of great transference. Vimalamitra lives on Mount Wutai Shan in China, while Guru Rinpoche lives on the Copper-Coloured Mountain.

So to say that the Chimé Phakmé Nyingtik teaching is the ultimate, unified wisdom intent of these three great masters means that this practice is connected with the Great Perfection, the Dzogchen tradition. Therefore, to avoid even touching upon Dzogchen as I explain this practice from refuge and bodhichitta onwards would not be honest of me. To present the practice without making the distinction between the relative and absolute levels, or explaining them individually just a little, would be deceptive. I am saying this not so much for the benefit of the audience I am speaking to today, but for the benefit of the recording which will remain. This is something I must also keep in mind.

The first preliminary practice is taking refuge, and I have now explained its two aspects—relative and absolute. This is how refuge should be explained for the Chimé Phakmé Nyingtik. For more ordinary practices, refuge would only be explained on the relative level and that an ultimate refuge exists and that practitioners should actualise it would only briefly be mentioned. It's important to give explanations that people can understand. The best approach of course is to avoid explaining anything at all and to remain silent! But if I do start to explain something, then I must explain it so that those who are listening can understand. I could say various things without really explaining anything at all! But I must bear in mind that the recording of whatever I say will be broadcast all over the place in the future.

3. Bodhichitta

Second, arouse bodhichitta in aspiration and action.

Bodhichitta has two aspects—the bodhichitta of aspiration and bodhichitta in action. "Bodhichitta of aspiration" is to make a strong wish to reach enlightenment so we can help all sentient beings, "I will do what all the victorious ones and their heirs have done before me—chief among them Jetsun Drolma—in order to benefit all sentient beings who wander in samsara." The second aspect of bodhichitta is to act on that aspiration by practising the Chimé Phakmé Nyingtik. These two aspects should be present in your practice, together and inseparably. Both aspects are invoked in the four-line prayer that's part of the bodhichitta section of the sadhana, so you must generate them both as you say that prayer. Again, Vajrayana is about recitation and meditation, so you must actualise the meaning as you say the words. Don't just chant mindlessly, oblivious to what you are saying.

> HO
> Sentient beings are as countless as space is vast,
> In order to free every one of them from the ocean of
> suffering
> By attaining immortality through this yoga of the Sublime
> Lady,
> I arouse the enlightened mind of bodhichitta.

Embraced by bodhichitta, your practice becomes a Mahayana, Great Vehicle, practice. If you don't generate the mind of enlightenment, your practice won't even count as a Mahayana practice, so to think of it as a Vajrayana practice would be out of the question.

It is very easy to say, "We must think about all sentient beings all the time", but it's very difficult to bear in mind every time we do something positive, even during our most benign positive activities. Those who can are very rare. Some of my older monks have spent up to fifteen years in retreat and have recited billions of Vajra Guru mantras. But I tell them, "If you don't say mantras with bodhichitta in your minds, all those recitations are useless!" If you recite hundreds of millions of Vajra Guru mantras but only think about yourself, if you only hope for a good, long life, free from illness for yourself, if you pray that only you won't fall back into samsara in your future life—however many mantras you recite, your practice won't be very beneficial.

Before you tackle sadhana practices, you must first complete the preliminary practices; you must do a *ngöndro*. This Chimé Phakmé Nyingtik teaching presupposes that you have received and practised a ngöndro which is why you won't find much about ngöndro in it—refuge and bodhichitta for example—or in most other sadhana commentaries.

4. Seven-Branch Offering

Third, the seven-branch offering.

Next, we accumulate merit and purify negativity. All the aspects of collecting merit and purifying obscurations and so on are included in the seven branches of offering which can be practised in a number of different ways.

a) Prostration

> I multiply my body as many times as there are atoms in the
> universe.
> Overflowing with devotion, I pay homage, body, speech
> and mind,

These two lines tell us to bring to mind the objects of refuge once again. Prostrations are offered with the following two lines,

> As I bow to the lotus beneath the feet of the buddhas and
> bodhisattvas of all directions and times,
> And to their sublime mother, Tara.

According to the Vajrayana, you offer a full prostration. As your five points—hands, knees and forehead—touch the ground, you must bring to mind their significance.[84] Alternatively, you can follow the Sutrayana approach and offer by emanating an infinite number of visualized forms of your own body to pay homage to the buddhas and bodhisattva through your body, speech and mind.

b) Offering

We offer with the following two lines,

> Here is an unsurpassable array of outer, inner and secret
> substances,
> Like the vast cloud-like offerings of Samantabhadra.

The practice text includes two lines for each of the first two branches, and the remaining five have one line each.

Offer the outer, inner and secret offerings—which will be discussed more fully later in the text—and every kind of offering that comes to mind. In this way you make infinite offerings beyond the conception of an ordinary mind, not just once but continuously throughout all eternity.

c) Confession

> I confess all negative actions, obscurations, faults and
> downfalls, . . .

Confession must always involve the four powers. Because we have so many vows to keep, it's inevitable that we'll break some of them. So to purify all these breakages and faults, we must confess using the four powers, which are the power of support, the lama; the power of practice; the power of heartfelt regret; and the power of strong resolve never to do it again even if one's life is at stake.

In the Nyingma tradition, we maintain all the vows associated with all three yanas together and at the same time, and so confession is relatively easy. When you receive an empowerment, you become a Vajrayana practitioner, a vajra holder, because you will then hold all three sets of vows—the vows of individual liberation, the bodhisattva vows of bodhichitta and the Vajrayana vows or samaya commitments. Each vow progresses from the previous vow, in essence though they are all the same. In order to follow the path, we must take these vows, but since they are not easy to keep we offer confession based on the four powers to purify the breakages.

d) Rejoicing

And rejoice in the practice of the two accumulations.

The two accumulations are all the merit and wisdom accumulated by sentient beings. "Merit" is positive action that's driven by mind, whereas "wisdom" is accumulated without mental activity or references, for example by resting in meditative equipoise. By rejoicing in someone else's positive activity, you will accumulate the same amount of merit as they accumulate. This is very important.

e) Request the Turning of the Wheel of Dharma

Continue turning the wheel of the dharma, . . .

f) Request the Buddhas and Bodhisattvas Not to Pass into Nirvana

And do not pass into nirvana, but remain here, we pray.

g) Dedicate the Merit

I dedicate our accumulation of merit towards the
attainment of the heart of enlightenment.
May we swiftly accomplish buddhahood for the benefit of
others.

Here, in the Chimé Phakmé Nyingtik, the seven-branch practice follows the approach common to Sutrayana and Tantrayana.

5. Dissolution of the Field of Refuge

The field of merit dissolves into you, inseparably.

Dissolve all the deities in the field of refuge into yourself and actualise the state of being inseparable from Wish-Fulfilling Wheel. It is crucial that we see ourselves as not being separate from the deity. Once we do, we will also be convinced that we embody all the qualities of the deity, which is why this dissolution is very important. Once the deity has dissolved into you, rest in the state of unity but not for too long. When thoughts begin to arise, feel once again the vajra pride of being the deity. Actually, a Mantra practitioner should bring the awareness of being the deity to mind in every moment. Then you arise as the activity deity,

> *In that state, arouse the vajra pride of being the wrathful activity deity.*

The wrathful activity deity is Hayagriva. He holds a lotus club in his right hand and a skull cup in his left. He wears the eight charnel ground ornaments of a wrathful deity, but not all the ten glorious ornaments. Here again, in an instant you visualize yourself as the deity, then hold the vajra pride of the view, thinking, "I am the deity."

6. Torma Offering to the Obstructing Forces: the Gektor

On the first day of a retreat, you must offer a torma to dispel obstructing forces—that torma is called a gektor. As you place the gektor in front of you, arise as Hayagriva and feel a complete confidence, or vajra pride, that you are Hayagriva. Out of emptiness arises compassion. From that compassion arises wrathful action which manifests in a wrathful form—not out of anger, but as the wrathful expression of compassion. From Hayagriva's heart emanate rays of light in the form of hooks which produce vast numbers of wrathful deities and more hooks and lassos and so on. These emanations summon all the malevolent beings who create obstacles to dharma practice, who gather in front of Hayagriva. It is to these malicious creatures that we must offer the gektor torma which takes the form of the inexhaustible five sensory stimulants and is therefore beautifully shaped, makes pleasant sounds, has a wonderful fragrance, has an excellent taste and is soft to the touch.

To purify the gektor torma, the three syllables RAM YAM KHAM emanate from your heart. RAM releases the fire of wisdom to burn away our grasping at the idea that the torma and so on exists, that it has true existence. YAM releases a wind that disperses all grasping. KHAM releases water to cleanse impurities so that all grasping is entirely removed. Then out of emptiness, the syllables OM AH HUNG manifest and bless the offerings which then become inexhaustible wisdom nectar and appear in the form of the five sensory stimulants. The gektor is offered as you bring together deity, mantra and mudra. Visualize yourself as the deity Hayagriva, perform the mudras of the sensory stimulants and use samadhi to visualize what I have just explained. The mantra is BALINGTE SOHA. Once the malevolent spirits have gathered in front of you, say the mantra BALINGTE SOHA, perform the appropriate mudra, then offer the blessed torma. This offering will delight and satisfy the obstructing forces who are now pacified and have abandoned any idea they might have had of obstructing dharma practice. Instead, they are happy, rejoice and then return to where they belong. This is what you actualise.

Those obstructing forces who do not leave must be expelled. So Hayagriva produces from his five centres and every pore in his body hundreds of thousands of Hayagriva wrathful deities in huge numbers, which deluge the obstructing forces with the five weapons, expelling them.

In the practice text, the following verse offers the torma and tells the obstructing forces what to do,

> HUNG
> Primordially, samsara and nirvana are inseparable,
> Yet temporary delusion manifests as negative forces and
>   obstacle makers.
> Accept this torma as an offering or a gift
> And depart for the dharmadhatu empty of inherent
>   existence.

HUNG is the Buddha's core seed syllable and the primordially pure nature of our mind. So at this level, there is no distinction between samsara and nirvana. "Depart for the dharmadhatu empty of inherent existence" means dissolve into emptiness. So the obstructing forces are sent to the basic space beyond nature, meaning they are naturally liberated and therefore disappear. In other gektor practices, obstructing forces are sent to the other side of the ocean.

Recite the fierce mantra, . . .

Here you should recite fierce mantras such as OM PEMA NATA KRITA HA YA GRI WA SARWA BIGHANEN HANA HANA HUNG PET and OM SUMBHANI SUMBHANI HUNG GRIHANA GRIHANA HUNG GRIHANAPAYA GRIHANAPAYA HUNG ANAYA HO BAGAWAN VIDYARADZA HUNG PET, which is the mantra that terminates the malevolent spirits.

. . . and throw power substances at them. Assume the gaze of the vajra view.

Substances that are feared by malevolent spirits should be offered at this point. These are for example the gugul and mustard seeds blessed and consecrated by Vajrapani who gave them to the Buddha to tame and chase away negative forces. You burn the gugul because the malevolent spirits can't stand its smell, and you throw the mustard seeds.

"Assume the gaze of vajra view" means actualising the view of emptiness. The vajra view isn't something you do with your eyes, you actualise it through meditation which sends away the negative forces, meaning they dissolve. The vajra is the symbol of indestructibility. A vajra cannot be cut, is indestructible, real, solid and stable. It therefore cannot be obstructed and is completely invincible. This is what emptiness is like. Emptiness is like space, which can't be altered or cut or burned in any way. You can't do anything at all to space. So here you introduce emptiness, which negative forces cannot overcome. As you abide in the view of emptiness, delusion doesn't have a chance; and in the absence of delusion, negative forces won't know how to obstruct you.

The *Lamrim Yeshe Nyingpo* says that according to Hindu mythology, Indra's hundred-spoked vajra has the power to destroy negative forces which is why the vajra is rotated during the recitation of the Sumbhani mantra. In fact, the *Lamrim Yeshe Nyingpo* says that the vajra has the power to effect four benefits, meaning it is certain to accomplish four specific functions. So it's a vajra that you throw at those who are hostile, because it will unfailingly hit its target, and the hostile being will certainly die. But a being who is killed by a vajra in this way will then be guided to a higher rebirth. So at this point in the practice, we make sure that all obstacles to our enlightenment which are the thoughts and concepts that arise in our minds—but nothing outside mind—are eliminated.

7. Protection Spheres

Fifth, meditate on the protection spheres.

A protection sphere is always completely sealed. Nothing—not air, not even mind—can pass into it. The protection sphere or tent forms a boundary inside which the mandala of deities is spontaneously present. This is the kind of protection sphere you must meditate on. There are different ways of visualizing a protection sphere, but at the very least it must always include egg-shaped layers of vajras, fire and wrathful deities that surround the palace and pure realm and the five elements on which they rest. Visualize an egg-shaped vajra protection tent with a double vajra at its top and base and layers—or walls—of many crossed vajras packed together so tightly that there's not even enough space for air. The tent is surrounded by fire and sometimes also by water and wind, and around the layer of fire is an infinite number of wrathful deities. The male wrathful deities face outwards to protect against incoming negative forces, and the female wrathful deities face inwards to protect against the loss of siddhis. They are sometimes surrounded by a stable, shining, five-layered dome made up of the five attributes of the five buddha families (wheels, vajras, jewels, lotus flowers and swords) sequentially arranged and countless in number which fill all directions (above and below, the cardinal and intermediate points and so on) with rings of fire. The apex of the dome is ornamented with a half-vajra.

Read the lines corresponding to the vajra tent in the text and visualize all its characteristics. At the very least, trust that everything is there.

As you say BENDZA JNANA RAKSHA OM AH HUNG, the protection sphere manifests, inconceivably vast and extremely solid. For the sphere to be as strong as possible, you must first realise emptiness.

8. Invocation and Descent of Blessings

Sixth, visualize yourself clearly as the Sublime Lady . . .

Think, "I am Jetsun Drolma." Again, don't fake being Tara, you truly are Tara. As I have already told you, if you're not sure what the view is and if you don't have confidence in it, you cannot practise Vajrayana. The view of pure perception will give you confidence that you really are the deity. Think, "My mind is the ground, buddha nature, which actually is the deity." Realise the truth of this! Once you do, the clear appearance of the deity will arise naturally.

. . . and chant the following invocation amidst a profusion of brilliant rays of light . . .

The clear visualization of yourself as the deity Jetsun Drolma now emanates innumerable rays of light, "a profusion of brilliant rays", that fill the whole of space, purifying the environment, all sentient beings and the offerings. Buddhas accomplish their activities with rays of light.

. . .with yearning songs, . . .

A "yearning song" is like the cry of a lonely child calling out for his mother and in this context refers to the mantras that follow the invocations: A LA LA HO SAMAYA HO SAMAYA STAM and OM TARE TUTTARE TURE SOHA JNANA BENDZA SAMAYA ABESHAYA A AH   HRING HRING PHENG PHENG HUNG HUNG HUNG   DZA HUNG BAM HO.

. . . incense and music.

The substances used here are good incense with an exquisite fragrance and lovely music.[85] As you offer the music, think to yourself that all sounds are in fact music and that as the music plays, everyone is summoned. It's like when you ring the lunch bell, everyone comes running, or when you gesture with your hand for someone to come towards you, they come. These are the kinds of convention we use to summon people. It's the same idea here.

> The three root deities of the ten directions and four times
> Are aroused as the mudras of the Sublime Lady's three
> secrets—
> Let them dissolve into me, the place, the ritual implements
> and substances,
> Which now blaze with the splendour of blessings.
> OM AH HUNG A LA LA HO SAMAYA HO SAMAYA STAM
> From the expanse of the ground, the dharmakaya palace,
> Arises the appearance of the ground, the discernment of
> everything,
> O bhagavati of the supreme lotus family,
> Wish-Fulfilling Wheel who increases longevity,
> Bless this place and bestow the supreme empowerment,
> Arouse primordial wisdom in our body, speech and mind,
> Increase our longevity, merit, wealth, experience and
> realization,
> And grant us the ordinary and supreme accomplishments.
> OM TARE TUTTARE TURE SOHA
> JNANA BENDZA SAMAYA ABESHAYA A AH
> HRING HRING PHENG PHENG HUNG HUNG HUNG DZA
> HUNG BAM HO

During the descent of blessings, realise that all the deities of the ten directions and four times—of past, present, future and the fourth time of great equality—and all the Three Roots deities——lama, yidam and khandro—are the Sublime Lady of Immortality's enlightened body, speech and mind, her three secrets. From the Dzogchen perspective, everything we perceive with our five sense faculties—or six if you include mind—is considered to be a thought. So the greatest kind of descent of blessings is when, the moment a thought arises, you are aware of it and recognize it, then it dissolves. But if you can't do that, then practise as explained. The descent of blessings is about recognizing natural purity—the original primordial purity—and great equality. It's like prospecting for gold: the point isn't to change the earth into gold, to change something impure into something pure, it's about recognizing what is already there.

To understand the Mantrayana, first you have to appreciate that the Vehicle of Characteristics is a complete and flawless path and that it came directly from the Buddha. The Vajrayana is the vehicle that takes fruition as the path and has four levels of approach: Kriya Yoga, Charya Yoga, Yoga Tantra and Unsurpassed Yoga Tantra. The Unsurpassed Yoga Tantra has nine divisions, which can also be classified as the three inner tantras of Mahayoga that emphasize kyerim, the Anuyoga practice of dzogrim, and Atiyoga or Dzogpachenpo which is beyond the conceptualization of the two previous vehicles. The Sarma schools speak of male, female and nondual tantras. Each of these three vehicles is divided into three sections, each emphasizing a specific form of practice: Maha-Maha, Anu-Maha, Ati-Mahayoga; Maha-, Anu- and Ati-Anuyoga; and Maha-, Anu- and Ati-Atiyoga. The Chimé Phakmé Nyingtik is an Ati-Mahayoga practice because it follows the kyerim method for generating the deity and because it involves many aspects of the Dzogchen or Atiyoga approach plus all the different levels or bhumis of progressing on the path.

The text of the descent of blessings says,

> The Three Roots deities of the ten directions and four
>   times
> Are aroused as the mudras of the Sublime Lady's three
>   secrets— . . .

All the deities of the Three Roots dwell in the ten directions which are all around you. The ten directions are the four cardinal points, east, south, west and north; the four intermediate points, southeast, southwest, northwest and northeast; and above and below. The four times are past, present, future and the inconceivable fourth time of the Nyingmapas. If you were to add up all the deities who live in all those directions and times, how many would it make? A lot, yes? And Jetsun Drolma is the expression of the activities of all these billions of deities, her nature is their enlightened activities. All their blessings and rays of light,

. . . dissolve into me, the place, the ritual implements and
   substances,
Which now blaze with the splendour of blessings.

As the blessings enter them, the ritual implements and substances blaze
with the splendour of blessings. The meaning of these words is encapsulated
in the three syllables OM AH HUNG since qualities and activities are merely
aspects of body (OM), speech (AH) and mind (HUNG).

Realising just how extraordinary these words are, you utter, "A LA LA
HO!" which means "incredible" or "beyond words". SAMAYA HO! invokes
the samayas of these inconceivable, inexpressible manifestations of wisdom.
What are their samaya pledges? To help sentient beings until samsara is
empty. So by invoking their samayas, what you're saying is, "Do this for me
too, now!"

There is so much to understand about these mantras. They weren't translated and so were left in Sanskrit because that language carries more blessings than Tibetan. Those who are well-versed in Sanskrit don't have to say
the prayer in Tibetan, the Sanskrit mantra is enough. In fact, those who
have superior capacities can do the whole practice without saying one word
of the Tibetan prayers; they just say the mantras. For example, such a practitioner would eliminate negative forces by instantly meditating on the deity
and, instead of saying the relevant Tibetan verse, directly actualise the meaning of that verse as they recite the mantras. They would then recite BENDZA
JNANA RAKSHA OM AH HUNG as they meditate on the protection spheres and
OM AH HUNG A LA LA HO SAMAYA HO SAMAYA STAM as they accomplish the
descent of blessings.

9. Blessing the Offerings

If you want to practise a little more elaborately, the descent of blessings and
blessing the offerings can be done separately. But in a less elaborate practice,
they can be done together because they have the same meaning.

Visualize yourself clearly as Jetsun Drolma. Rays of light emanate from
your heart as you call out to the deities in a song of yearning and offer
incense and music to indicate that you want them to come to you. The
text goes on to say that all the jnanasattvas in the mandala led by Jetsun

Drolma—including her body, speech, mind, qualities and activities, power and ability—arrive in my outer environment and transform it into a pure buddha field. Think, "They dissolve into the space in which I practise, transforming it into the unfathomable palace, then into my body so I truly become the deity. They dissolve into my speech, transforming my words into vajra speech, endowed with the quality of the melodious voice of Brahma. They dissolve into my mind so that my thoughts have no effect upon my mind, and its dharmakaya nature manifests." Impure body, speech and mind become the pure three vajras so you must trust that they have transformed into vajra body, vajra speech and vajra mind. This is how to practise the descent of blessings.

You bless the offerings by blessing all material objects arranged before you, as well as the vast offerings you have created in your mind which are just like the clouds of offerings that were offered by Samantabhadra. Use everything you have. Spread a beautiful cloth on the table, present the offerings in your loveliest bowls and arrange everything as exquisitely as possible. Recite the mantras. You can add the eight offerings mantras, for example ARGHAM for drinking water and so on. Perform mudras and rest in samadhi to bless the offerings. The mantra in the text is,

OM AH HUNG SARWA PUDZA MEGHA SAMAYA HUNG

OM AH HUNG represent enlightened body, speech and mind, respectively. SARWA means all, PUDZA means offer and MEGHA means clouds. So the meaning of the mantra is that you offer everything possible in an extremely vast offering.

You will need the three special blessed substances of amrita, torma and rakta. "Sky treasury" means inexhaustible, so when we open the sky treasury, the offerings we make will become inexhaustible.

Usually sadhanas have seven preliminary sections, seven sections in the main practice and seven concluding sections. We have now covered the seven preliminary sections. Next, we come to the seven sections of the main part of the practice—kyerim practice.

C. The Main Practice

1. The Generation of the Samayasattvas

First, generate the samayasattvas.

OM MAHA SHUNYATA JNANA BENDZA SOBHAVA EMAKO HANG

MAHA means great. SHUNYATA means emptiness. JNANA means wisdom. Here, you actualise the dissolution of all phenomena into great emptiness as you recite this mantra. Out of that emptiness arises the deity.

The three samadhis of kyerim practice are very profound. Our nature is primordial purity, you should be clear about that. If we don't recognize the dharmakaya for what it really is—buddha nature, the true nature of our mind—we are deluded. Since we are deluded, we form concepts, and it is because we have concepts that we are sentient beings, as opposed to buddhas. The primordial purity of our true nature is called "rigpa", and the display of rigpa now arises in the form of compassionate energy which is the natural expression of primordial purity. The outer display or outer clarity is the delusion that characterizes sentient beings. The inner display or inner clarity is Buddha which is the wisdom that is free from concept and thought.

For sentient beings like us, our inner display is very weak, whereas our outer display is very strong. From the outer clarity, karma arises as do destructive emotions and thoughts. Each of our actions strengthens our karma which becomes stronger and stronger. This is how we form our habits and tendencies, and as a result our karma and destructive emotions completely obscure the dharmakaya and we suffer. At the same time, as Longchenpa said, "Our buddha nature is like a diamond that's been stuck in the mud for a thousand years. Once the diamond is dug up, it is exactly as beautiful as it was a thousand years ago, unspoilt by the mud with all its qualities intact. Similarly, our buddha nature, however obscured, always remains perfect and incorruptible."

Since buddha nature is obscured by karma and destructive emotions, we are reborn in samsara again and again. There are only four ways of taking birth: from an egg, a womb, heat and moisture, and miraculous birth. Having been reborn in samsara, we are once again deluded sentient beings. And it's impossible to count the number of times we've been reborn or the number of times we've died. To stop being ceaselessly reborn in samsara, we must eliminate the causes of rebirth which are karma and habitual tendencies. How do we do this? Through the practice of kyerim. Kyerim is a special teaching from the Secret Mantra Vajrayana that purifies and eliminates the habitual tendencies that cause us to be reborn in one of four ways.

Egg birth is the most elaborate form of birth. It is called "double birth" because it involves two births—an egg is born from the mother, then the being is born from the egg. Not just birds, but many beings are born from eggs. To purify this kind of birth, we need a similarly elaborate method which involves the practice of the five manifest enlightenments.

To purify birth from the womb, we generate through the four vajras. The parents have sex, a consciousness enters the mother's womb and a baby develops over nine months. Ask your doctor for the details. Once the baby emerges from the womb, he or she grows up to be an adult. This is true for all beings born from a womb. It's just details like length of time they spend in the womb and so on that differ.

The three-vajra generation is practised to purify birth from heat and moisture. This type of birth requires a little heat and moisture to create the right vessel for a consciousness to enter and a being to develop.

Miraculous birth is used by those who just have to think about taking birth for it to happen. They don't need a father, a mother or heat and moisture. They don't need anything at all and are born in an instant. The cause for their birth is mind. This is the most common type of birth; most of the beings who fill the hell realms were born miraculously. That's how they are able to take birth in fire, stones and so on. Instantaneous visualization purifies the habitual tendencies associated with miraculous birth and doesn't require causes and conditions like reciting prayers and so on. The visualization simply appears in an instant.

There is a great deal of explanation in the tantras about the five manifest enlightenments, the four-vajra generation, the three-vajra generation and instantaneous visualization.[86] When we die, all the concepts we developed in this life cease and we enter the intermediate state between two lives, the bardo. Beings who pass through the bardo are reborn using one of the four methods of birth. Therefore, to free ourselves from the cycle of rebirth in samsara, we must purify the habitual tendencies that lead us to samsaric rebirth, for example our desire to enter a womb and to then be born nine months and ten days later. In the Chimé Phakmé Nyingtik, the kyerim practice is based on the four vajras which purifies the habit of being reborn from a womb.

The stages of generation through the four vajras are:

—Meditation on emptiness and bodhichitta; mind manifests as the seed syllable of the deity, for example HUNG.
—The HUNG descends onto the deity's seat such as sun and moon disc seats, purifying mind of its tendency to enter a womb.
—To purify the baby growing in the mother's womb, the seed syllable transforms into the body of the deity.
—The placement of the three seed syllables at the three places of the body of the deity.

The Three Samadhis

All things in samsara and nirvana are
The primordial, luminous space of suchness in which arises
The power of all-illuminating compassion. Their union
Is the causal samadhi, a white TAM,
Appearing like a rainbow from the sky and . . .

The three samadhis are the most important aspect of both an explanation of kyerim and of its practice. A practitioner must plant the structure of the three samadhis. We practise the three samadhis by reciting the words of the sadhana and meditating on their meaning. Secret Mantra Vajrayana uses both recitation and meditation. So we recite the sadhana using our mouths while our minds actualise the meaning of the words. The dharmakaya buddha, sambhogakaya buddha and nirmanakaya buddhas are linked to the three samadhis. There are a great many teachings about this subject, but at the very least you should know that the sambhogakaya arises from the dharmakaya, that the nirmanakaya arises from the sambhogakaya and that all three kayas arise to help sentient beings. The three samadhis follow the same sequence.

The first samadhi, the samadhi of suchness, is the dharmakaya, the primordial luminous space of suchness. Ideally, the practitioner maintains the clarity of rigpa and rests in emptiness. However, what you manage to do will depend on the level of your practice. Best is to actualise the meaning, not conceptually but directly. Breathe out at least twenty-one times, fourteen or a minimum of seven times as you rest in the view.

The second samadhi, the samadhi of universal manifestation, is the sambhogakaya. As a thought arises, meditate on vast compassion indivisible from emptiness. This is how you apply the second samadhi. Our thoughts always end up deluding us, and our delusions lead us to negative actions. Think about how this always happens and develop tremendous compassion for all those who fall into this same cycle of suffering. Just as the light of the sun instantly dispels all trace of darkness, great compassion arising from shunyata instantly dispels delusion.

The third samadhi, the causal samadhi, is the nirmanakaya. The seed syllable arises from great compassion. Indivisible emptiness and compassion become a brilliant white seed syllable TAM that appears from space like a rainbow. Infinite light radiates from the TAM, symbolizing the infinite qualities of the buddhas. The light that shines from the TAM should be dazzling. Why? Because dazzling, brilliant light signifies the inconceivable qualities of the buddhas, for example the thirty-two major and eighty minor marks, the eighteen unshared qualities and the sixty aspects of melodious speech. Visualize the syllables in whichever script you prefer. Jamyang Khyentse Wangpo said it's better for Chinese people to visualize the syllables as a Chinese script, for Tibetans to visualize Tibetan script and for Indians to visualize an Indic script.

> Sending out light that purifies clinging to reality in the
> world and amongst beings.

At the moment, we see the whole universe impurely. We see houses, earth, stones, fire, wind, water and so on. This samadhi is the way to purify those kinds of impure perceptions. If you are able to perceive as described in the text, you have pure perception. However, it is only pure perception in the context of kyerim training. From the dzogrim perspective, even kyerim's pure perception is still impure. Through kyerim practice, the whole universe and all sentient beings are purified into primordial wisdom. All our grasping at the world's reality and any sense we have of solidity are purified into nothingness. It doesn't exist.

Within the expanse of the five elements, the consorts, . . .

There are two stages of generation: the generation of the support (the environment and the palace) and the generation of the deities. The environment and palace are visualized from the outside in, while the deities are visualized from the inside out. The five consorts—the five female buddhas—arise from space and are the embodiment of the five elements, and so they form the environment. They are also the five wisdoms and are therefore related to the five aggregates.

Visualize the syllable TAM in space, enclosed within the protection sphere. The TAM emanates the seed syllables associated with the five elements. E represents the element of space; it also represents mind in the body. YAM represents wind; it also represents the air in the body. RAM represents fire and warmth, BAM represents water and blood, LAM represents earth and flesh, and SUM represents Mount Meru and the bones. There are also kyerim practices that lead you through a visualization of the vajra body mandala, but that's not the case here.

The following syllables now emanate from the TAM: E, YAM, RAM, BAM, LAM, SUM. An E syllable arises first and transforms into the element of space which takes the form of a dark-blue triangle that appears to rest upside down in space, with one point aimed directly downwards. In some practices this syllable is white or the shape of a ball of light, but in all practices it is immeasurably big. YAM, the element of wind, descends into the inverted triangle, and as it approaches the triangle's lowest point, it transforms into a dark-green crossed vajra radiating dark green light. What you have now is blue light shining from the bottom of the inverted triangle and a sphere of dark-green light surrounding the crossed vajra.

The other syllables now descend into the space of the vast triangle which is visualized this way because the elements and everything that they form always appear in space. Next is the red RAM (fire) which transforms into a bright red triangle radiating red light that forms a sphere around it. From the TAM emerges BAM (water) which transforms into a white disc radiating white light. Then LAM (earth) emerges and transforms into a golden square radiating yellow light. Then SUM descends to rest on top of the golden square and transforms into Mount Meru with its four sides made of the four precious substances, larger at the top than at its base. There are four terraces at the top of Mount Meru, and everything up to the terraces is inside the element of space. The other vajra tent begins at the level of the terraces. Inside it is an iron ring. Inside the iron ring are the eight great charnel grounds, one in each of the eight directions. At the centre of the ring is an unopened, one-thousand-petalled lotus bud which encloses a crossed vajra. Each of its prongs extends to a cardinal direction: the yellow prongs point south, the red point west, the green point north and the white point east.[87] Each stage of visualization purifies one of the habitual tendencies associated with the outer environment.

Visualization of the Palace

All sentient beings live somewhere, and to purify the habitual tendencies associated with our homes, we meditate on the palace.

> Within the expanse of the five elements, the consorts, . . .

All five elements are now as pure as the five wisdoms. When you practise in retreat, you visualize the building where you do your retreat as the palace, not an ordinary house, and by doing so you purify your ordinary perception.

> . . . Stands the celestial mansion of great liberation,
> Formed of precious crystal,
> Complete with four sides, four doors and all its features.
> A wish-fulfilling jewel beautifully ornaments its summit.
> It has toranas, dharma wheels, deer and parasols,
> And is adorned with the yellow brick frieze, festooned
>   garlands,
> *Sharbu* ornaments and pagoda roofs.
> It is encircled by offering goddesses who stand on the
>   pleasure terraces,
> And all this is surrounded by the worldly protectors.

The syllable DROOM descends to the centre of the crossed vajra and transforms into the celestial mansion of great liberation made of precious crystal. So the crossed vajra forms the foundation of the palace. The Chimé Phakmé Nyingtik palace doesn't have any unique characteristics apart from being made of crystal, so we follow the general description of palaces given in the *Secret Essence Tantra*. The palace has four sides, but the four gateways mean it isn't a perfect square. Its characteristics are beyond what we can imagine, and its dimensions are immeasurable. It is protected by worldly protectors.

The four gateways represent the four immeasurables. The porticos that form the gateways stand in front of each of the four doors and have four pillars—two inner and two outer—and four steps leading up to the door. Here, each portico or torana is made of eight ornamental friezes, although as Jamyang Khyentse Wangpo pointed out, simple visualization practices only include four. All eight are visualized if you follow the more elaborate approach, but both methods are good. Above the ornamental friezes at each door is a dharma wheel with a deer and doe on either side and a parasol above it. The tops of the gateways are open so rays of light can shine out to accomplish the activities.

Inside the palace stand eight pillars. From the top of the palace wall to each of the pillars are eight beams that support a roof that is open at its centre. A phumba stands above the empty circle in the roof and is curved like a stupa. It represents great equality. Above the phumba, several levels like those you see on top of a stupa, including the thirteen rings, extend skywards. They are surmounted and beautifully ornamented by a sun, a moon and a wish-fulfilling jewel.

The knee-high red pleasure terraces extend from and surround the palace. The palace is white in colour. Around the top of the palace walls are strata of decorative friezes. The lowest is the yellow brick frieze above which stand very short columns linked by beautiful, festooned garlands. Above the columns hang the *sharbu* ornaments over which slope a yellow pagoda roof with gargoyles in each of the four directions. The top of the pagoda roof is embellished with, for example, the four vases, and ornaments hang from poles such as the four banners, mirrors and so on. On the red pleasure terrace stand four offering goddesses in each direction, so a total of sixteen encircle the palace. Outside in the charnel grounds, the worldly protectors of the ten directions surround the palace. The square floor of the palace is made of crystal and is surrounded by a vajra canal which directs water to flow over the spokes of the crossed vajra as it leaves the palace.

If you can find a three-dimensional model of this kind of palace, the best way to help you visualize is to look at that. However much I talk about the shape, colour and features of this palace, modern people don't seem able to understand. At least, that's my experience. Other lamas like Dzongsar Khyentse Rinpoche have said the same thing: that modern people just don't get it. The words for porticos, dharma wheels, deer and parasols, yellow brick friezes, festooned garlands, *sharbu* ornaments and pagoda roofs are all very poor translations because the names of what we're visualizing don't exist in western languages. So it's best to find a picture of each of the features to look at as you go through your practice text. Just talking about these things is of no use at all. The Sakyapas go into great detail about this visualization and include things like measurements and proportions. Dilgo Khyentse Rinpoche didn't explain the palace when he taught westerners. He told them simply to think of a beautiful but incredible building made of precious substances that is beyond the bounds of possibility. By doing so, he said you purify your habitual tendencies. Alternatively, you could try imagining your own house made of jewels and light with no outside or inside.

The palace is the natural manifestation of the deity; there is no difference between a single one of its pillars and the deity. In fact, the whole palace is the deity. If you want to know more details about the palace and their significance, you should read the commentaries or ask people who know about these things.

The descriptions of the deities themselves—for example one face, two hands and so on—are easy to understand from the text. Or you can look at a thangka.

The Seats

Generally, people need a house to live in. But to build a house, you will need land, an environment. In the house, you need seats to sit on. Right now, our chairs, sofas and benches are impure perceptions whereas a lotus, sun and moon disc are pure. But of course, such seats don't function within the ordinary realm of possibility. Just try sitting on the sun, you'd burn up instantly!

> In its centre on a four-petalled lotus are
> Skilful means and wisdom—sun and moon fused
> together— . . .

Lotuses grow in mud, yet lotus flowers are unstained by that mud. Likewise, the deity who sits on the lotus is certainly present in samsara, yet is unstained by it. The sun and moon together represent skilful means and wisdom, and both are necessary. In the light of the sun and the moon, darkness is entirely eliminated. In the presence of the sun and the moon, the mind of the deity does not experience the smallest delusion, thought or concept. So the mind of the deity who sits on a sun and moon disc seat will be entirely free of delusion.

> In the centre of which is the syllable TAM, as their union.

TAM which is the causal samadhi that we have mentioned earlier and is indivisible from your own mind descends to rest on the sun and moon discs that form its seat. "Fused together" refers to the union of skilful means and wisdom.

> Light emanates from TAM as an offering to the noble ones,
> . . .

From TAM, rays of lights shoot out to make offerings to all the noble beings in every direction and to benefit all sentient beings.

> Gathering and bringing back the quintessence of samsara
> and nirvana, . . .

"Samsara" means all sentient beings, and "nirvana" means all the tathagatas. When the light returns to the TAM, it brings the essence of all sentient beings and all buddhas which is what is meant by "the quintessence of samsara and nirvana".

The Deities

Now meditate on the main deities.

> Which transforms into the magical body of wisdom,
> Embodiment of the enlightened activity of the buddhas,
>   past, present and future,
> Wish-Fulfilling Wheel, bestower of immortality.
> Brilliant white, with one face and two hands,
> Her right hand in the mudra of supreme generosity,
> Her left grants refuge, symbolizing the Three Jewels,
> And holds an utpala flower on which rests the vase of
>   longevity.
> Peaceful, smiling, with seven eyes of wisdom,
> She is lovely. Adorned with silks and jewelled ornaments,
> Her two legs are crossed in vajra posture,
> She sits on her lotus and moon disc seat.

With her right hand, Tara, the Wish-Fulfilling Wheel, makes the gesture that symbolizes granting refuge. She has seven eyes: two eyes like everyone has, plus one in the middle of her forehead and one in each hand and foot. She wears the five silk and eight jewel ornaments.

> As her natural radiance, the supreme skilful means, the
>   Lord of the Dance,
> Holds a lotus flower and long-life vase and embraces her in
>   union.

She is in union with the Lord of Dance (Avalokiteshvara and Amitayus)[88] who manifests as her natural radiance, meaning the rays of light that constantly radiate from her.

This is the meditation on the main deity. If you cannot lay the foundation of this practice properly using the structure of the three samadhis, you are not practising kyerim correctly. Nowadays, few really understand the three samadhis. In fact, many monks and lamas don't understand them at all. But to practise kyerim without relating to the samadhi of suchness and the samadhi of universal manifestation will only add one delusion to another. The three samadhis are the mandatory prerequisite for all kyerim practices that involve meditation on a deity, not just the Chimé Phakmé Nyingtik, and encompass the most important points of kyerim.

However rushed you may feel, make sure that you meditate on the three samadhis properly. Of course, at first you won't be able to practise exactly as described in the text, so practise on an aspirational level—at least try! You should bring to mind your understanding of the three samadhis. To do that, you must first learn what they are. Then visualize the deities as you follow the text.

Having visualized the main deity in union, you then visualize the retinue who are no different from the main deity,

> She passionately abides in undistracted great bliss and the
>   four joys,
> While her secret space emits
> The bodhichitta seed syllables TAM, DROOM, HRIH and
>   HUNG.

From her secret space comes the four seed syllables, the nature of which is bodhichitta, which transform into the four Taras. The syllables emanate and reabsorb rays of light. As they reabsorb the light,

> In the east, TAM transforms into dark-blue Vajra Tara
> Holding an utpala flower and a vajra, in the mudra of
>   supreme generosity.
> In the south, DROOM transforms into yellow Ratna Tara
> Holding an utpala flower and a jewel, in the mudra of
>   supreme generosity.
> In the west, HRIH transforms into red Padma Tara
> Holding an utpala flower and an iron hook, in the mudra
>   of supreme generosity.
> In the north, HUNG transforms into black Karma Tara
> Holding an utpala flower and a sword, in the mudra of
>   supreme generosity.
> They are all adorned with the silks and jewelled ornaments,
> Wearing the pacifying, increasing, magnetising and
>   wrathful expressions.

> Each sits on a lotus and moon disc in the half-vajra
>   posture.

Each syllable in turn emanates and reabsorbs rays of light, then transforms into one of the four Taras. In the east is blue Vajra Tara. She holds an utpala flower and a vajra. In essence she is Akshobhya, purified anger, and accomplishes the pacifying activities. In the south is yellow Ratna Tara. She holds an utpala flower and a jewel. In essence she is Ratnasambhava, purified avarice, and accomplishes enriching activities. In the west is red Padma Tara. She holds an utpala flower and an iron hook. In essence she is Amitabha, purified discriminating thoughts, and accomplishes magnetising activities. In the north is black Karma Tara. She holds an utpala flower and a sword. In essence she is Amoghasiddhi, purified karmic formations, and accomplishes wrathful activities.

> Again, the Sublime Lady emanates DZA, HUNG, BAM
>   and HO.
> These syllables are sent to the four doors where, on lotus
>   and sun disc seats,
> They transform into Vajra Hook Tara, Lasso Tara,
> Iron Chain Tara and Bell Tara,
> White, yellow, red and green respectively, with semi-
>   wrathful expressions,
> And each holding her own hand implement and an utpala
>   flower.
> Dancing, with one leg stretched and the other bent, they
>   suppress the four maras,
> And are adorned with the silks and jewelled ornaments.

The main deity emanates the syllables DZA HUNG BAM HO. The syllables rest on seats by each of the four doors, emanate and reabsorb rays of light and transform into the four Gatekeeper Taras who are all dancing. In the east, a white Tara gatekeeper holds an utpala flower and an iron hook; she has mastery over the pacifying activities. In the south, a yellow Tara gatekeeper holds an utpala flower and a lasso; she has mastery over the increasing activities. In the west, a red Tara gatekeeper holds an utpala flower and an iron chain; she has mastery over the magnetising activities. In the north, a green Tara gatekeeper holds an utpala flower and a bell; she has mastery over the subjugating activities. Visualize these eight deities clearly.

Many other deities are actualised on an aspirational level, so just consider them to be present. They are not described in the text, but their presence is required.

> A host of the Three Roots deities and dharma protectors fill
>   the whole of space
> As a great net of magical emanations
> That is the self-radiance of primordial wisdom arising from
>   basic space,
> Akin to the sun's rays and the sun itself.
> Gathering in great family assemblies,
> The deities—the great arising as the ground of all that
>   appears and exists—
> Manifest clearly, unborn yet primordially perfect.

The deities of each family including dakinis and protectors fill the whole of space, having manifested from the Sublime Lady, Wish-Fulfilling Wheel. They all have the same nature, primordial wisdom. And they all appear at once, a great net of magical emanations like the rays of the sun.

> The crowns of their heads, their throats and hearts
> Are marked with the syllables of the three vajras, . . .

"Their" means all the deities of the mandala, the main female and male deities and all the deities in the retinue. "The syllables of the three vajras" are white OM, red AH and dark-blue HUNG at their foreheads, throats and hearts respectively. Or alternatively, the three vajras can be visualized as white Vairochana for the enlightened body, red Amitabha for the enlightened speech and blue Akshobhya for the enlightened mind. If you practise elaborately, you visualize the body of the deities; if you practise more simply, you visualize the hand implements, and the simplest form of practice is to visualize the syllables. Which you practise depends on what you can manage.

From which rays of light stream out and
Invite the jnanasattvas.

All the deities emanate rays of light from their three places. The rays of light look like hooks and reach out to the wisdom deities in their respective buddha fields to invite them to come to the visualized mandala, the samayasattva.

2. Invitation to the Jnanasattvas

We now invite the jnanasattvas into the samayasattva mandala. To invoke the jnanasattvas, we offer incense, beautiful music and songs of devotion and yearning like we did for the descent of blessings earlier. If you can't play any musical instruments, just use a damaru and bell and light some incense, which don't present any problems in India. In the absence of devotion or faith though, the deities will not come. In other words, as we meditate on the deities from a state of pure perception, if there is no pure perception, there is no meditation on the deity. The invitation begins,

> HRIH
> Long-life Goddess with supreme discerning wisdom, . . .

The wisdom of discernment is one of the five wisdoms, and this wisdom is the essence of the lotus family. The natural expression of the wisdom of discernment manifests in the form of the wisdom deity White Tara in union with her consort Nateshvara[89] Amitayus. White Tara who is the lord or sovereign of her buddha family is,

> . . . crowned by Amitabha, the Buddha of Limitless Light.

As mentioned earlier, she is the embodiment of all the enlightened activities of the buddhas,

> Lady who is the enlightened activity
> Of the buddhas of past, present and future,
> Approach! You who manifest as the Wish-Fulfilling Wheel
>   . . .

This sentence is very straightforward; it means "please come here, you who have a wish-fulfilling wheel". She manifests with,

> . . . the retinue of assembled families that you emanate— . . .

These are the four Taras of pacifying, enriching, magnetising and subjugating activities, the four gatekeepers and so on.

> Rupakayas that magically arise
> From the dharmakaya beyond arising,
> Your samaya of great compassion obliges you
> To confer the supreme siddhi on this practitioner,
> Direct your wisdom mind into this mandala of the
>   samayasattva
> And arouse in me indestructible vajra wisdom!

They all arise from the unborn expanse of the dharmakaya as a magical display of birth in the form of rupakayas. Why do they arise? As a result of their passionate concern for sentient beings. They are summoned by great compassion and are invoked through their samaya, their sacred pledge. What was their sacred pledge? That Jetsun Tara will confer the supreme and ordinary siddhis on the practitioner who brings her to mind, prays to her and accomplishes the practice. They are also liberated from the cycle of existence of samsara by merely hearing her name. Her compassion is extremely swift, isn't it? So in order to bestow the supreme siddhi on this practitioner, upon this samayasattva mandala, the visualized mandala, the practitioner asks her to generate indestructible vajra wisdom, grant empowerments and blessings and bring about realization.

Then you recite the mantra. SAMAYA HO is a way of reminding the wisdom deities of the sacred promise they made in the past. SAMAYA STAM asks that they grant us everything they promised. E A RA LI exhorts them to do everything they're asked to do with joy and delight and not grudgingly. HRING HRING DZA means to bring or to give. JNANASATTVA means wisdom being. We request the jnanasattvas to enter the samaya mandala. A AH means now rest in that state.

3. Request the Jnanasattvas to Take Their Places

The jnanasattvas invited from the dharmadhatu
Are drawn into and bound to the samaya mandala,
Where they stay, rejoicing in the great equality of one taste.

The jnanasattvas are invoked and reminded of the sacred pledge. Then once seated, they become one with the samayasattva mandala with great joy and in one taste.

OM . . .

"OM" is a syllable we see a lot of, don't we? That's because OM is the essence of the five wisdoms and is therefore placed at the head of most mantras. The Nyingma tradition explains how the OM syllable embodies the five wisdoms. The instruction is to say OM slowly, lingering on the end of the syllable. Sadhus know how to chant in this way, but don't ask the Tibetans because they have no idea at all! They just gibber, "OM OM OM" very quickly. Tibetans generally aren't much good at speaking Sanskrit. Once during Atisha's visit to Tibet, he had a headache and asked some monks to recite the mantra of Dorje Namjom for him, but they couldn't pronounce it properly and to Atisha it sounded like, "Break his head! Break his head!" After reciting OM, the seed syllable of the five wisdoms that opens the mantra, continue with,

Enlightened body, speech and mind mudras
Of the unsurpassable vajra wisdom,
Come and remain securely in great inseparability,
Forever indivisible from the host of deities made manifest
through samadhi.

This verse requests that the deities remain and is followed by the mantra,

BENDZA JNANA DZA HUNG BAM HO SAMAYA TISHTA LHEN

This part is the most important to explain. The words of the prayer are quite straightforward, and since you have the translation you will be able to understand what the words mean. Unless it was translated by one of those great writers who, as Dalai Lama says, uses such beautiful turns of phrase that when they reread what they've written, even they wonder what it was they were trying to say. I don't know anything about translation, but Khenpo Petse once went to France to teach the *Secret Essence Tantra* to Sogyal Rinpoche's students. There were about three or four hundred people present and I was also at Lerab Ling to do some practices. Sometimes, on my way to the toilet, I would stop outside the tent to listen to the teachings and heard Khenpo Petse explaining the words, the meaning, everything, in such an extraordinary way. It was an incredible teaching! I couldn't believe it; it was amazing! But I have no idea what the translator was doing with it. Whatever Khenpo Petse said would immediately be translated with what seemed to me to be rather too much ease. I went to Khenpo Petse one day and said, "Your explanations are so extraordinary, so profound, that even in Tibetan it's not easy to understand and grasp the extent of what you're saying. Yet your translator appears to give an immediate translation with the greatest of ease. I wonder if he is translating what you're saying correctly. What do you think?" Khenpo replied, "I've been asked to explain the text so that's what I'm doing. Is it translated correctly? I have no clue!"

Kyerim: An Overview

To return to our subject, I will now give an overview of kyerim practice. As I mentioned earlier, visualize the samayasattva mandala palace slowly, moving from the outside to the inside, and visualize the deities slowly, moving from inside to outside. An experienced practitioner is able to bring to mind and visualize the entire Chimé Phakmé Nyingtik mandala extremely clearly and in great detail, the palace and all nine deities (the main deity and all the retinue deities). The entire visualization immediately arises very vividly in their minds as if they were standing in front of a mirror. This kind of practitioner practises by bringing the complete visualization to mind instantaneously and actualises it fully as they go through the text.

For example, Patrul Rinpoche was able to visualize in detail the entire mandala of the peaceful and wrathful deities in the time it takes to mount a horse. Actually, he thought kyerim was very easy. Why? Because he had something to meditate upon. If you have something to meditate upon, there is something to train your mind to do [as opposed to Dzogchen meditation]. A practitioner of average capacity who hasn't quite reached that level is able to actualise the details as they recite the description of the visualization like "one face, two hands . . ." and so on. At this level the quality of the visualization, its clarity and so on will vary, and so the practice must be repeated again and again until a really clear image appears in your mind.

Phungong Tulku was one of Dudjom Rinpoche's root teachers. When they practised together, he would sometimes stop the chant master, saying, "Repeat that section! I didn't do it very well." What didn't he do well? He didn't actualise the kyerim visualization clearly.

Those with the least capacity who find they are unable to visualize much at all should simply try to feel the deities are really there. Practising by merely reciting the text while allowing mind to wander all over the place—anywhere, in fact, but on the description of the visualization you are chanting—is utterly useless. Simply mouthing empty words cannot be described as kyerim practice. But if you follow the words and try to actualise their meaning as you say them—even if your understanding of what you're saying is very limited—you are practising kyerim.

Visualize the palace first followed by the seats on which the deity will sit and then the main deity in union. The main deity is such an important part of the visualization that you must go over it again and again until it's absolutely clear in your mind. How to visualize will be explained a bit later on.

Having done your best to visualize the main deity, if it's possible for you to visualize the individual deities in the retinue clearly, that's very good. If you cannot, just try to sense their presence on an aspirational level which the teachings say is fine. Why? What's the rationale behind aspirational practice? As the text says, if the main deity is like the sun, all the retinue deities manifest like the rays of the sun and are indivisible from one another. So once you have meditated upon the main deity, just having a sense that the deities in the retinue are there will be enough. We Buddhists use many traditional examples, so you may need to stretch your minds a little to imagine what life was like in ancient times. For example, what would happen if you invited a king to stay with you? You didn't have to think about inviting all his attendants, bodyguards and servants because wherever he went, they would all automatically follow. Similarly, wherever the main deity of a mandala appears, their entire retinue will automatically also be there.

When you visualize the main deity, sometimes start at the top of the head and work down to the seat on which the deity sits and sometimes do it the other way around. Slowly scan the deity, actualising each detail with great clarity. You must train your mind like this until the visualization appears very vividly and clearly.

Here I have explained the kyerim practice quite simply without going into too much detail to give you an idea of what you need to aim for as you do this kind of practice. It's my response to the question, "How can I practise when I don't know all the details?" This is what you should do.

In the kyerim practice for generating the palace that we are concerned with here, the deities of Chimé Phakmé Nyingtik are only peaceful, but some practices involve both peaceful and wrathful deities, and others only wrathful deities, for example Vajrakilaya and Vajrabhairava. In such practices the palace is completely different, and the method of meditating on the deity is different too. Another approach is that of meditating on the body mandala, and yet another associates the palace and the deities with different aspects of the body. The method used in Chimé Phakmé Nyingtik is different from the simple body mandala practice just mentioned, and I won't go into that right now.

How to Visualize the Jnanasattva
Becoming One with the Samayasattva

After extending invitations to the jnanasattvas to become one with the samayasattvas, we ask the deities to take their places in the mandala and remain there. First visualize the deities, then invite the jnanasattvas to become one with the samayasattvas. I will now give an overview of how this is done.

As you meditate on yourself as the samayasattva, actualise the entire mandala from the vajra fence of the protective sphere to the tiered mandalas, the palace, the main deity and the retinue within it. Think about the entire samayasattva mandala. Now visualize a mandala identical to the samayasattva mandala—this is the jnanasattva mandala. The example often used is that it is like lighting one butter lamp with another. The method for visualizing it is as follows: protection spheres surround each of the samayasattva and jnanasattva mandalas, and the extreme outer limits of these spheres are encircled by fire. The two circles of fire touch, and the mandalas inside face each other. Actualise in your visualization a host of jnanasattvas that suddenly manifest from the expanse of the Buddha's dharmakaya like snowflakes in a blizzard. They dissolve into the clearly visualized samayasattva mandala, bringing with them the blessings of enlightened body, speech, knowledge, love and power. Samayasattvas and jnanasattvas become indivisible in one taste like pouring water into water.

BENDZA JNANA DZA HUNG BAM HO

BENDZA JNANA means vajra wisdom and is analogous to the host of jnanasattvas.

DZA HUNG BAM HO

I should say a few words about DZA HUNG BAM HO since it appears in numerous practices. As you say DZA, Hook Goddess—so-called because she holds a hook—emanates from the heart of the main deity and exits through the eastern door of the mandala to request that the jnanasattvas return with her to become one with samayasattvas. She returns to the mandala accompanied by them and enters through the eastern door. "The eastern door" here does not refer to the geographical east, but the east that is the direction the main deity faces. One of the qualities of the deity is that from whichever direction it is approached, that direction is east which makes the deity very different from ordinary people. If any one of us were to sit in a room with four doors marking the four cardinal points, we would only be able to face one of those doors. But the faces and arms of deities are totally unimpeded, so wherever they appear if someone approaches them, their faces and arms manifest so the deity is approached face on. As you say the syllable DZA, Hook Goddess is emanated, leaves through the eastern door and hooks wisdom deities back into the mandala through that eastern door.

After DZA comes HUNG, emanating Lasso Goddess. Now each jnanasattva deity merges indivisibly with the corresponding samayasattva deity. The hook is to grab and the lasso to bind. You actualise the jnana and samaya deities merging indivisibly. BAM emanates Iron Chain Goddess, and you actualise the merging of the jnana and samaya deities so they become inseparable beyond separation and reunion. Ho emanates Bell Goddess and since the jnana and samaya deities have merged inseparably, Ho is an expression of joy that this has happened.

That's the explanation of DZA HUNG BAM HO from one tradition, but you can do a shorter version if you prefer. This mantra concludes all the prayers that invite the wisdom deities, and these four seed syllables—plus associated mudras—represent four things for the practitioner to actualise. On a very simple level:

—With DZA, Hook Goddess invokes the sacred pledge of the jnanasattvas
—With HUNG, Lasso Goddess invites the jnanasattvas
—With BAM, it's as if Iron Chain Goddess draws the jnanasattvas from their dwelling by saying, "Please come here immediately!" There's a subtle difference in the meaning between HUNG and BAM. When we say HUNG, we invite the deities by saying, "Please come." BAM, on the other hand, brings with it a great sense of urgency, "Please come now!"
—With HO, we rejoice with Bell Goddess at the indivisibility of the wisdom and samaya deities.

There is a crucial point to understand here. Buddha nature—the basic element in all sentient beings—is the basis of the entire mandala of wisdom deities. It is also the basic element in me. Because buddha nature is primordially pure, to manifest that purity, I must meditate on the samayasattvas. The jnanasattvas are the primordially pure kayas of all the buddhas. This means that samayasattvas and jnanasattvas are primordially one taste beyond separation and reunion and are beyond time, since primordial purity did not happen at a specific point in time. As Jigme Lingpa and numerous other great masters have said, the intention behind the repetition of this process in our practice is to refresh a state that has always been. If therefore you imagine that two deities are merging together outside yourself like two people melting into each other, you are completely wrong. If on top of that you imagine the wisdom deity to be better than the samaysattva deity already in the mandala, you're making an even worse mistake! But that's how ordinary people like us think, we imagine the jnanasattvas are superior to us.

To eliminate this dualistic tendency, in our practice we go through the process of inviting the wisdom deities to become one with the visualized deities. As this principle is explained, you will have a sense of what the teacher is trying to tell you. However, to genuinely overcome your habits and give rise to a realization of nonduality is extremely difficult. This is how it usually works: a lama explains the principles of invitation to you and you hear what he says, think about it and understand it. But you will also definitely wonder and think about it, and overcoming those thoughts is the invitation. The meaning of DZA HUNG BAM HO is vast, but here I have explained it very briefly.

The easiest way to present the four mudras of hook, lasso, iron chain and bell is to show them. Elaborate practices include a prayer for requesting the deities to be seated, and some may contain very elaborate invitation sections. In the practice we are discussing here, once the wisdom deities— the jnanasattvas—have been invited, you actualise the visualization of them standing in the courtyard surrounding the palace, then ask them to be seated. They sit, indivisible and in one taste with the samaya deities. Here the request to be seated is concise,

SAMAYA TISHTA LEN

4. Homage

HRIH
To the deities of the mandala of the Sublime Lady of
    Immortality,
Primordially innate within me and
Free from dualistic clinging, I offer the homage of the view
In the expanse of the purity and equality of dharmakaya.
AH LA LA HO ATI PU HO PRATITSA HO

There are four different kinds of homage, and among them the ultimate homage of the view is offered by maintaining the view beyond the duality of subject and object. It is offered within the basic space of dharmakaya, the great purity and equality.

AH LA LA HO are words of amazement at the extraordinary qualities of the Buddha, and with AH TI PU HO you visualize an activity deity emanating from the main deity and prostrating with folded hands to the main deity. As you pay homage and prostrate, think of all of the deities' extraordinary qualities. There are sixteen offering goddesses on the red terrace of sensory pleasure right outside the palace walls, and it is also possible to offer prostration through these goddesses. If you visualize an activity deity similar to the main deity and emanating from the heart of that main deity, she must eventually dissolve back into the main deity's heart once she has prostrated. The point of paying the homage of the view is to realise that yourself—the samayasattva—and the jnanasattva are indivisible. In the teachings, it should be mentioned at that point that the lama should offer prostrations naked.

5. Offerings

The text of the terma says,

> I send out hosts of vajra goddesses
> Who fill the sky,
> And great clouds of offerings pervade the whole of space.

Actualise this as you make the offerings. There are four kinds of offerings—outer, inner, secret and the offering of suchness. Inner offerings are considered superior to outer offerings, secret offerings are superior to inner offerings and the offering of suchness is supreme. The unsurpassable Mantrayana contains practices that include lower offerings like the outer offerings and so on and others that don't. But the highest offerings are always included.

There are several different traditions for making offerings. As you will remember, right outside the wall of the mandala is the red terrace of sensory pleasure where sixteen offering goddesses stand, four in each direction. These goddesses are emanated by the main deity to present offerings to the main deity. You will also remember that the entire mandala right down to the vajra fence and vajra protection sphere is the display of primordial wisdom. Therefore, the offering goddesses are not separate from the main deity. This is one way of making the offering, but there are many other ways too. For example, at this point in the practice you are the samayasattva indivisible from the jnanasattva—this has already been accomplished. When it's time to make the offerings, an activity deity emanates from your heart as the indivisible samayasattva and jnanasattva and stands at the entrance of the mandala. As you perform mudras like the lotus circling mudra, an infinite number of deities radiate out and present offerings to all the deities of the mandalas. This is another way of making offerings.

How the activity deity functions is very similar to how things work in our ordinary lives. If you want to eat, somebody has to cook; if you need clothes, somebody has to make them. In this case, if you want to make an offering, you need an activity deity to do it for you. Once the offering has been made, the activity deity dissolves back into the heart of the main deity.

The Chimé Phakmé Nyingtik employs yet another approach to making offerings. As you are visualizing yourself as the main deity of Chimé Phakmé Nyingtik, you emanate rays of light from your three centres—forehead, throat and heart—which transform into an infinite amount of vajra goddesses who fill the sky completely, making all the outer offerings of drinking water, cleansing water, flowers, incense, light, scented water, food offerings and music. They also present the inner offerings of beautiful physical forms, smells, sound, taste and tactile sensations. This method of offering follows the text of the Chimé Phakmé Nyingtik terma most closely.

> OM
> Whether actually present or manifested by the mind,
> All the offerings in infinite universes, inner, outer and
>   secret
> I offer to you, noble Wish-Fulfilling Wheel:
> Accept them and grant me the siddhi of immortality!

The four lines start with, "Whether actually present or manifested by the mind, . . ." The actual offerings are those you have prepared, the imagined offerings are all those you can bring to mind like the clouds of offerings of Samantabhadra. It is said that there is no difference between the real offerings and those made by the mind. "Infinite universes" implies that the universes are so vast that they pervade the whole of space. To offer all these, "I offer to you, noble Wish-Fulfilling Wheel" means the offering is made to all the deities of the mandala. Their body, speech and mind are all fully satisfied and as a result grant all blessings and siddhis, including the siddhi of immortality which is the one you are requesting.

a) Outer Offerings

The verse for the outer offering is very short, just a few words, but it is complete. How can it be complete when it's so short? Because the text says, "All the offerings in infinite universes" and is followed by the mantras beginning with OM ARYA TARA meaning "Jetsun Drolma", SAPARIWARA meaning "all", then the list of offerings, ARGHAM, PADAM and so on.

Jamgön Kongtrul Lodrö Taye noted down how Jamyang Khyentse Wangpo made offerings when he did this practice using the more detailed method; this text is called the *Elaborate Garland of Offering*, and it is at the end of your text.[90] Each offering is described as "infinite universes of" drinking water or cleansing water and so on, and it is a good method to use when you practise elaborately. Why? Because when you do ritual practices like this one, offerings are important.

The text devotes four lines to each offering—outer, inner and so on—and indicates what the practitioner should actualise for each offering. To have to visualize everything in the time it takes to recite just one or two lines would be a bit difficult, wouldn't it?

(i) Drinking Water

These days, practitioners in retreat start by placing drinking water, cleansing water, flowers and so on on their shrines, but as the King of Bhutan discovered, there is a limit to their knowledge about these offerings. Once when the King visited one of his monasteries, he stopped to admire the beautifully laid out eight offerings. He asked what they were and a monk explained that they were offering substances. "What," asked the King, "are they for?" But the monk had to admit that he didn't know.

If you practise slightly elaborately, ARGHAM refers to drinking water which is water that is extremely pure and has the eight qualities. Hindus probably consider that the water of the Ganges has these eight qualities, whereas most of us think the Ganges is perhaps the filthiest river in the world! The tantras mention a river to the west of Oddiyana where the water has these eight qualities, and the commentaries say that Indians would collect its water and take it all the way back to India to use in the preparations for a great banquet. I don't know if this is true or not, but nowadays we don't see anything like that. The eight qualities of pure water are lightness, coolness, sweetness and so on. All Hindus know them. In any case, you will need clean water. In the advice about substances, it is said you should put some roasted rice in it. Ideally from a Tibetan perspective, water should be hot, but the tantras come from India where water is always spoken of as cooling and refreshing. In this case, you are not making a small offering but a really vast one, so it is said that you should offer an ocean of pure water.

(ii) Cleansing Water

The second offering is cleansing water. It is said that your offering should be like the continuous flow of the Ganges which is the greatest river in India. In terms of substances to use, add some white flowers to the cleansing water and a little bark from different trees.

(iii) Flowers

The next offerings are divine flowers filling the entire sky. Flowers from the realm of the gods are offered because they are far superior to those from the human realm. Even though flowers from the human realm are beautiful and have extraordinary qualities, they can't compare with flowers from the god realm which are made of precious substances. And you don't just offer a few but fill the entire sky with them. The practice manuals say you must offer different kinds of flowers—flowers from mountains, from meadows and plains, water flowers, rock flowers and so on.

(iv) Incense

Then there's the offering of fragrant incense. The tantras and instruction manuals explain that you should offer the kind of incense that has the most excellent fragrance which is generally considered to be that of white sandalwood. White sandalwood isn't just any sandalwood like the stuff we find today but is of the very best quality. The agar tree is also mentioned along with a few medicinal substances. The tantras make no mention at all of French perfume! I say this because whenever I travel, westerners show me their "must-have" offering of tiny perfume bottles, and such an offering is not proscribed since all pleasant fragrances are considered good. Some substances produce a fragrance when they burn like incense, others naturally emanate their fragrance without being lit and both can be offered.

(v) Lights

The purpose of offering butter lamps and light is to eliminate darkness, and as mentioned in the tantras many substances can be used as fuel for light offerings, for example seed oil, butter from herbivores, essential oils, the sun and the moon and so on. In France, a woman once asked Dilgo Khyentse Rinpoche if she could use electric light as an offering. Khyentse Rinpoche said "yes" and that actually electric light was very good. Therefore, I think it's fine to use electric light as an offering.

(vi) Scented Water

It is said in the tantras that you should collect water from sacred places like the twenty-four sacred lands where the water is very special and naturally very good. So to prepare fragrant water for this offering, start by collecting special water from sacred places. There are also several medicinal substances to be gathered which you chop up into tiny pieces, wrap in cloth and boil in water until most of the water has boiled away. Add a little more water and boil again, repeating this process several times. This is how to prepare the offering of scented water according to the tantras. If you cannot do it, just add saffron to water.

(vii) Food

Tibetans make offering tormas from dough. Strictly speaking, the food offering should be edible and have a hundred tastes and a thousand potencies. This gives us something to think about because a substance with a hundred different tastes and a thousand different potencies is not easy to find. Some say that our human tongues cannot taste a hundred different tastes. I don't know how many we can discern—perhaps sweet, sour, astringent and a few more—but the divine food offering we make here should have a hundred different tastes. The thousand different potencies are revealed once the food has been ingested. Nowadays, as we sentient beings lack merit, most of the food we eat neither tastes good, nor is it nourishing or beneficial. Often it has quite the opposite effect and actually harms us. For example, those who indulge too much in sweet food end up with diabetes, and those who eat too much fat have liver problems like jaundice and other debilitating diseases. The buddhas on the other hand can taste a hundred different exquisite tastes and one thousand potencies in all the food they eat because they have great merit.

Offering goddesses present these food offerings, but they don't mix them up into a kind of soup and present a huge container of the stuff to the deities. We cannot make offerings like that! We must arrange them beautifully, separating them out as we do for a splendid buffet.

Practices for presenting offerings begin with the different kinds of water followed by the other kinds of food offerings, then the *tambula* (betel nut) and sweets, typically concluding with a fire offering practice. So in your meditation, imagine offering goddesses bring each ingredient one after another.

(viii) Music

Basically, offer all the sounds in the world and all the pleasant resonances of the universe.

When offerings are placed on the shrine, many people put small Tibetan cymbals called *tingshaks* or some other small musical instrument in a bowl of rice. However, as Jamgön Kongtrul explained since *tingshaks* in a bowl alone do not produce any sound, this arrangement doesn't qualify as a music offering. You must play the instrument for it to be an actual music offering.

If you can't play a musical instrument or don't have one, ringing a bell also counts as a music offering. Once Patrul Rinpoche and Nyoshul Lungtok were staying on a mountain in the snow above Dzogchen Monastery. On the 10th days they did *Rigdzin Düpa* and on the 25th days *Yumka Dechen Gyalmo* with a tsok offering. At that time, they only had a very bad damaru that sounded flat and rattled, "Tok, tok, tok." They didn't even have a bell. So Patrul Rinpoche told Nyoshul Lungtok to hit two flat stones together, and this also qualifies as a music offering!

If you are practising elaborately, do the mudras as you recite the mantra at the end of each four-line prayer. Before you begin each mudra, with a snap your fingers actualise in your visualization the manifestation of all the offering goddesses. Then say the mantra for each offering—ARGHAM, PADAM and so on—and do the corresponding mudra as you imagine the offering goddesses present that particular offering. At the end, snap your fingers again and the offering goddesses dissolve back into you. The offering goddesses have different characteristics. Those presenting drinking water are white, those offering cleansing water are blue and so on, and each holds a container appropriate to the offering they are presenting. However, Jigme Lingpa and other masters like him have said that since the offering goddesses are the natural display of primordial wisdom, the specifics are not that crucial. That's why today I won't go into detail.

Present all the offerings successively, but at the end recognize that there is no offering and no one whatsoever making the offering. You are simply manifesting yourself, you offer to yourself. Yet since it is all the play of interdependence, as you present the offerings consider you are perfecting the accumulation of merit and that you have been granted all the supreme and ordinary siddhis. These two aspects of offering are not in conflict with one another.

b) Inner Offerings

The inner offerings are present in the following four lines of the text,

> OM
> These objects stimulate the senses

And this duality arises as great bliss;
Accept this offering of vajra form, sound, smell, taste and
     touch
As the great mudra of offering.

(i) Rupa

For the first offering—the offering of vajra form—the offering goddess
holds a mirror and offers the deities all the beautiful forms in the world
which are reflected in the mirror. The mirror is offered, and it is called RUPA
in Sanskrit.

(ii) Shapta

The next is SHAPTA—the offering of sound—and the offering goddess plays
the vina or the flute. Basically, all pure sounds are offered, but the tantras
mention that the vina produces a thousand different sounds from a thousand chords very pleasantly. When Dilgo Khyentse Rinpoche commented
on this point, he said that the sound of the vina is such that even those
experiencing the terrible sorrow of having lost their father are filled with joy
and happiness the moment they hear its sound. In other words, Khyentse
Rinpoche was saying that the instant you hear the vina, it removes even the
extreme pain and suffering we experience at the death of our fathers.

(iii) Gende

The next offering is the offering of smell—GENDE. An offering goddess holds
a conch with a right turning swirl and containing pure water and presents
it as the offering of smell. The outer offering of scented water made earlier
was about pleasant fragrance, whereas here when the scented water offered
in the conch is sprinkled on your chest, you will immediately experience the
wisdom of great bliss.

(iv) Rasa

RASA is the offering of taste and involves the tastes of the outer offerings
plus those of the inner offerings like the great flesh and so on. So everything

that is edible, food offerings, fruit and so on is offered in a vessel made of precious substances and presented to the deities. They experience this incredible offering by emanating rays of light from the tips of their tongues that form hollow tubes like a straw through which they experience the taste of the food.

(v) Parshe

Finally, the PARSHE is offered by the vajra goddess of touch and is presented as a soft cloth. Tibetans offer white scarves called *kataks*, but they are not specifically mentioned as offerings. Here, we offer all beautiful cloth and "the strong yet soft and light garments of the gods". These divine garments are also transparent. In Tibet, often the only kind of cloth available was animal skin—sheepskin for example—and the only thin fabric they had was the silk of the *kataks* they imported from China. This is probably why the Tibetan tradition is to present a *katak*, held high above their heads when they make an offering representing touch.

So the five inner offerings are form, sound, smell, taste and touch. Here again, if you want to practise more elaborately, you can use the additional text Jamgön Kongtrul has written which contains five four-line verses to guide you through each of the five offerings. At the end of the practice, the offering goddesses who had originally emanated from yourself dissolve back into you. Don't just leave them hanging around out there!

c) Secret Offerings

The secret offerings are amrita, rakta and torma. The terma text says,

> OM
> Amrita of eight root and one thousand minor ingredients,
> Rakta, the essence of the liberation of the three worlds
> And the balingta that pleases the five senses,
> May these offerings please the host of mandala deities!

This prayer gives just one line for each of the three offerings.

(i) Amrita

Amrita of eight root and one thousand minor ingredients,

. . .

The offering is presented in a kapala or "container of great bliss" which is a human skull. If you don't have one, you can use something that looks like a kapala. In any case, place the amrita which is made of the eight root medicinal substances that are quite easy to find in the container. There are also one thousand secondary substances—two hundred and fifty from the earth, two hundred and fifty from stones, two hundred and fifty from medicinal substances and two hundred and fifty from sentient beings. The thousand secondary substances are a bit more difficult to find. On top of that, a precise and specific measurement of each secondary substance is blended into the amrita. Having gathered all the substances, grind them up. Nowadays, it is not unusual for *mendrup* to be used when practitioners cannot make the amrita properly, but amrita is not *mendrup*. *Mendrup* must be blessed through practice, whereas amrita is prepared in its own specific ritual. In any case, mix the substances with alcohol.

Make this offering accompanied by a vast visualization of five nectars, five meats, five medicines, five grains and so on. Visualize the syllables OM AH HUNG emanating rays of light that return, melt into light, then dissolve into the amrita and so on. This section is quite elaborate and there are many more such details to visualize at this point, but I won't explain them all right now. Amrita is imbued with the good qualities of the five sensory objects that satisfy the five senses of all sentient beings, and it is also inexhaustible. Anything mixed with it immediately becomes a substance with the capacity to satisfy all five senses of beings. Put a little on your tongue and by the time it has been ingested by your body, it will have purified all breakages of samaya and in the process you will immediately receive all ordinary and supreme siddhis.

(ii) Rakta

Rakta is made of thirty-five substances, and its preparation also involves a thousand different kinds of blood. But we won't discuss this right now—the police will come and arrest us if we talk too much about that kind of thing! This offering is a gathering of all the destructive emotions in the world— most importantly desire—and this is what we should actualise in our visualization. All the desire in the world and all five poisons are gathered, liberated and eliminated, and their very essence is extracted through the liberation to produce the rakta. So rakta is the pure essence of the liberation of all destructive emotions, and you must put a little into the offering. A few lamas have warned me that we shouldn't talk about blood, but rakta is in fact the Sanskrit word for blood.

(iii) Torma

The next offering is *torma* in Tibetan, *balingta* in Sanskrit, and it satisfies the five senses, fulfilling all unfulfilled samayas.

(iv) How to Offer Amrita, Rakta and Torma

Place a little amrita, torma and rakta in front of you as you practise, as the support for your visualization which multiplies them so they become extremely vast. It is said that they fill "a container as vast as the three-thousandfold universe", so the offerings of amrita and rakta are as immense as oceans. Emanated in the amrita are an infinite number of amrita offering goddesses; in the rakta are infinite rakta goddesses pouring an ocean of blood from their secret places and the torma is like Mount Meru with the ability to satisfy all five senses of beings. As you offer amrita to the deities of the mandala, a vajra straw like a rainbow appears from each of their mouths to taste the amrita.

Form the amrita offering mudra as you make the offering. Usually, you use the thumb and ring finger together like a ladle made of the sun and moon to offer the amrita to all the deities. If you make this offering elaborately, read or recite the name of each recipient starting with the masters of the lineage at the top of the mandala, the deities of the mandala who are in the middle and the dharma protectors who are at the base. This offering satisfies their enlightened body, speech and mind, and as a result they send their blessings in the form of small syllables—white OM for body, red AH for speech and blue HUNG for mind. These syllables balance on the tip of your ring finger, and as you place that finger on your three centres—forehead, throat and heart—you receive the blessings of the enlightened body, speech and mind. Drink the remaining amrita and receive the siddhis.

Present the rakta three times to empty the three realms of existence, the entire universe. Basically, offer rakta until the entire universe is empty.

As you offer the torma, it emanates offering goddesses in infinite number who present offerings to the deities of the mandala, satisfying their enlightened body, speech and mind. As a result, all blessings and siddhis are gathered and dissolve into the torma and the practitioner.

Don't empty the vessel holding the amrita, a little should be left as a blessing, but the vessel holding the rakta should be completely emptied. The blessings dissolve into you and into the torma, and at the end of the retreat you receive the siddhis from the torma by placing it on your three places. This concludes a brief presentation of amrita, rakta and torma. Usually, when I go into detail about these substances, people get scared!

d) Innermost Offering

For the innermost offering of suchness, the text says,

> A
> Natural clear light bodhichitta
> Is beyond the elaboration of the three spheres
> Of offering substances, the offerer, the act of offering and
>   so on—
> Please, accept it as the great, supreme offering.

If you think about it carefully, the offering of substances, the benefactor who presents the offering (the practitioner, you), the deities who are the recipients and all those involved in the practice don't really exist in the state free of conceptual elaboration. The nature of this state is clear light, and when unimpeded appearances manifest, we call it "bodhichitta". To rest in that state of recognition is said to be "the great supreme offering". A detailed explanation can be found in the Dzogchen teachings which dwell in particular on the aspect of primordial purity. It is in this state that you are supposed to rest. Just talking about Dzogchen is not the great supreme offering of suchness, resting in the state of primordial purity is.

6. Offering Praise

In this practice, we offer praise. Visualize in the sky before you all the victorious buddhas of all directions and times raining down flowers, and gods and goddesses—like Brahma, Indra and the ten protectors of the world—in the courtyard around the mandala palace playing music on vina, flute, drums, hand drums and so on. As you actualise this visualization, offer the words of the practice.

Offering of praise has three levels: the symbolic level, the level of the meaning and the level of the signs. The symbols are one head, two hands and so on; so even though buddhas have no appearance, they manifest with symbolic features, each of which can be explained. The signs correspond to the ornaments and garments they wear. Actualising the meaning of the symbols and signs while chanting the words of praise is the level of meaning. You should chant the words of praise while you actualise what had just been explained, and you will be able to understand what you're saying by reading the translation.

General offering of praise,

> OM
> You were born from the tears of
> The lord of the world and master of compassion.
> Mother of the buddhas of past, present and future,
> Wish-Fulfilling Wheel, to you I pay homage and offer
>   praise!

Offering of praise to the vajra body,

> The colour of the stainless moon, jewel of the sky,
> You hold an utpala flower in the mudra of supreme
>   generosity,
> Peaceful and smiling, blazing with the splendour of the
>   signs and marks—
> To your vajra body, I pay homage and offer praise!

Offering of praise to enlightened speech,

> Your melodious speech, an ocean of qualities,
> Sprinkles a soothing and refreshing shower of amrita

That awakens the buddha nature in sentient beings—
To your Brahma speech, I pay homage and offer praise!

Offering of praise to the enlightened mind,

With your wisdom of knowledge and love, you see
everything,
From the perspective of the samadhi of equanimity,
Without moving from the space of the inconceivable great
seal—
To your mind of clear light, I offer praise and homage.

Offering of praise to enlightened qualities,

Whoever prays to you,
You bless instantly and
Grant them the accomplishments and everything they
desire—
To your infinite enlightened qualities, I pay homage and
offer praise!

Offering of praise to enlightened activities,

With your names and array of forms,
With the various secret mantras of awareness,
You pacify, enrich, magnetise and subjugate—
To your spontaneously accomplished enlightened activities,
I pay homage and offer praise!

Paying homage to all the deities,

Unmoving from unique dharmata,
Yet in accord with the capacity of beings to be trained,
You display a net of magical emanations—
To all the deities of the mandala, I pay homage!

According to the tantras and to the text by Jamyang Khyentse Wangpo,
you offer praise as you perform the relevant mudra for each of the buddhas
of the five families.

The Three Crucial Points of Kyerim Practice

This concludes the section on the generation of the deity—the kyerim practice. To summarize, the important point here is that all three crucial elements of kyerim practices are present in your practice—the vivid visualization of the features of the deity which we have been talking about until now, firm confidence or vajra pride and remembering the purity. If you practise these three crucial aspects, you are practising correctly.

The first crucial aspect is clear visualization. This means that your visualization of the deity should be pristinely clear, not dull, hazy or confused—that's not how you should visualize. A clear visualization is one that is really vivid and alive, just as if you are actually seeing a real person in front of you and all their features are easily discernible. This is what your visualization of the deity should be like. An important point is that if to start with, you are unable to visualize the whole deity precisely and with great clarity, first visualize the top of the deity's head and work down. As you do so if you forget the face while you concentrate on the torso for example, it's fine to go back and visualize again the feature you have forgotten. So if at first you find you cannot visualize all the details of the entire deity, it's fine to focus on just the head or even just the eyes or nose, then work down to the lotus seat. If you practise this way, eventually you will be able to visualize the entire deity clearly.

The key point is to visualize the deity in its entirety and vividly as if a real person is standing in front of you. However, if you can't visualize all the aspects of the deity at once, visualize the different parts one by one. Don't imagine you are not allowed to focus on individual features. Focus on each detail separately until eventually you can visualize the entire deity all in one go. So the method is to scan the deity from the top to the bottom, slowly actualising each detail. Sometimes try working up from bottom to top, sometimes from left to right and sometimes from right to left. That's how to train yourself, and if you do, eventually you'll be able to visualize the entire deity clearly and in detail.

Jigme Lingpa said that if you practise a peaceful deity and focus on the moon disc seat, the clarity of your visualization will be enhanced. If you practise a wrathful deity, you will enhance the clarity of the visualization by focusing on the wisdom eye. But you lot aren't likely to do this. However, as Dzongsar Khyentse Rinpoche told me to teach, I must at least mention such things.

If you truly intend to train gradually in the practice of visualizing the deity, you should use a thangka. Thangkas are not just decorations, they are samaya substances to support your practice and representations of the enlightened body. Actually, you are supposed to keep them hidden and not show them to anyone. The same goes for statues, especially of the Vajrayana deities. Representations of the enlightened body should have perfect proportions and perfect characteristics. The details of what those proportions and characteristics are can be found in the tantras, along with instructions about how to draw thangkas and make statues. If you don't know how to do it, ask someone who does, like a thangka painter. Once you have a perfectly made thangka or statue, you should consecrate it with a *rabne* practice that will make it fit for use as a support for your practice. This is what you should prepare before you practise. Then put the image in the room where you practise so no one else can see it and sit right in front of it.

First pray to your teachers that you may perfectly accomplish the path of kyerim. Then focus your mind and gaze one-pointedly at the thangka or statue without moving your body. Just focus on the image. Then you close your eyes. Having stared intently at the thangka or statue, when you close your eyes its image will appear in your mind. If it appears in your mind clearly and perfectly, focus your mind on that image. But usually it's not that simple. The image does not appear so easily and you have to repeat the process many times, opening your eyes to look at the thangka or statue, then closing them again to see the image in your mind's eye. Train yourself in this way again and again. Visualize the deity for a short time, close your eyes and picture the deity in your mind's eye. Then repeat the process many times over.

What's the point of doing this? Just focusing your eyes on the image isn't good enough. What you must train yourself to do is to focus your mind on it as well. But the problem with the mind is that it tends to be easily distracted and will think about anything but the image. So even if mind wanders here and there, try not to let it move away from the image in the thangka. Focus on different parts of the deity—the protuberance on the head, the right eye and so on—so mind is always focused on something related to the image. And once you are at least a little used to doing that, the image will start to appear with some clarity in your mind.

If you practise like this, you will have seven experiences one after the other. The first is that mind won't stay focused one-pointedly on the image even for a single moment, but will move around very quickly like a waterfall cascading down a steep mountain. This experience will probably surprise you. In fact, you'll find it hard to believe just how distracted your mind can be. But there's no need to be afraid. By simply taking a little care of your mind and continuing to practise to try gaining even a little control of it, you will find it will naturally settle and that in time you'll be able to focus better. Think for example of the part of a river where the water flows in torrents, so fast that you can't see the stones and fish at the bottom of river. Just a little further downstream the current slows, and suddenly you can see the riverbed quite clearly. When your mind is busy with many thoughts, it isn't focused so you must continue to practise focusing your mind on the object. Once you've gained some experience of this kind of practice, you'll begin to know when mind is resting and when it's distracted. Once you reach this point—like waves that come from the ocean then dissolve back into it—you must continue to focus mind on the object.

Practise in sessions like you would on a retreat. By practising intensely in this way, the distractions will pass like the wind gusting between two rocks on a mountain. Suppose a strong wind blows between the two rocks, then suddenly dies and never revives. The gust that blows in the next moment is quite a different wind from the first. Likewise, distracting thoughts appear in your mind, then die and never appear again. Once your visualization is quite clear, you should sometimes try to visualize the deity much bigger, as big as Mount Meru. At other times, visualize it so small that it would fit inside a sesame seed. Maintain your awareness of the deity at all times in whatever you do—eating, sleeping, sitting, resting or whatever it is you are doing—and your visualization will become like a completely still lake. Because the water is unmoving, the moon, the stars and everything will be reflected perfectly on its surface.

Having reached this level of stability in your visualization practice, you can begin to emanate and reabsorb rays of light without affecting the clarity of the main deity. Whatever you do with those rays of light, however far you send and reabsorb them, you will still be able to maintain the clarity of your visualization of the main deity. If you don't establish stability first, when you concentrate on the activity of the rays of light you will forget the deity and will not maintain a clear and complete visualization. Once you're able to maintain the stability of the visualization whilst also accomplishing the different activities like emanating and reabsorbing rays of light, your visualization will be as stable as a mountain. The rocks, trees and animals that can be found on a huge mountain are a little like its ornaments. They bring nothing extra to it, nor can they move or change the mountain in any way. As you practise using this method, you'll experience what it is to perfect your visualization practice which the teachings liken to the sky.

If you focus too intently—fixing your eyes, mind and inner air (*lung*) on the object with exaggerated concentration—so many thoughts will arise that you might think you're going crazy. This is when you should take a break. Rest, change your posture and relax for a while. If you just let go a bit, your mind will relax. If you rest for too long, you'll forget everything. So don't rest for too long before coming back to the practice and refocusing your mind. Even so when you relax, it is important to maintain the awareness that you are the deity and to continue to visualize yourself clearly as the deity. Focus as much as you can on the features you see less clearly.

If you find you can't visualize any part of the deity clearly, do cleansing practices for purification and endeavour to confess your non-virtuous actions through confession practices. If you suffer from problems of your inner air when you practise—for example you cannot sleep—it is said you should eat good, nutritious food. If on the other hand you feel sleepy and dull during your practice or your mind is foggy, the advice is that you should not eat too much; eat sparingly and wear light clothing, not warm clothing. I don't think anyone follows this advice these days; nevertheless, I am obliged to tell you about it.

I could talk about meditation experiences in relation to progressive stages of the Vajrayana paths and bhumis, but there's not much point. Once you start to attain bhumis or reach a state of realization, you'll know. Right now, there's no point going into it because you won't understand. What I can say is that you will automatically come to know the qualities of the Buddha, for example absence of movement, clarity, vividness and so on. By continuously practising the deity, the result you will attain is that even your own outer appearance will be transformed, and when others look at you, they will see you as the deity like for example the time Acharya Hungkara entered a village in India and everybody started shouting that Vajrasattva had arrived. The inner sign of accomplishment is that the form of the deity will appear naturally on your bones and so on. But if it happens to you and you show your doctor, I'm sure he'll say you have cancer and will want to cut it out! In any case, if you genuinely want to practise kyerim, that's how to do it. There is an even more elaborate way of practising kyerim, but I've said enough for today.

This is what we call "clear visualization". The measure of the clarity of your visualization is that it is like the sun, moon and stars reflected in the still waters of a lake or a clean mirror. You should be able to visualize all the details perfectly, right down to the black and white of the eyes. The thirty-two major and eighty minor marks should also appear vividly and clearly in your mind. Once that happens, you can say that you have accomplished a clear visualization.

The Four Nails

The Nyingmapa tradition teaches a special pith instruction, a *mengak* taught by Guru Rinpoche called the "four nails" that bind the life force of the practice, and strictly speaking it's not a teaching that should be shared widely. But these days, even Dzogchen teachings are given to all and sundry! The big difficulty seems to be more about finding people who want to listen than finding people who want to talk about the secret tantra teachings. Today I will talk about the four nails that bind the life force of the practice with only Khyentse Rinpoche in mind. So whatever transgressions, downfalls, obstacles or problems that may arise as a result of sharing this *mengak* with a wide audience will be for Khyentse Rinpoche to deal with. I won't accept the consequences.

First of all, what is a "nail"? In this context, it has a similar function to nails used in carpentry and building. Samsara is separate from the state of complete enlightenment—buddhahood. Why? Because if there is no delusion, that is "buddha"; if there is delusion, there are "sentient beings". So there's one ground, but two different paths which must be nailed back onto the ground. This is the kind of nail we are talking about here. Unless you use the four nails that bind the life force of the practice to eliminate all delusion, the two (impure and pure) won't stay together. In the state of buddhahood the ground is pure, and in samsara the ground is impure. The path is a mixture of pure and impure that lies somewhere between the two. To return this mixture of impure and pure to the state of pristine purity and maintain it, you need the four nails.

In this context, "life force" refers to the life force of the Buddha—the non-conceptual, non-dualistic wisdom that is the wisdom mind of the Buddha. Once the whole of samsara is nailed with the nail of non-conceptual wisdom, it is pure, it is "buddha".

The first of the four nails is the *nail of all appearance as the deity.* All worldly appearances are impure, but without applying any kind of external antidotes and relying solely on appearances themselves, you transform them into the pure manifestation of the deities. This is the nail of all appearance as the deity, and this is what we have been discussing so far. As you practise this nail, you should not harbour any ideas or concepts about the deity being pure and everything else impure and so on. In fact, there must be no distinction at all between pure and impure. Within the realm where the deity appears purely, however hard you try to find impurities, you wouldn't succeed. And I have been telling you this all along. Everything in the mandala—all the manifestations from the palace right down to the vajra fence and so on, even the encircling fire—is the manifestation of primordial wisdom. So that's the first nail, the nail of all appearance as the deity.

What is this second nail? It is the *nail of unchanging wisdom mind* which is the realization that the nature of the deities, palace and nothing that appears truly exists. Why are all appearances empty? As I've been saying since the beginning, they are all the manifestation—the expression—of three aspects of the nature of the mind whose essence is empty, whose nature is cognisant and whose energy is unimpeded compassion; everything arises out of the nature of mind. This means that the very essence of all that appears is empty and primordially pure. "Empty in essence, nature cognisant" means that the very essence of appearance is empty.

"Empty in essence" is a term common to all traditions, but Nyingmapas specifically use the word *kadak*, primordial purity. All that manifests from that primordial purity, the display of the empty essence, is generally described as "clarity" or "cognisance", while the Nyingmapas call it "spontaneous presence". Buddha said, "Mind is devoid of mind, the nature of mind is clear light."[91] All the lamas explain this quotation in the same way. "Mind is devoid of mind" refers to primordial purity or empty in essence; "the nature of mind is clear light" refers to the aspect of clarity, cognisant nature or spontaneous presence. Everything manifests as an expression of the spontaneous presence that arises from primordial purity without any separation of that spontaneous presence from primordial purity. Recognition of this is the nail of unchanging wisdom mind, meaning all that manifests has never been separate from primordial purity. The only way you can hammer in the nail of unchanging wisdom mind is by actualising the view. The Nyingmapas say that with the mere recognition of the nature of mind, the nail of unchanging wisdom mind is hammered in. This goes without saying for someone who is able to rest in that state, or those who have gained stability in or perfected it. They say in that moment of recognition, the nail of unchanging wisdom mind is fixed. And that's all you need to do.

The third, *the nail of all sound as mantra*, will be explained when we come to mantra recitation. We will also talk about *the nail of the activity of emanation and reabsorption* when we come to mantra recitation. Briefly, we emanate and reabsorb rays of light to accomplish different enlightened activities of buddhas.

So these are the four nails. Once you know how to apply or hammer in these four nails, you will know the crucial points of kyerim and dzogrim. Until then, it will be difficult for you to genuinely practise either.

When we started talking about kyerim practice, I mentioned the three samadhis—the samadhi of suchness, the samadhi of universal manifestation and the causal samadhi. The nail of unchanging wisdom mind is the same as the first samadhi, the samadhi of suchness. Of the first two, the samadhi of suchness and the samadhi of universal manifestation, the most important is the second, the samadhi of universal manifestation.

In the causal vehicle of characteristics, Buddha talks about the indivisible unity of emptiness and compassion. Emptiness without compassion is useless. Here in the Vajrayana the nail of emanation and reabsorption of rays of light accomplishes the enlightened activities of the buddhas, and the nail of all sound as mantra is the activities we engage in out of compassion for sentient beings. Buddhas manifest enlightened activities out of compassion to benefit sentient beings, likewise the appearance of the deity is the expression of the compassion of the buddhas. This is why I emphasize that you should begin to build the framework of your visualization practice with the three samadhis. Without compassion, all the activities of emanating and reabsorbing rays of light will be entirely useless—just a lot of extra work. Which is why the samadhi of universal manifestation is the more important one. The commentaries explain that if you just visualize the causal samadhi and practise kyerim without compassion, when you visualize a deity with nine heads you risk ending up being reborn as a monster with nine heads.

All these practical instructions (*mengak*) on the four nails that bind the life force of the practice are based on the samadhi of suchness and the samadhi of universal manifestation. So far, I have explained the first two, the nail of all appearance as the deity and the nail of unchanging wisdom mind. Of these two nails, it is the nail of unchanging wisdom mind that you must hammer into every aspect of your practice of kyerim from beginning to end. If you do, you can't go wrong. If you don't, however much you practise, however clear your visualizations, however well you know the different aspects of the practice, you will fail to accomplish much benefit. This is why Patrul Rinpoche considered these four nails to be of such crucial importance. So much so that he wrote a commentary specifically explaining those points. It is called *The Melody of Brahma*,[92] and Nyingmapas make very small copies of it and keep them in their amulets so it is with them wherever they go.

7. Mantra Recitation

Next we will talk about *the nail of all sounds as mantra* which is addressing the aspect of the enlightened speech of the deity now that we have covered the enlightened body.

There are three main steps in the Chimé Phakmé Nyingtik practice that are applied to mantra recitation: approach, accomplishment and activities. In most of the practices transmitted through the kama lineage, as well as some practices that appear in termas, mantra recitation has four phases: approach, close approach, accomplishment and great accomplishment.

a) Approach Practice

Generally speaking, the first step of approach is to remove our tendency to grasp at the idea that we ourselves and the deity are separate. At the beginning of the practice, we see ourselves and the deity as two separate entities, and the method we use to remove that tendency to grasp is approach practice. The methods for doing this that we find in the teachings are based on how we operate in our ordinary lives. If you want to get to know a stranger, the first thing you find out is their name. Once you know their name, if you use it gradually the stranger will become more familiar to you and you will become better acquainted with each other. By the time you know each other well, you will have created a bond and will have become quite close to someone who had once been a stranger. This example shows how the practice works.

Here, the deity we want to accomplish is White Tara, so we invoke her by repeating the mantra OM TARE TUTTARE TURE SOHA which basically is her name—apart from the OM at the beginning and SOHA at the end. Therefore, as we repeat the mantra, we are actually repeating her name which has the power to bring her closer to us. At the same time, it eliminates any grasping at the duality of her and us. By repeating this mantra, you invoke the power of this kind of blessing.

There are a couple of important points here. In all Sarma tantra practices, you do the ritual for self-visualization before you recite the mantra, then you perform a separate ritual for the front-visualization and again recite the mantra. There is also a specific ritual for visualizing the mandala in the practice vase. This is how the elaborate practices are laid out. The Nyingma tradition also includes elaborate practices involving different rituals for self-visualization, front visualization and vase visualization. In most of the Nyingma Highest Yoga Tantra practices, the first step of the approach practice is a self-visualization practice, but you don't need to do a front visualization. For the next steps of accomplishment and activity, you emanate another mandala from the mandala of self-visualization although you don't need to do a separate ritual for this front visualization, simply say the mantra for "dividing the house of mantra". You only need a front visualization ritual for the self-empowerment practice and when you are giving empowerments. In the present case, the vase instantaneously arises as the mandala, and the deities appear clearly in the vase like the reflections of the planets and stars on the surface of a lake.

However, since we are talking about how to do this practice in retreat, when it comes to the approach section, you don't need to generate a separate self-visualization and front visualization. At the end of the offering of praise section, all the deities offering praise dissolve back into the deities of the mandala. At this point in kyerim practice, we have visualized ourselves as the deity (samayasattva) in a palace surrounded by deities and we have invoked the jnanasattvas who have dissolved into us, but we haven't dealt with the aspect of enlightened speech that corresponds to approach, accomplishment and activity. At this point, we are just visualizing ourselves as the deity and meditating on that visualization. We visualize ourselves as the deity to purify the habitual tendency common to all sentient beings of seeing ourselves with a body.

The practise of dzogrim involves what we call the "vajra body" or "body mandala", and through this practice you see the entire mandala present within your own body. Since we are not quite so far along the path, we visualize ourselves as the deity to create a good habit that will mature so we can eventually practise the body mandala. The fruition of the practice is the attainment of the enlightened body of a buddha with the thirty-two major and eighty minor marks and all the qualities.

We practise mantra because, right now, all the sounds we produce and hear are impure, so we must purify our speech by reciting mantra. This is how we actualise the enlightened qualities and enlightened speech of a buddha and develop a voice that has sixty qualities and is the inexhaustible wheel of enlightened speech.

We mature mind to become an enlightened mind in the dissolution practice of dzogrim. If you apply the nail of unchanging wisdom mind in your practice, enlightened mind will automatically be there and will mature through the practice.

Kyerim—as we now know—involves the three samadhis: the samadhi of suchness, the samadhi of universal manifestation and the causal samadhi. The first samadhi, the samadhi of suchness, is basically the view, and the samadhi of universal manifestation and the nail of unchanging wisdom are the meditation, while action accompanied by compassion is indirectly present in that meditation. Enlightened qualities and enlightened activity are associated with and taken care of by applying the nail of all appearance as the deity, the nail of all sound as mantra and the nail of the emanation and reabsorption of rays of light. We've already spoken about the body, speech and mind.

To practise in this way is called the union of kyerim and dzogrim, and to be able to practise both authentically should be part of your practice. To be able to walk properly you need two legs—having just one makes walking difficult. In this case, if you only practice kyerim and not dzogrim, however perfect your visualization you will not attain enlightenment. This is why these crucial points are so important to your practice. Practising like this is really important!

The Importance of Enlightened Speech

It is said that the mantra is the inexhaustible wheel of enlightened speech. This is a very significant statement. The buddhas benefit sentient beings with their enlightened body, mind and speech. Of the three, the most beneficial to sentient beings is enlightened speech. Why? The benefit buddhas bring through their enlightened bodies lasts a very limited amount of time. Although the enlightened mind that nothing can alter, change or destroy is crucial, on its own it cannot benefit beings directly. But the enlightened speech of the buddhas is how the wheel of the dharma is turned, and it is turned in many different ways that also involve both enlightened body and mind. The dharmakaya is the enlightened mind and omniscient wisdom of the Buddha, and this is what we must actualise. But to do so, we must rely on the instructions relayed to us through enlightened speech which is why enlightened speech is so important.

Enlightened speech is described, for example, at the beginning of the *Secret Essence Tantra* as the wheel of clouds of syllables, and the first syllable AH is explained as being the original sound and foundation on which all other syllables are formed. AH is therefore the basis of all mantras, and from AH came the vowels and consonants that then led to the mandalas of mantras which are so important. The principles of mantra are as follow:

—Mantra is the deity—by reciting the mantra you'll accomplish
    the deity
—Mantra is the mandala—the entire mandala unfolds out of the
    seed syllable—and is the same as the deity
—Mantra is a cloud of offerings—as you recite the mantra, you
    please and satisfy the deities of an infinite number of mandalas,
    so effectively mantra is an offering you make to them
—Mantra is the accomplishment of siddhis because by reciting
    mantras you accomplish siddhis
—Mantra eliminates obscurations—by the power of reciting
    mantra, you will purify obscurations
—Mantra is enlightened activity because by reciting mantras you
    will be able to accomplish all the different activities—pacifying,
    enriching, magnetising and subjugating
—Mantra is a blessing because by reciting the mantra, you will
    receive the blessings of the buddhas and deities.

There are nine points in all. I don't remember them all because the last
time I looked at the *Secret Essence Tantra* was about thirty years ago! In any
case, if you do some research, you'll be able to find all nine.[93] And as you
now know that mantra is so important, you know that you must recite mantras! As you recite the mantra, actualise the visualization associated with it.
So what is the visualization?

> I am sublime Tara. In my heart
> Is the jnanasattva Amitayus, . . .

This is quite clear and is what we have discussed so far, you visualize
yourself as the Sublime Lady of Immortality.

There is one point that can be confusing. Although Jetsun Drolma is
in union with her consort Amitayus, the seed syllable is visualized in the
Sublime Lady's heart; but we don't visualize anything at the Lord of the
Dance Amitayus' heart centre. On a lotus seat at the heart of Jetsun Drolma, the Sublime Lady, is the wisdom being Amitayus. The text describes
him,

. . . Brilliant white and holding a long-life vase in the
    mudra of meditation,
Beautiful with his silk and jewelled ornaments,
In vajra posture on a lotus and moon disc seat,
Shining and resplendent amidst brilliant rays of light.
In the centre of his heart is a lotus, sun and moon discs,
In the middle of which is TAM encircled by the mantra
    mala.

Most of the time, Nyingma sadhana practices involve what we call the
three nested sattvas through which we consider one sattva, or being, to be
inside another. This is also very important. Here at the heart of the samayasattva Jetsun Phakma, we have Amitayus as the jnanasattva, and at his heart
is the syllable TAM which is the samadhisattva. Circled around the syllable
TAM are the syllables of the mantra OM TARE TUTTARE TURE SOHA as fine as if
written by a single hair. The lamas say that the smaller your visualization of
the syllables, the easier it is to see them really clearly.

Both kama and terma teachings and practices of the Nyingma tradition
say we do four recitations, one for each of the four aspects of practice: approach, close approach, accomplishment and great accomplishment. During
approach practice, the mantras are visualized very clearly, as clearly as the
moon and the stars in the sky. You visualize the seed syllable surrounded
by the mantra syllables like the moon is surrounded by the stars. Then as
you recite the mantra, visualize the main deity, the samayasattva, at whose
heart is the jnanasattva; at the heart of the jnanasattva is the seed syllable,
the samadhisattva, surrounded by the syllables of the mantra. As you focus
one-pointedly on the appearance of the syllables being as clear as the moon
and the stars, you recite the mantra. This is how to do the approach practice.

The important point here is that the samadhisattva and mantra syllables
are not moving. They remain static but appear very clearly at the heart of the
jnanasattva. It is far more difficult to visualize the mantra's syllables when
they move around, rotating, emanating rays of light and reabsorbing them.
It is said that the head of the syllable curls slightly inwards. So that you can,
when necessary, make the mantra syllables revolve clockwise, you must visualize them standing counterclockwise around the TAM. But we don't move

the mantra at this point, we just make sure the syllables are set clockwise around the TAM.[94]

Now you need to recite the mantra OM TARE TUTARE TURE SOHA. There are so many methods for reciting mantras, including a general method, va-jra recitation and so on. Do whichever you like. When you recite mantras, chant neither too loudly, nor so quietly that you cannot be heard, neither too fast, nor too slow and so on. There are ten points you should know and bear in mind to recite mantras properly. Don't yell the mantra too loudly, but you should be audible. Similarly, if you recite the mantra too slowly, you will never finish; but if you go too fast, not all the syllables will sound as you will not pronounce all of them properly, which isn't appropriate. There are ten faults of mantra recitation that you should avoid.[95]

Basically, recite the mantra just loud enough for you to hear it yourself. There are times in wrathful practices when it's appropriate to recite mantras very loudly, but that's not the case here. There is also what is called the mental recitation when you actualise the mantra in your mind and literally recite the mantra mentally. But that's quite difficult! Vajra recitation involves retaining the intermediate breath in the vase while reciting the mantra and so on. It is said to be extremely beneficial but very difficult. In this case, start reciting the mantra and do maybe three hundred as you focus your mind using the methods explained above. Then visualize and actualise,

> Reciting the mantra evokes his wisdom mind, causing
> A stream of boundless light to burst out
> From the top of the jewel on the ushnisha at the crown of
>   my head,
> From which appears the sublime Vijaya,
> The colour of crystal. Her right hand,
> In the mudra of granting refuge, holds a hook;
> Her left, in the mudra of supreme giving, holds a long-life
>   vase.
> She radiates light and rays of light, and
> Limitless forms of herself stream out like specks of dust in
>   sunbeams.
> They draw in all the wisdom, love and power of

All the deities of the mandala,
All the buddhas and bodhisattvas of the ten directions,
All the yidams, dakas and dakinis and
All the protectors of the Vajrayana teachings.
They also draw in all the subtle vital essence of samsara and
  nirvana, the animate and inanimate universe,
In the form of the quicksilver that accomplishes all
Marked with forms of great bliss.
It dissolves into me and the practice articles,
Granting me the siddhi of immortal life
And intensifying the wisdom of great bliss.

You have the translation, so this isn't difficult. It says that from the mantra garland at Amitayus' heart centre, rays of light emanate and fill Jetsun Drolma's entire body, then pour out of the ushnisha on top of her head and transform into infinite Ushnisha Vijayas holding vases of longevity in their left hands and hooks in their right. The hooks emanate rays of light and are used to gather the nectar of longevity into the vase. The nectar dissolves back into the Sublime Lady, and all the blessings and accomplishments are drawn into her. That's a brief version of the visualization. Specific to the Chimé Phakmé Nyingtik visualization is that the three deities of long life are practised together: yourself as the Sublime Lady, the samayasattva; white Amitayus, the jnanasattva, visualized at the heart of the samayasattva; and Ushnisha Vijaya, who performs the activities. The text is quite clear, and this visualization is pretty straightforward.

The many Ushnisha Vijayas gather the nectar of longevity with their hooks, and in this practice nectar is called the "quicksilver that accomplishes all". What is this nectar made of? Basically, the Ushnisha Vijayas' hooks gather all the blessings of the wisdom mind and the love, compassion and power of all the buddhas and bodhisattvas of all directions in the form of nectar. They also gather all the positive qualities of sentient beings and all the power of the elements and the universe. Everything that's gathered appears as a nectar that is brilliant white in colour and the consistency of quicksilver. It's also very bright and emanates rays of light. It is so powerful that if a little is sprinkled on a dead tree for example, it will immediately burst into life, sprouting leaves, blossoms, fruits and so on. If this nectar is drunk, it will give you the strength of a thousand elephants and is said to give you the same life span as the sun and the moon. This is what you actualise and maintain in your visualization, and you mustn't be distracted. Apply the nail of recognizing all sound as mantra by reciting the mantra without interruption—don't let your recitation fade or go silent, just continuously recite the mantra.

Generally speaking, the visualization of the *mikpa* (how to direct the practice) involves the emanation and reabsorption of rays of light. First you emanate rays of light to make offerings to the buddhas, then they send the light back and it dissolves into your heart, bringing blessings, empowerments and so on.

Chimé Phakmé Nyingtik is a long-life practice, that's its main purpose. It is not possible to attain the supreme accomplishment unless you have first received the siddhi of longevity. Guru Rinpoche said that before undertaking any activity, first you should do the practice of longevity because if you live a long life, you will be able to accomplish everything you set out to do in this life and you will also accomplish the purpose of all your lives.

Spend most of your time reciting the ten-syllable mantra OM TARE TUTTARE TURE SOHA. Then recite the mantra that combines all three deities of longevity, OM TARE TUTTARE TURE HRIH DROOM BENDZA JNANA AYUKE SOHA. Because it begins with the syllable OM and continues TARE TUTTARE TURE, this part of the mantra invokes Tara; HRIH is the seed syllable of Amitayus; DROOM is the seed syllable of Ushnisha Vijaya; BENDZA JNANA is the indestructible vajra wisdom; and AYUKE is for long life. We recite this mantra to accomplish our wishes.

This will draw in the accomplishments you wish.

Then recite the mantras of the jnanasattva, Amitayus, and the nirmanasattva, Ushnisha Vijaya. The mantra of Amitayus is OM AMARANI DZIWANTIYE SOHA. The mantra of Ushnisha Vijaya is OM AMRITA AYURDADE SOHA.

Your visualization as you recite the mantras should be along the same lines but will change to be consistent with whichever mantra you recite. For example, when you recite the mantra of Amitayus, replace the mantra of Tara around the seed syllable with the mantra of Amitayus, while the seed syllable TAM is replaced with HRIH. Similarly, for the mantra that combines all three deities, since you already have the syllables OM TARE TUTTARE TURE SOHA, leave them as they are and just add the remaining syllables HRIH DROOM BENDZA JNANA AYUKE between TURE and SOHA. So the mantra of all three deities combined is OM TARE TUTTARE TURE HRIH DROOM BENDZA JNANA AYUKE SOHA. The text says that,

> *If you practise this diligently for three weeks, you will actually see the face of the mandala deities in meditation or in your dreams; you will hear them and accomplish the warmth of samadhi. You will dream of the sun and moon rising and flowers blooming. The bandha will actually overflow, the pills will increase in number and wonderful perfumes will be emitted. These and other such signs will occur. Samaya*

It's not extraordinary for us to see the sun or the moon shine; we see the sun shine every day, don't we? This means that to dream of the sun or moon rising is a sign of accomplishment. So that was the method for approach practice.

<h2 style="text-align:center">b) Accomplishment Practice</h2>

Before beginning accomplishment practice, it would be good to renew the offerings or at least replenish the offerings you have already made.

When you focus on the accomplishment stage, the practice itself remains the same. The only difference is that before beginning the approach section, which is the beginning of the mantra recitation, you divide up the mandalas by visualizing both the self-visualized and the front mandala which emanates from the self-visualized mandala. So first recite the mantra for separating the self-visualized mandala from the front mandala; you'll find it in the *Retreat Manual*.[96] The main deities manifest from the corresponding syllables TAM, DROOM, HRIH, HUNG and so on, to become the front mandala. It is possible to visualize the two mandalas surrounded by just one enormous protection sphere, but the fire encircling the immeasurable palace of the self-visualized mandala should still make contact with the fire encircling the palace of the front mandala.

Then and before you go through the practice text of the accomplishment section, you must actualise briefly the approach section, directing the practice as I have just explained, and recite about one hundred of each of the approach mantras:

—OM TARE TUTTARE TURE SOHA

—OM TARE TUTTARE TURE HRIH DROOM BENDZA JNANA AYUKE SOHA

—OM AMARANI DZIWANTIYE SOHA

—OM AMRITA AYURDADE SOHA.

The accomplishment section begins,

> Again, great cloud-like rays of light emanate and return,
> And dissolve into the heart of the mandala deities
> Who experience untainted great bliss.
> Indestructible, supreme primordial wisdom arises,
> And all worlds and beings within the three realms
> Appear as the play of bliss and emptiness.
> The outer environment are the five spaces and the mandala
> of the dharmadhatu,
> The beings within it are awareness in the form of deities,
> The sounds are the indestructible mantras.
> They are all the miracles of the single samadhi
> Of supreme, unchanging clear light—
> All phenomena of samsara and nirvana that appear and
> exist
> Become the wheel of the net of magical manifestation.

Mantra Recitation

Jamgön Kongtrul's *Retreat Manual* says,

> When the visualization is clear, add the visualization of the
> emanation and reabsorption of rays of light from the heart
> of the main deity to invoke her retinue. First concentrate
> on accumulating Vajra Tara's mantra and recite the three

others only briefly at the end of the session. Once you have completed the accumulation of Vajra Tara's mantra, you only need to recite it a few times before concentrating on accumulating Ratna Tara's mantra, which you do for most of your practice session. And so on.

There are four main Taras surrounding Jetsun Drolma. First concentrate on accumulating the mantra of Vajra Tara and recite the three other mantras at the end of the session, but keep them brief. Once you have accomplished the Vajra Tara mantra, repeat it a few times before you accumulate the Ratna Tara mantra as the main focus of your session. Practise the same way for each mantra.

Visualization

The *Retreat Manual* continues:

> The visualization is as follows. In the heart of each of the Taras of the four families is a lotus and a moon. On top of the moon within Vajra Tara is a dark-blue syllable TAM; in Ratna Tara, a yellow DROOM; in Padma Tara, a red HRIH and Karma Tara, a black HUNG. Their respective mantra malas revolve around the syllable.

In the heart of each Tara is a lotus, on top of which stands their respective seed syllable and around which revolves their respective mantra mala.

Vajra Tara	dark-blue TAM	OM TARE TAM SOHA
Ratna Tara	yellow DROOM	OM TARE DROOM SOHA
Padma Tara	red HRIH	OM TARE HRIH SOHA
Karma Tara	black HUNG	OM TARE HUNG SOHA

The *Retreat Manual* adds,

> Conclude the session in the same way you concluded the approach stage, except that here it is important to offer a tsok every day.

You conclude the session in the same way you concluded the approach section, and it is said that it is important when you focus on the accomplishment phase to offer a tsok every day.

I explained when we were talking about approach practice that mantras are visualized very clearly like the moon and the stars appear in the sky, but they don't move. Here in the close approach, the example used is of a king and his emissaries. When a king wants to get something done, he sends an emissary to do it for him, and once the task has been completed, the emissary returns to report to the king. Likewise in the accomplishment stage, the main deity, Tara, emanates rays of light that touch the hearts of the deities in her retinue—Karma Tara for example—invoking each deity's wisdom mind to accomplish her task. Having accomplished all her activities, the rays of light return to the main deity, bringing with them blessings and accomplishments.

I think I'll repeat this part very simply, so you can understand. From the heart of the main deity, rays of light emanate, touching the heart and invoking the wisdom mind of one of the deities in the retinue, for example Karma Tara. That deity then emanates rays of light and so on, which accomplish the activity she has been charged with. These rays of light then return to the retinue deity, and having accomplished her task, she emanates rays of light that reconverge into the heart of the main deity, bringing blessings and siddhis.

This visualization is also described in the *Retreat Manual* by Jamgön Kongtrul. At the heart of each of the Taras in the retinue—Vajra Tara, Ratna Tara, Padma Tara and Karma Tara—stand their respective seed syllables surrounded by their respective mantras. The colour of the seed syllable and mantra is the same as the colour of that deity.

That was the accomplishment practice. During approach practice, we acquaint ourselves with the deity and become quite close. During the accomplishment practice, we try to accomplish the deity, meaning we try to become one with or indivisible from the deity. This is the accomplishment we want to achieve.

c) Activity Practice

You can only apply activity practice once you have accomplished and therefore become one with the deity through accomplishment practice. Until you are one with the deity there are no activities for you to accomplish. However, when we do sadhana practice, we must complete all three phases of approach, accomplishment and activity, which means that even if you have not completely accomplished the deity, you must still do the recitations associated with activity practice. Here, the activities are carried out by the four Taras who act as the gatekeepers. Do you remember the four deities at the gates? They accomplish four activities—pacifying, enriching, magnetising and subjugating. The way to direct the practice is as indicated in the text of the activity section,

> Myself the samayasattva, with the jnanasattva
> And the nirmanasattva,
> Send forth a brilliant profusion of rays of compassion
> That invoke the wisdom mind of the Taras of the four
>   families.
> In turn, they send out rays of light
> That invoke the wisdom mind of the gatekeepers who
>   accomplish activities.

Rays of light emanate from the main deities to the next ones, touching each other in turn. Clearly actualise the visualization of the four seed syllables in their respective colours surrounded by their mantra malas as you recite the practice. Rays of light stream out from the five deities and the retinue to invoke Hook Tara. The five deities are the main deity and the four Taras. Basically, rays of light radiate from one deity to the next. From the three main deities Arya Tara, Amitayus and Ushnisha Vijaya, rays of light stream out and touch each of the four Taras in turn, starting with Vajra Tara. Then light streams out from the four Taras' hearts, invoking the wisdom minds of the four Gatekeeper Taras. The *Retreat Manual* adds,

> The rays of light stream out [. . .] to invoke Hook Tara.
> Hook Tara manifests many emanations, rays of light and
> infinite displays which accomplish the activity of pacifying

all obstructing forces such as illness, negative spirits,
negative actions, obscurations and so on. Accumulate only
her mantra throughout the session. The conclusion is as
before.

So we begin with Hook Tara to accomplish the pacifying activities. The
Retreat Manual continues,

Now alternate as follows.

During morning session, practise only Noose Tara's mantra
and visualization, accomplishing the enriching activities.

In the afternoon session, practise Iron Chain Tara's
mantra and visualization and accomplish the magnetising
activities.

During the evening session, practise Bell Tara's mantra and
visualization and accomplish the subjugating activities.

Practise each activity by creating the relevant visualization of deities and
rays of light to accomplish each specific activity. How you direct the practice
is explained in the sadhana text,

Deities resound with the sound of their own mantras,
    which
Fill the sky and pervade the ten directions.
With infinite ways of training those beings who are ready,
They pacify all disease, harmful forces, negativities and
    obscurations within dharmadhatu,
They increase longevity, merit, wealth and intelligence,
Bring the three realms, inner air and mind under control
    and
Destroy enemies, obstacle makers and duality.
These supreme and common activities,
Through the magic of the samadhi of emanating and
    reabsorbing rays of light,
Are all accomplished as I envision them.

At the hearts of each of the Gatekeeper Taras stand the relevant sylla-bles—DZA, HUNG, BAM and HO—surrounded by their respective mantras.

This is how the activities are accomplished: from the heart of the main deity, rays of light invoke the surrounding four Taras, then emanate from their hearts to touch the hearts of the four Gatekeeper Taras who accomplish the activities. First, rays of light touch the heart of the Hook Tara accomplishing pacifying activities, then the hearts of the other gatekeepers successively to accomplish the activities of enriching, magnetising and subjugation. All these activities are accomplished through the emanation of rays of light.

An important aspect of this practice is that each deity resounds with the sound of their own mantra. So for example, at the hearts of the main deity and the jnanasattva is the mantra OM TARE TUTARE TURE SOHA. Each syllable produces its own sound: OM produces the sound "om"; TARE produces the sound "tare" and so on. And at the same time, each deity recites his or her re-spective mantra which is why the example used to illustrate the activity stage visualization is of bees buzzing around a broken hive. If you break the hive of a colony of bees, they will swarm around it, making their own buzzing sounds; likewise in this visualization, each syllable buzzes with its own sound.

The Four Activities

The four different activities of pacifying, enriching, magnetising and subju-gating are quite straightforward and laid out clearly in the text. Illness, spir-its, forms of negativity and obscurations are each mentioned and addressed through the activity of pacifying.

Through our practice we enrich, enhance or make more abundant lon-gevity, merit, wealth and wisdom. Gelugpa lamas sometimes scold the Ny-ingmapas and accuse them of enhancing their own worldly wealth through such Nyingma visualization practices, which would be very bad. At the same time, being wealthy can be quite useful and very beneficial. In terms of wealth, there is no one wealthier than the Buddha! Buddha can manifest whatever he wants from the sky treasury—basically he can pluck material objects from primordial space. As Guru Rinpoche said, "I don't need other people's gold; all that appears and exists is gold to me." Just by touching something someone like Guru Rinpoche could turn everything to gold.

Next, with the magnetising activities, everything is brought under your control. So you bring all sentient beings of the three realms of existence under control and, more importantly, your own inner air, or *lung*, that is ridden by the mind, and the mind itself. By the time your mind and *lung* are completely under control, you will have reached enlightenment.

Jetsun Milarepa achieved enlightenment by bringing his mind and *lung* under control through *tsalung* practice. All yogic exercises that work with the channels and inner air, for example the Six Yogas of Naropa, are practised to bring our inner air, karmic wind and mind under control. Our bodies are like countries criss-crossed with roads (the channels), along which the inner air travels like a horse, ridden by the mind which is like the horse rider. If we cannot bring mind and inner air under control, the horse will run wild as if it had no rider at all. This is the situation most of us face at the moment. Another example is of a blind horse ridden by someone without legs. The blind horse wanders around but has no idea where it is going. Similarly, our inner air like the horse wanders everywhere in our bodies but has no idea where it's really going, and the mind is like the legless rider who has no choice but to go wherever the horse goes. Through *tsalung* practice you can take control of and direct your inner air like a tame and well-trained horse and therefore direct the mind to go wherever you want it to. Once your *lung* is completely under your control, then all the concepts, thoughts and ideas disappear, never again to appear in your mind.

Subjugation or wrathful activity is basically to kill the enemy you want eliminated, and that enemy is the delusion of duality or dualistic clinging.

By relying on the common accomplishment of the activities of pacifying, enriching, magnetising and subjugating which we accomplish through the power of samadhi, we are able to reach the state of complete enlightenment, the supreme accomplishment. How are these common activities accomplished? By the magic of the emanating and reabsorbing samadhi. All our activities, everything, will be accomplished as if by a wish-fulfilling jewel, a precious gem that grants all wishes and prayers instantly; it doesn't have to think about granting your wish, you just make your request and it is instantly fulfilled. And everything you want will be accomplished through the power of samadhi as you practise these four activities.

d) How Long Should I Practise For?

The questions that always comes up around how to do the practice are, "How many mantras should I recite" and "How long should I practise for?" Even those of you who haven't actually asked these questions are, I'm sure, waiting for the answers. So I'll tell you!

There are three options: time, number and signs. *Time* refers to the length of time you do the practice, the number of days or months. *Number* means you decide to recite a specific number of mantras. *Signs* mean you decide to practise until certain signs of accomplishment manifest.

(i) Time

All Guru Rinpoche's instructions about how much time should be spent on this practice were intended for students of superior capacity like Vairotsana, King Trison Deutsen and Yeshe Tsogyal, and were therefore extremely short. This is why the instruction manual says that those of superior capacity should do the approach practice for three weeks, because that's how long practitioners of superior capacity usually need to experience signs of accomplishment; accomplishment practice for one week; and activity practice for a single day. With just one day for the activity practice, do the pacifying activity in the early morning session, the enriching activity in the morning session, the magnetising activity in the afternoon session and the subjugating activity in the evening.

(ii) Number

Jamgön Kongtrul spoke briefly about how many mantras we should recite, and the instruction manual specifies that you must practise for three months simply for familiarization with the practice.

To determine the number of mantras you recite, since the main mantra OM TARE TUTTARE TURE SOHA has ten syllables, it is said you should recite one hundred thousand for each of the ten syllables, making a total of one million, plus an extra hundred thousand to make up for any omissions or additions you make as you practise. The mantra of the combined practice OM TARE TUTTARE TURE HRIH DROOM BENDZA JNANA AYUKE SOHA has nineteen syllables, and you should recite seven hundred thousand, plus seventy thousand to make up for your mistakes. Recite the jnanasattva Amitayus' mantra OM AMARANI DZIWANTIYE SOHA four hundred thousand times, and also do four hundred thousand recitations of the nirmanasattva Ushnisha Vijaya's mantra OM AMRITA AYURDADE SOHA.

According to the Nyingma tradition, in the accomplishment practice, you usually recite one tenth of the number of mantras you do in approach practice. For example, in this practice you recite one million mantras during the approach practice which means you say one hundred thousand during the accomplishment practice. So recite one hundred thousand mantras for each of the four Taras and forty thousand mantras for each of the four Gatekeeper Taras. Here again, for the practice to be complete, you must add another ten percent, four thousand, to make a total of forty-four thousand. Jamgön Kongtrul says this number of mantras is appropriate for a practitioner of medium capacity.

If you want to do the practice more elaborately, multiply the number of mantras by four, so for example instead of one hundred thousand recitations, you do four hundred thousand. Jigme Lingpa said that what practitioners of the past were able to accomplish in one hundred thousand recitations would take four times as long in his time because they were already living in the degenerate time and the qualities of sentient beings were not as great.

(iii) Signs

If you don't concentrate as you practise, it doesn't matter how many million mantras you recite, your practice will be pointless. These days many people seem able to recite one hundred million mantras—I've met many monks who have recited more—but they tell me they don't achieve any signs of accomplishment. This is because they can't meditate or focus their minds as they recite the practice. The kinds of signs you might achieve are mentioned in the text. The best is to have a face-to-face meeting with the deity during which you hear him or her speak to you directly. The second best is to experience dreams during which you meet the deity—for Westerners, it seems, this happens quite easily! But most of these dreams aren't authentic signs of accomplishment. Actually, they're useless. I remember, when I was on my way to France once with Tulku Pema Wangyal, he told me that because Westerners' samayas are so pure and they have genuine devotion for and faith in the teachings, they immediately achieve signs of accomplishments in their dreams. At the time I thought that this was probably the case. But then as time went on, I realised that most of the Westerners were actually just crazy! What they experienced weren't real signs! I haven't met anyone who achieved genuine signs of accomplishment. Experiences are like mist in the morning, they come and go, and generally the idea of experiences of all kinds seem to pop into their minds, but it doesn't mean much. If you think to yourself, "I must have an indication, a sign! I must have some dreams! I'm sure I will have some really good dreams!" you're bound to dream something, but the so-called signs you see in your dream won't be real signs at all.

If you do achieve genuine signs of accomplishment, it is said that you should receive the siddhis immediately, even if the signs appear in the middle of your retreat. If you don't, the siddhis will fade away. The retreat manual clearly explains about receiving the siddhis which generally comes towards the end of the practices.

8. Tsok

There's nothing special about the tsok in this practice. *Tsok* means "gathering", so start by gathering excellent food and offering substances, in particular those that represent skilful means (something to eat) and wisdom (something to drink). Without these two kinds of offering the tsok will be incomplete. Similarly, the gathering of practitioners should include both men and women. A gathering of only male practitioners doesn't qualify as a genuine ganachakra feast. Without women present, the practice is only a simple tsok offering.

Start by blessing the offering substances, then immediately invite your guests. The tsok in the Chimé Phakmé Nyingtik practice contains a specific invitation. Follow the stages described in the text. Having invited the guests, make the offerings. This is what you do in the tsok offering. The purpose of this visualization is to emanate offering gods, goddesses and tsok substances, and for the gods and goddesses to offer the five sensory pleasures to the invited guests who include countless deities of the Three Roots, buddhas and bodhisattvas of the ten directions, and the dakas and dakinis of the twenty-four sacred places and the thirty-two sacred lands. They are pleased—body, speech and mind—with the infinite offerings you present to them.

During the tsok, you must make offering for confession and fulfillment, this is the second tsok offering. The visualization for both offering the tsok and the fulfillment practice is the same. The only difference between these two parts of the practice is that you make more food offerings for the tsok and offer more objects in the fulfillment practice. Through the fulfillment practice, you offer all the offering substances, own up to all your faults, errors and mistakes and confess at the end of the practice. Having done so, it is important to be confident that all your mistakes and so on have been completely purified. The Chimé Phakmé Nyingtik doesn't include a *dralwa* practice (sometimes translated as liberation or annihilation) which is usually found towards the end of a tsok to liberate or annihilate all the enemies related to ego clinging.

The Chimé Phakmé Nyingtik includes quite an elaborate practice of self-empowerment.[97] Should you skip this section and not receive the self-empowerment, there is also a method for blessing the tsok by gathering the siddhis of longevity and dissolving them into the tsok substances.

Now it is time to enjoy the tsok. The men should start eating by using their right hands first, and women should use their left; the men should start by drinking and the women should start by eating. You should then nurture the experience of great bliss. It is said that if the practitioners wish to, they can now perform vajra songs and vajra dances. Next, gather the remaining tsok offerings and take them out to offer to the remainder deities and elemental spirits. Make prayers of aspiration, then make torma offerings to all the dharma protectors (male, female and neuter), rinse the plate you offered the torma on with amrita and offer the rinsing water to the twelve Tenma protectors of the land of Tibet who were tamed by Guru Rinpoche. The two plates that were used for the covenant, or cheto, and Tenma tormas are then placed upside down, and all the samaya breakers and obstacle makers are summoned and trapped beneath them, never to rise again. At the end, make a brief offering of praise to the mandala deities. Confess how inadequate your offerings were, all your transgressions, incorrect visualizations and recitations and so on, and recite the hundred-syllable mantra three times.

Vajra Pride

Vajra pride is the second crucial point of kyerim practice. Your visualization of the deity must be clear. So far, what we've been doing is maintaining a clear visualization of the deities as we meditate on the main deity, the samayasattva in union with the consort, the jnanasattva, the seed syllable, the nirmanasattvas, the four Taras accompanying the main deity, the retinue and the four Gatekeeper Taras who accomplish the four activities. This is how we have been practising visualization and what we've been talking about over the past couple of days.

But even more important than maintaining the clarity of our visualization is vajra pride or vajra confidence. Even if you achieve the clearest visualization possible, it is also vital for you to have a strong sense that you are the deity—this is vajra pride. Without it, even if you visualize yourself as the deity perfectly, that visualization will be no more than an image like a statue or a thangka. It will be a representation or picture of the deity, not the deity itself. Unless you have a strong sense that you are the deity, your visualization will not be the deity. A worse mistake would be to fake it by trying to make yourself look like something you know you're not. In other words, to make yourself look like the deity, thinking, "Even though I am not the deity, I will try to see myself as the deity." This is not how to approach this practice. Neither is, "Even though right now I am not the deity, through the practice I will become the deity."

When we were talking about the view, specifically the ground, I explained that the nature of our mind is the dharmakaya and that the dharmakaya of the Buddha is no different from the dharmakaya that is our own minds. So as we visualize ourselves as the deity, the appearance we actualise is in fact a manifestation of this wisdom, this dharmakaya. Our visualization is wisdom manifesting with one face, two hands and so on. It's no less than the manifestation of primordial wisdom, which is the very nature of your mind. The dharmakaya, the Buddha and this deity are no different from who you are or from your mind. Therefore at this point, it is vital to have absolute certainty, confidence and pride in this truth.

Longchen Rabjam said that whether or not your visualization is clear, the moment you start to think of the deity it is imperative that you feel this vajra pride. If you practise thinking, "Even though I am not the deity, I will try to actualise myself as the deity in order to accomplish really being the deity", you will never accomplish anything. It just doesn't work like that. Even though your body is not the body of the deity, your mind is the deity, and there is not one single doubt that this is so! Which is why you really must arouse that strong sense of confidence and pride in being the deity and why it is said that vajra pride is even more important than clear visualization. Even if you manage to create an extremely clear visualization, without vajra pride all you've done is create an empty image. This is why you need vajra pride. This is extremely important, as we can see from numerous quotations masters cite in the sacred texts and through reasoning.

Along with a clear visualization and vajra pride, you must also practise a third element which is to remember the purity. If these three elements are part of your practice, you are practising kyerim.

Remember the Purity

This third point, remembering the purity, is basically to remember that everything you do in your meditation practice—the deity you visualize, the appearance of the palace and so on—is no different from the dharmakaya. They all manifest without ever separating or moving out of the space of the dharmakaya, which is why all these different aspects of practice must be embraced by the view of emptiness. This is the essential method for remembering the purity.

More elaborately, the significance of each aspect of the deities and palace—one face, two hands, two legs, the five silk ornaments, the eight jewel ornaments and so on—are specifically related to the enlightened qualities of a buddha. Therefore, you must bring to mind the purity of each of these aspects. But usually, people don't understand, the meaning is not clear to them. Unless you study the commentaries and have followed a shedra type of training, you won't really be able to understand these enlightened qualities. In Buddhism we talk of the four immeasurables, the four genuine restraints and four bases of miraculous powers that are among the thirty-seven elements that lead to enlightenment, the four means of gathering students, the seven branches of enlightenment, the six perfections and so on. Even though you hear and may even understand the words, you may find the meaning difficult to grasp. Actually, they are all related to different aspects of the deities, and if you want to know more, look at the different commentaries and practice instructions. Briefly though, it comes down to remembering the purity, and what I have explained today will suffice.

9. Dzogrim

Now we turn to the extraordinary teachings on dzogrim, the Dzogchen practice that's part of the Chimé Phakmé Nyingtik. Dilgo Khyentse Rinpoche wrote an elaborate commentary on the guru yoga sadhana based on the three great vidyadharas of longevity—Vimalamitra, Shri Singha and Guru Rinpoche—in which all the profound and crucial points of Dzogchen meditation are mentioned and is a part of the Chimé Phakmé Nyingtik cycle. You will find it in his *Collected Works*.

As I explained earlier, the practice of Chimé Phakmé Nyingtik purifies all the samsaric processes of beings and begins at the intermediate state or bardo. All sentient beings go through different stages of life. They take birth, grow up and become adults and accomplish various impure activities. The process of kyerim transforms all the impure aspects of a sentient being's life into the pure characteristics of the deity. This is what we train ourselves to do in kyerim practice.

Kyerim therefore has the power to eliminate all habitual tendencies that lead us to take rebirth in cyclic existence, samsara. There are two obscurations that cover our enlightened primordial wisdom—cognitive and habitual obscurations. Of these two, the obscurations of habitual tendencies are more difficult to remove than the cognitive, but kyerim purifies them both.

From the moment we are born, all sentient beings know one thing—we will eventually die. Even the Buddha passed into parinirvana. This is why there is a section in the practice for dissolving the mandala.

> A! The samayasattvas, rigpa's natural display,
> Are one taste, beyond any possible separation or reunion,
> Within the expanse of the basic space of self-arising
>   primordial wisdom,

> So all their features like face and hands, all dissolve into
> all-pervading space.

I won't explain the words. As we chant the syllable A, the dissolution process begins. At the beginning of the practice when we first visualize the main deity, we work from the inside out; during the dissolution, we visualize from outside in. So the fire encircling the vajra fence dissolves into the vajra sphere, which dissolves into the environment, which dissolves into the palace, which dissolves into the retinue deities, who dissolve into the main deity. Similarly, the seats dissolve into each other, then into the main deity. At this point, all that's left is the main deity. The samayasattva dissolves into the jnanasattva, who dissolves into the TAM syllable which is the samadhisattva. Then the samadhisattva dissolves from bottom to top. In the end, all that's left is the circle above the syllable, and even that dissolves into light and vanishes into the ultimate space. The dissolution process we go through at death is reflected in the process of dissolution we find in kyerim practice. Then you rest in that state.

Those bound by cyclic existence are reborn into samsara, but a buddha manifests as a nirmanakaya for the sake of sentient beings. So next is the reappearance or arising which is like a rebirth. By saying the syllable TAM, you provide the circumstances necessary for the arising to unfold.

> TAM
> Once again, like a rainbow appearing from the sky,
> I arise in the form of the Lady of Immortality;
> Appearances, sounds and thoughts,
> Arise as deity and mantra, as the play of great wisdom.
> OM AH HUNG

When you arise again, it's fine to visualize yourself as the main deity; you don't have to visualize the entire retinue and the deity reappears to benefit all sentient beings.

There is another key point here. If you do this practice in retreat, don't dissolve the outer protective sphere. In retreat, you must maintain a continuous awareness of it. Each time you practise, re-establish it in your visualization, actualise its presence and only at the very end of the retreat do you dissolve it.

10. Requesting the Deities to Remain

Before you dedicate, if you have been practising in the presence of a representation of the enlightened body, speech or mind of the deity, you must
do a consecration or "request that the deities remain in the representations".
Ask the deities to remain in the images until they are destroyed by natural
disasters brought on by the four elements—earth, water, fire and wind. A
while ago there was a fire here in this shrine room at Deer Park and the main
statue was almost burnt. If the fire had destroyed it, the wisdom deity would
also have gone.

If you went through the elaborate practice of preparing a sand mandala
to support your practice (something I doubt you'll ever do), you have already asked the deity to remain until the sand mandala is dismantled. At the
end of the practice, you ask them to leave through a ritual for requesting the
wisdom deities to depart from the mandala.

11. Dedication and Prayers of Aspiration

Next are the dedication and aspiration prayers. All Sutra and Tantra texts
say that dedication and aspiration are extremely important elements in all
practices.

The dedication,

> HO
> The accumulations of the wisdom of primordial purity,
> And the accumulation of merit based on interdependent
>   origination,
> I dedicate within the space of the essence of enlightenment,
> The uncompounded expanse in which the two
>   accumulations are indivisible.

The prayer of aspiration,

> From now on and in all my lives,
> May I always be in your care, exalted Lady,
> And with the siddhis of longevity and wisdom,
> May I spontaneously accomplish all that truly benefits
>   myself and others.

Your practice should be accompanied by the dedication of merit and aspiration prayers. As you say the prayers of auspiciousness, visualize the buddhas and bodhisattvas filling all of space and showering you with mandarava flowers as they sing songs of auspiciousness. If you have received many empowerments, you must know about the elaborate visualizations you are supposed to actualise as you recite prayers of auspiciousness. Also, offerings of blessing rice and grain, flowers, incense, music and so on are scattered. Anyone who's received empowerments will have seen that too. At that point, you play cymbals and damaru.

> OM
> Holders of the dynamic energy of awareness in the mind
>   direct, symbolic and aural lineages,
> Vidyadhara lamas, let auspiciousness abound!
> You who appear in infinite mudras of peaceful and
>   wrathful deities,
> Yidam deities, let auspiciousness abound!
> You who assist the yogis in increasing great bliss,
> Outer and inner dakinis, let auspiciousness abound!
> You who judge good and bad and dispel obstacles,
> Ocean of dharma protectors, let auspiciousness abound!
> May all be auspicious for the short-term activities of four
>   types
> To fulfill the twofold benefits,
> While ultimately, may all be auspicious for the direct
>   experience
> Of the immortal wisdom body.

All the verses of auspiciousness in this sadhana are composed with such sweet words that have a truly excellent meaning! We would say here "Sarwa Mangalam" which is Sanskrit, and you could say it too. Then,

> *Scatter flowers in all directions as you recite this prayer. Then celebrate . . .*

To clarify, basically you can now throw a party and enjoy yourselves!

And increase the two accumulations.

This means that you should accumulate as much merit and wisdom as you can and do whatever possible to accumulate even more merit and wisdom.

At the end in the last paragraph of the text, there is a short prophecy plus a brief history of the practice that details its benefits. It is very clear, you just have to read it to understand it. King Trison Deutsen and his son, Gyalse Lharje, are mentioned, and the five recipients of the practice are listed as King Trison Deutsen, his friend Yeshe Tsogyal, his subjects Vairotsana, Gyalwa Chöyang and Nubchen Sangye Yeshe.

> *To you, the sovereign father and son,*
> *And the subjects and friend—five in all.*

Father and son are Trison Deutsen and Gyalse Lharje.

> *Conceal it in the expanse of the great bindu,*
> *For the benefit of future generations.*
> *When the time is ripe and the right interdependent*
> *circumstances come together,*
> *May it appear and benefit others on a vast scale!*

This precious teaching was given to these five people, then hidden as a terma in their minds to be revealed in future for the benefit of sentient beings. The five recipients of these teachings also manifested in the future: King Trison Deutsen and Gyalse Lharje manifested as Jamyang Khyentse Wangpo; Vairotsana returned in the form of Jamgön Kongtrul; Gyalse Lharje Chokdrup Gyalpo's incarnation was Chokgyur Lingpa; and Tertön Sogyal, Shechen Gyaltsab Pema Namgyal, Karmapa Tekchok Dorje, Khakhyab Dorje and Dodrupchen Jigme Tenpe Nyima are all believed to have been emanations of Gyalse Lharje Chokdrup Gyalpo. It's interesting when a good prophecy is made just how many people are eager to say, "Yes, he was pointing at me! I'm the one who will accomplish this. I was the one he was writing about!"

Jamgön Kongtrul said over and again that Jamyang Khyentse Wangpo's terma revelations are unique and extraordinary revelations. They contain few words but carry an extremely profound meaning and great blessings. He said the five main emanations of King Trison Deutsen were all great tertöns, the five king-like tertöns. The body emanation was Nyang Ral Nyima Özer, the speech emanation was Guru Chökyi Wangchuk, the mind emanation was Tashi Tobgyal, the activity emanation was the Great Fifth Dalai Lama and the quality emanation was Ngari Panchen. But according to Jamgön Kongtrul, Jamyang Khyentse Wangpo was greater than any of the five king-like tertöns. Jamyang Khyentse Wangpo had five students who were also great tertöns which is why Khyentse Wangpo is considered to be the universal monarch of the profound terma tradition. He revealed the terma of the Chimé Phakmé Nyingtik, wrote it down, practised it, and after about a week Guru Rinpoche, Shri Singha, Vimalamitra and all the deities of the mandala appeared to him directly and he received their blessings. Khyentse Wangpo gave the Chimé Phakmé Nyingtik empowerment to Chokgyur Lingpa, and immediately Chokgyur Lingpa saw very clearly the main deity's seven eyes—two in the deity's feet, two in her hands and three on her face. He saw them very clearly for quite a long time.

CHAPTER 9:

How to Direct the Practice of Chimé Phakmé Nyingtik for Someone Else

by Tulku Orgyen Tobgyal

In the Chimé Phakmé Nyingtik, we meditate on the deity Jetsun Tara, Wish-Fulfilling Wheel, who has seven eyes. On her lap sits her male consort, the Lord of Dance Amitayus,[98] who is white suffused with red. Jetsun Tara and Amitayus in union are the samayasattva. We don't have time to go into their ornaments and ritual objects, but as this assembly—everyone gathered here in Lerab Ling—is made up almost exclusively of great Chimé Phakmé Nyingtik practitioners, that kind of explanation isn't so necessary.

In the centre of Tara's heart sits Amitayus, the Buddha of Limitless Life. He is brilliant white and wears all the silks and jewel ornaments of a sambhogakaya. He sits on a lotus and moon disc seat holding a vase of longevity, his hands form the mudra of meditation and in his heart is the samadhisattva, which in this case is a white syllable TAM. These are the three nested sattvas.

What I will explain today is how to direct the practice of Chimé Phakmé Nyingtik so that it extends the life of Sogyal Rinpoche. This will be my main point.

When we do this practice of long life for an ordinary person, we visualize that person in the belly of the TAM. When we practise for a master from whom we've received empowerments, we visualize him in the circle at the top of the white syllable TAM, sitting in the upright posture. Visualize his features very clearly as you meditate. Revolving clockwise around the TAM are the ten syllables of the Tara mantra, each resonating with its own sound. By reciting the mantra, we invoke Amitayus' wisdom mind. From the syllable TAM and the mantra mala, inconceivably numerous rays of light shine from the crown of Amitayus' head, flaring up through Tara's body and out through the ushnisha at the top of her head. The light manifests as countless

Ushnisha Vijayas as infinite as specks of dust in sunbeams, who stream out in every direction filling the universe. With their iron hooks, they draw the five outer elements, the five inner aggregates and the secret wisdom, love and power of all the buddhas and their heirs like iron filings to a magnet and deposit it all in their vases. As the empowerment is granted, all this nectar dissolves into the body of the master who is visualized in the syllable TAM. Consider without any doubt that the master's body, speech and mind are now beyond change or decay and that he has gained the indestructible vajra body of immortality. This is the visualization we do when we practise for our master.

I'll now say a few words about the nectar gathered by the Ushnisha Vijayas, the quicksilver of accomplishment which is pure white. What is it made up of? What gives it its power? This nectar is the quintessence of the wisdom, love and power of the buddhas of the ten directions and their heirs. It is the quintessence of longevity and immortality and of the buddha's enlightened body, speech and mind. It is the quintessence of all five elements and of the vitality of all sentient beings, gods, nagas, human beings and so on. These are the pure essences that fill Ushnisha Vijayas' vases. Generally, we think of the five elements of earth, water, fire, air and space as being the elements that form this world. But actually, they extend much farther than that. The five elements we are talking about here form the basis of billions of universes extending to the far reaches of space, and the Ushnisha Vijayas gather the elemental essence of all these universes. The quicksilver of accomplishment is so powerful that if you taste even a single drop and it then dissolves into your body, it will restore the loss of your vitality, the strength of your mind will increase as long as space endures and you will be endowed with,

> . . . the strength of an elephant; scattered on a dead tree, it would immediately burst into life with leaves, flowers and fruit . . .

Later in the practice at the point in the text when you recite the mantras of the four Taras of the four families and also when you visualize the prayer for summoning longevity (*tseguk*),[99] focus on dissolving the nectar of longevity into the body of the lama. The four Taras pacify, enrich, magnetise and subjugate: they pacify all diseases, harmful forces, negativity and obscurations within dharmadhatu; they increase the length of the lama's life, his merit, wealth and intelligence; they help the lama control the channels, inner air and bindus in his body;[100] and they destroy all the harm caused by enemies, obstacle makers, spells, curses or the demons of the Lord of Death.

At the end, you seal the practice. The dharmata, your true nature which is the same for everyone, will not die as long as space exists. So the dharmata, the mind of the lama and your own mind—the ground of all three is the same—are bound together as one. At this point, you rest in that state in meditative equipoise and attain immortal life.

When Longchenpa was given a sign that he was about to die, he still had things to do and he didn't want to die right away. So he inhaled and held his breath, and all the portents of death were eliminated. So holding the breath is also very powerful.

CHAPTER 10:

Origins of Chimé Phakmé Nyingtik Drupchen

by Tulku Orgyen Tobgyal

The Chimé Phakmé Nyingtik is one of Jamyang Khyentse Wangpo's terma teachings. Dzongsar Jamyang Khyentse Chökyi Lodrö wrote the *Drupchen Manual*[101] for the Chimé Phakmé Nyingtik at the request of the Queen of Nangchen—who was the wife of a minor king who ruled over the region of Nangchen in Kham. Since then, Adeu Rinpoche's monastery had intended to do a Chimé Phakmé Nyingtik drupchen annually, but I don't know how many years they managed it, maybe two, before the Chinese came. Before the *Drupchen Manual* was written, there do not seem to be any reports about a Chimé Phakmé Nyingtik drupchen having been performed. But we can't say for sure that it wasn't. It might have been, but who knows? The biographies of Jamyang Khyentse Wangpo and Jamgön Kongtrul mention the Chimé Phakmé Nyingtik a lot, but nowhere do they suggest that a drupchen was performed.

The question all of you need to know the answer to is, "Where does the practice tradition for the Chimé Phakmé Nyingtik drupchen we follow here at Lerab Ling come from?" In 1958, Dzongsar Jamyang Khyentse Chökyi Lodrö was very ill and so a Chimé Phakmé Nyingtik drupchen was performed. Many of his students were there, including Sogyal Rinpoche. Pema Tashi, our monastery's chant master who died a few years ago, was appointed chant leader for the ceremony and my father had to be the vajra master. At that time, Pema Tashi, the chant master, had never performed this drupchen, so he asked Khyentse Chökyi Lodrö how to do it and he learned directly from him. Khyentse Chökyi Lodrö went through the entire text and pointed out when to do what and what to chant when. He explained the entire drupchen to Pema Tashi and he also told him to chant according to the Chokling tradition. Pema Tashi was surprised and asked, "Can we really do that?" "Of course," replied Khyentse Chökyi Lodrö, "there is no tradition greater than Chokling."

So Pema Tashi led the Chimé Phakmé Nyingtik drupchen which took place in the upstairs temple of the palace in Sikkim. Each afternoon, Khyentse Rinpoche would join them briefly, but he was very ill.

Later in Bhutan, one of Sakya Trichen's divinations said that it would be good to do a Chimé Phakmé Nyingtik drupchen and offer a long-life ceremony to Dilgo Khyentse Rinpoche. The present Neten Chokling incarnation was there, as was the present Dzongsar Khyentse Rinpoche and all the others. The chant master was the same as before, Pema Tashi. Before the drupchen began, he asked Dilgo Khyentse Rinpoche to clarify how the drupchen should be done, and Dilgo Khyentse Rinpoche said exactly the same as Khyentse Chökyi Lodrö. Then at the end of the drupchen, the long-life ceremony was offered. This is the tradition that has now reached Lerab Ling.

During Jamyang Khyentse Wangpo's time, there was no tradition of doing this drupchen. But in the latter part of Jamyang Khyentse Chökyi Lodrö's life and similarly the latter part of Dilgo Khyentse Rinpoche's life, drupchens were performed more often. When the long-life ceremony was offered to Dilgo Khyentse Rinpoche in Bhutan, he wrote them a letter which said,

> "I have practised the special deity of Chimé Phakmé Nyingtik throughout my life and have accumulated many approach and accomplishment practices, but I have never had the opportunity to do a Chimé Phakmé Nyingtik drupchen before. So I would like to thank the Rinpoches who organised this drupchen. According to the prophecies, one of the Khyentse incarnations will have a long life. It'll probably be me because I am now more than eighty years old."

We are doing the same drupchen practice of Chimé Phakmé Nyingtik. Many people now do this drupchen all over the world. It is important to clarify this, otherwise if you're ever asked where the tradition of doing Chimé Phakmé Nyingtik drupchen came from, you'd probably just say that you didn't know or, "I think Tulku Orgyen Tobgyal made it up."

CHAPTER 11:

The Chimé Phakmé Nyingtik Torma

by Tulku Orgyen Tobgyal

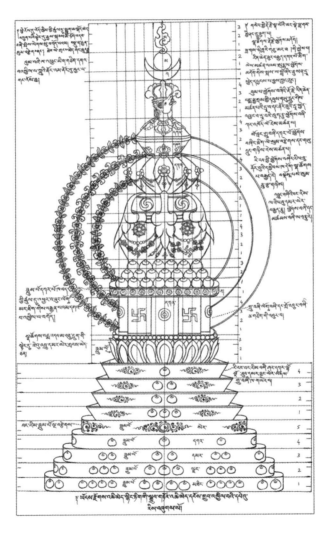

Drawing of the great Chimé Phakmé Nyingtik torma with explanations
for its preparation, from the *Treasury of Precious Termas*.

There's a part of the Chimé Phakmé Nyingtik that I haven't yet explained, and it's one of the most important. I'll explain it today; then tomorrow, you can practise it.

Generally speaking, sadhana practices involve three visualizations—self-visualization, front visualization and vase visualization. Practices in the Nyingma terma tradition were written with practitioners of the highest capacity in mind which is why front and self-visualizations are practised together and only one mandala is visualized. The vase visualization was also written for the most capable practitioners, and that's why the entire mandala of Chimé Phakmé Nyingtik is instantly visualized inside the vase. Less capable practitioners who are not at that level should follow a text that leads them step-by-step through the self-visualization of the deity, followed by the front visualization of the deity and then the vase visualization. But as Guru Rinpoche's termas were intended for the best kind of practitioner, we meditate on the self-visualization and front visualization together. Having done so, with the recitation of a mantra the front and self-visualizations separate like one candle lighting another, and in an instant two mandalas are visualized. If you practise essentially, the vase visualization should also appear instantly. This is true for all such practices.

A unique characteristic of the Chimé Phakmé Nyingtik is that the entire mandala is also visualized in the torma. Most Tibetan lamas don't know about this, but the *Drupchen Manual*[102] says,

> If you have the "essence of immortality" which is the
> torma support for this practice, you should add the deity
> generation practice called the *Heart Essence of Complete
> Immortality* in order to visualize the torma as the deities.
> This is how the venerable master used to practise . . .

The *Heart Essence of Complete Immortality* is a terma that was revealed by Chokgyur Lingpa, and when Jamyang Khyentse Wangpo who is the "venerable master" practised the Chimé Phakmé Nyingtik, he would add the generation of the deity from the *Heart of Essence of Complete Immortality*[103] to the practice. This approach is a special feature of this teaching which means that at this point, we must meditate on the deities in the torma. So how do we do it? We recite the lines,

HUNG HRIH
>Spontaneously, out of basic space, arises the great stupa of
>   immortality . . .

These verses tell us how to meditate on the entire mandala of deities
in the torma. Right now, I don't think anyone here is meditating on the
torma as the entire mandala, apart perhaps from Chokling Rinpoche and
the monks. Anyway here "basic space" means the great simplicity free from
elaboration, and the great stupa of immortality arises naturally from this
space to benefit sentient beings. It's like the stupa of Ushnisha Vijaya.

>   . . . so vast it pervades the dharmadhatu, the expanse of
>   space . . .

This stupa is so vast that, like space, it fills the dharmadhatu, and that's
how you should meditate on it. It's also like the palaces we describe when
we practise the *Narak Kong Shak*, "without inside and outside". This is the
expanse which is as vast as the dharmadhatu itself.

>   . . . in which stands the torma, made of the spontaneously
>   present five essences.

The five essences[104] are spontaneously present and therefore not made or
produced by anyone.

Now for the shape of the torma,

>   On the firm base, where the five mothers appear as five
>   steps . . .

The "five mothers" are the five elements: space, wind, fire, water and
earth. They are represented on the torma by five circular steps. The first step
is blue which is space. The next step is green which appears in your visualization as a crossed vajra and represents the wind element. The wind element
stands on and is supported by the empty expanse of space, the blue step.
Above the crossed vajra in your visualization is a red triangle, the mandala
of fire, which appears as the red step on the torma. The next step is white
representing the white water mandala, and it appears in your visualization as
a white disc. Above that is the yellow step, the earth mandala, which appears

in your visualization as a yellow square. All these elements, the five mothers, form the "firm base" which can only be altered by the kind of fire that blazes at the end of a kalpa.

Above these five circular steps are four square steps. The top of each square is divided into four triangles, which mark the four directions with four colours. Each colour represents the accomplishment of one of the enlightened activities of pacifying, enriching, magnetising or subjugating. In your visualization, gods and goddesses stand on these steps emanating the five kinds of sensory stimulants.

> On the firm base, where the five mothers appear as five
>   steps,
> Are self-arising bindus containing the sixteen awareness
>   consorts,
> Who emanate offering clouds of abundant sensory
>   delights.

The text about how to make this torma[105] explains that eighty norbus—called "bindus" in the visualization—are placed on the circular steps to represent the eighty minor marks and that the square steps are ornamented with thirty-two norbus to represent the thirty-two major marks. Each of these spherical norbus contains hundreds of thousands of offering goddesses, the sixteen awareness-consorts described in the Nyingtik.[106] Four goddesses appear on each step—one in each of the four directions—emanating cloud-like offerings of all the sensory stimulants. Above the square steps,

> The lotus possessing billions of petals . . .

The anthers appear in yellow on the torma, above the lotus petals.

> . . . bears hundreds of thousands of bindus containing
>   cities of immortals
> And vidyadharas with power over life.

The bindus contain hundreds of thousands of cities of immortals filled with deities, goddesses and vidyadharas. Each city doesn't contain just a few immortal vidyadharas, but millions and millions, all of whom have attained power over life just like Guru Rinpoche and Vimalamitra. This is what you should meditate on.

> The natural radiance of the five families appears as the
> excellent mansion of complete victory,
> Beautifully adorned with the five precious ornaments.

Above the bindus is the excellent mansion of complete victory, the nature of which is the five buddha families. It is adorned with many precious ornaments represented on the torma by bindus, svastikas and coils of joy.

> Here reside the attending four swift goddesses of longevity,
> . . .

Various deities reside in this mansion, starting with the four swift goddesses of longevity at the four doors.

> . . . and the goddess of power, Chandali the destroyer.

Inside is the magnetising deity Chandali the destroyer, known as Mother of Life Chandali, who completely destroys all obstacles to life. She holds a long-life arrow in her right hand and an excellent vase in her left. She is inside the mansion, and so she should be visualized inside the mansion. Actualise all this in your practice. Above the mansion,

> The excellent vase of dharmakaya that fulfills all needs,
> Is rich with blazing, everlasting *dagams*,[107]
> Adorned with bindus and the five insignia swathed with
> nets.
> From a wish-granting tree's foliage and blooming utpala
> flowers
> Rain down the excellent fruit of the desired
> accomplishments.

What is the significance? The vase gives us all the blessings and accomplishments, everything we need, and sensory stimulants fall like rain. Above the vase,

294   SUBLIME LADY OF IMMORTALITY

> In the adorned eight-faceted wish-fulfilling jewel,
> The *dagams* with an opening to the sky, are Hayagriva and
>   consort Varahi;
> The crowning sun and moon ornaments blaze with wisdom
>   fire.

The *dagams* are the eight segments that make up the eight-faceted jewel, and at the top of this jewel is a hole that opens into the sky. The deities you visualize inside the jewel are Hayagriva and Vajravarahi. And then above that,

> On the precious knot of eternity, the radiant net,
> Abide the sixteen peaceful and wrathful lords and ladies of
>   longevity.

The precious knot of eternity or radiant net is inside the eight-faceted jewel with sixteen peaceful and wrathful lords of life in union. The sixteen are the five buddhas in union with the five female buddhas, the five wrathful ones in union with the five wrathful female buddhas and also the six munis. Above them is a locket made from the semi-spherical sun and moon. And above that is a crossed vajra.

> Top and bottom clasped by the crossed vajra, bound by the
>   chain of syllables,
> The locket unites skilful means and wisdom. In its expanse
> Is the invincible, indestructible blazing vajra of the ten
>   strengths.

The upper part of the locket is the moon which represents skilful means; and the lower part is wisdom, represented by the sun. Together they represent the union of skilful means and wisdom. Half of the "indestructible blazing vajra" is inside the locket and half we can see is outside the locket above the semi-spherical moon. It has the ten strengths of a vajra which include invincibility and indestructibility.

> In the upper prongs are Oddiyana Amitayus,
> With consort Mandarava and a retinue of vidyadharas.

The deities are inside the upper prongs of the vajra.

> In the lower prongs is the sovereign of longevity, Ushnisha
>   Vijaya.
> In the hub, in bindus of the five essences,
> Are the five kings and five queens of immortality
> Manifesting in kayas arising naturally and primordially
>   from basic space.

In the middle of the vajra in the hub, visualize five spheres of light in five different colours; these are the five essences. Inside the bindus, visualize male and female buddhas of the five families who arise naturally and primordially from basic space.

> In the space around the torma, inside the large and small
>   bindus,
> Lamas, yidams, buddhas, bodhisattvas,
> Dakas, dakinis, dharma protectors and swift goddesses
> All emanate rays of light and regather it.

Any empty space left in and around the torma is filled from bottom to top with large and small bindus containing deities.

> . . . appear like dust motes in rays of sunlight, in a
> complete mandala that pervades space . . .

These bindus are like motes of dust in shafts of light and pervade the whole of space—they are everywhere. All the deities emanate rays of light and regather it, which is what deities do.

> . . . in a great mandala of these sixty thousand buddhas.

The text says there are sixty thousand buddhas in the torma, but the number of deities isn't limited to just sixty thousand. Actually, there are billions and billions of buddhas, of wisdom kayas, in this mandala—an inconceivable number.

> In hundreds of thousands, millions, billions and so on
> Of inconceivable buddha fields, appear kayas, wisdoms,

> Qualities and activities, limitless, beyond measure.
> The samayasattvas and jnanasattvas are primordially
>   inseparable, . . .

The samayasattvas, jnanasattvas and deities inside the torma are primordially inseparable—they are one and the same.

> . . . a perfect ornament of Samantabhadra's cloud-like
>   offerings.

There are four ways of relating to the torma, including the torma as the deity or mandala, the torma as clouds of offerings and so on.[108] Here, as described in the text, you consider this torma to be like a cloud of offerings and also the deities and so on.

Having done the self-, front and vase visualizations, you do the torma visualization. The addition of the torma visualization is a special feature of this practice. At this point actualise the visualization, recite the text and repeat the mantra. The explanation of this torma is more than fifteen pages long[109] and includes a line drawing of the torma that details its proportions and is set out just like a diagram of a stupa. There are also instructions about how to fill this special torma with rolls of mantras (*zung*) for each of the deities we've mentioned.

On top of the torma is a green horse's head, Hayagriva, to eliminate all obstacles. Above the horse's head is the lamp of wisdom in the form of a sun and moon. The flame of wisdom blazes from the lamp of wisdom to dispel the darkness of ignorance. There's a vertical white line on the horse's forehead, and the middle of its forelock should be red.

This torma is the main practice support for the Chimé Phakmé Nyingtik and is placed on the shrine. The visualization of the deities is accompanied by the usual emanation and regathering of rays of light. On the last day of the drupchen, we receive siddhis from the supports of the enlightened body, speech, mind, qualities and activities, and the last we receive are from this torma.

If I didn't tell you this, you wouldn't know, right? I didn't know any of it either until someone told me. In 1980, Dilgo Khyentse Rinpoche did a six-month Chimé Phakmé Nyingtik retreat at Phuntsok Ling in Bhutan and asked me to make a Chimé Phakmé Nyingtik torma. I already knew how to make tormas and I also knew that to make a specific torma all you do is copy an example. But on that occasion, he told me which deities relate to the different parts of the torma. That's when I received this meditation instruction from him.

The best kyerim practitioners can probably visualize one thousand buddhas in each grain of wheat used to make the torma—at least, that's what people say. But let's be clear about this: for myself, I really don't know. All we can do is try our best to bring these details to mind. *Meditating* on them might be a bit difficult, but we can at least think about this visualization. We may not be able to actualise "hundreds of thousands, millions, billions and so on" of deities, but we can evoke a sense of them. When Dilgo Khyentse Rinpoche gave me the instruction on torma, I asked, "Can we really meditate like that?" "Yes, of course!" he replied.

APPENDICES

Brief Answers to Questions on Chimé Phakmé Nyingtik, Beginning with Approach and Accomplishment

by Jamyang Khyentse Wangpo

Om svasti siddhi

When you arrive at the approach practice in the Chimé Phakmé Nyingtik, there are many ways of structuring the different phases of practice such as the ordinary approach practice uniting approach, accomplishment and activities for those who meditate mostly on an aspirational level, or drawing from the chest of the four branches of approach and accomplishment for the extraordinary practice on the level of flawless perfection[110] and so on. However, the long sadhana of the Chimé Phakmé Nyingtik briefly mentions the three phases of approach, accomplishment and activities.

Length of Practice

The sadhana also speaks of the three ways to measure them: time, number and signs. The text says that practitioners of greatest capacity should practise approach for three weeks, accomplishment for one week and activity for one day which, including receiving the siddhis, makes one month. Those of medium capacity should multiply that by three, making a total of three months. Practitioners with lesser capacity should therefore practise for six months.

In terms of numbers, we also distinguish practitioners of superior, medium and lesser capacities. Although it roughly takes the same amount of time, generally when you focus on the number of mantras you accumulate, the minimum should be one hundred thousand for each of the ten syllables of the main deity mantra, making one million; seven hundred thousand of the nineteen-syllable approach mantra of the combined practice; four hundred thousand of the jnanasattva and four hundred thousand of the nirmanasattva mantras; one hundred thousand of each of the accomplishment mantras of the four Taras; and forty thousand of each of the mantras of the four Gatekeeper Taras for the activity. This is the minimum number of mantras practitioners of medium capacity should recite, and that should take three months to accomplish. So the number of recitations for those of superior and lesser capacity are easy to work out.

For mere familiarization with the practice, you should recite four hundred thousand for the main deity's ten-syllable mantra; one hundred thousand for the combined practice; forty thousand for the jnanasattva and forty thousand for the nirmanasattva mantras; ten thousand of each for the accomplishment mantras; and however much you can manage in one day for each of the mantras of the four Gatekeeper Taras for activity. These numbers are based on the speed of those of superior capacity.

In terms of signs, the best, next best and least good are as usual.

Receiving the Siddhis

Concerning the way to receive the siddhis, you can rely on the specific sequence of the drupchen arrangement. More simply, place on your shrine a new offering torma (*chötor*) and so on, and assemble siddhi substances early the next morning after completing the number of activity mantras. After the mantra recitation, say the offering and praise for a thousand recitations. The mantra to invoke the siddhis is the combined practice mantra followed by KAYA WAKA TSITTA and so on, which you should recite an appropriate number of times. Then offer confession with the *Inexpressible Ultimate Confession (Yeshe Kuchok)*. Say the descent of blessings that is in the sadhana text and the elaborate offering and praise prayers. Finally, recite the prayer called "requesting siddhis" in the sadhana that starts with, "OM Sublime Lady . . ." Actualising the usual visualizations, place the phumba on your head and take some of its water; place the nectar at your throat and drink some; place the long-life torma at your heart; eat some of the substances in the kapala and keep consuming what remains for a long time as usual. Then offer a large tsok and conclude the practice.

. . .

The Mandala

The mandala is the usual peaceful mandala with eight-level toranas. On the red pleasure terrace stand the sixteen offering goddesses. Even though the protectors of virtues such as the seventy-five glorious protectors gather in the worldly deities' perimeter that surrounds the mandala inside the vajra fence, when drawing the mandala you only need to draw the perimeter and you don't have to draw the implements of the deities.

. . .

The Lord of the Dance

As for the colour of the body of the male consort, the Lord of the Dance, the text says,

> As her natural radiance the supreme skilful means, the
> Lord of the Dance . . .

Accordingly, the appearing aspect of skilful means arises from her light. So fundamentally he is white. However, here the male and female deities are together in reversed union; and as it is explained that the desire of the male is greater than that of the female, he should be visualized as red in colour, because he is full of desire. When painting the deities, this colour should also be used.

. . .

Ushnisha Vijaya

Ushnisha Vijaya's right hand is in the gesture of granting refuge and is poised on her right knee, forming the threatening mudra and holding the hook that gathers nectar. Her left hand in the mudra of supreme giving at the level of her heart holds a long-life vase from which she pours a stream of nectar. Her feet are loosely crossed in the sattvasana.[111]

Should you wish to draw or carve the deity, you can place in the hand in the mudra of supreme giving the stem of an utpala flower that blossoms at ear level, but you can also raise the hand which forms the mudra of supreme giving.

• • •

The Four Gatekeeper Taras

The four Taras, one at each of the four gates, are in a dancing posture with their right legs bent in the half-lotus dancing posture. Their right arms are extended, their right hands rest on their right knees in the gesture of bestowing refuge and they brandish their respective hand implements (iron hook and so on) with the threatening mudra. Their left hands in the gesture of supreme generosity are at their hearts holding the stems of utpala flowers which blossom at the level of their left ears.

• • •

Rotation of the Mantra Garland

Generally, we visualize the encircling mantra mala as follows: during the approach practice, we focus on visualizing the arrangement of the mantra mala; during the close approach practice, we visualize the mantra rotating; during the accomplishment stage, we visualize the palanquin; and during the great accomplishment stage, we visualize the emanation and reabsorption of rays of light. Yet it is enough to only visualize its arrangement when practising essentially. In most of the Mother Tantra cycles and when you practise female deities, the syllables are usually arranged counterclockwise. But in this sadhana, the mantra should be arranged in a clockwise direction just like the sadhanas of the Sarma tantras. The root mantra, the combined mantra, the jnanasattva mantra and the nirmanasattva mantra are all arranged in a clockwise direction.[112]

First concentrate on this visualization until it is completely familiar. Then you can start visualizing the emanation and reabsorption while reciting the mantra. Once the visualization of the mantra arrangement is extremely clear, we can imagine it turning. Visualize just the root mantra when reciting it. For the combined practice, visualize the root mantra with the rest of the combined mantra appended at the end. During the recitation of the jnanasattva mantra, keep the same visualization and change the core seed syllable: TAM becomes HRIH, encircled by Amitayus' mantra. At the heart of the nirmanasattva, at the centre of the sun and moon locket, visualize the syllable DROOM surrounded by her mantra mala. For the approach and activity mantras also, it is sufficient to visualize the individual core seed syllable of each deity (TAM, DROOM, HRIH, HUNG and DZA, HUNG, BAM, HO) at their hearts on a lotus and a moon in the colour of their respective deity and surrounded by the mantra garland.

· · ·

Mantra Recitation

For the approach, focus only on the approach visualization. You don't need to actualise the accomplishment and activity visualizations. In terms of mantra also, begin with only accumulating the ten-syllable mantra. At the end of the session, add the recitation of a few of the other approach mantras.

For the accomplishment, briefly recite the mantras of the main deity, jnanasattva and nirmanasattva. Once you visualize each deity clearly, add the visualization of the emanation and reabsorption of rays of light from the heart of the main deity to invoke her retinue. First concentrate on accumulating Vajra Tara's mantra for most of your practice session and recite the three others only briefly at the end of the session. Once you have completed the accumulation of Vajra Tara's mantra, you only need to recite it a few times before concentrating on accumulating Ratna Tara's mantra. And so on. You don't need to meditate on the activity phase. At this point, you can recite the combined mantra if you want to.

For the activity, divide the day into four sessions. Following your daily schedule, during the early morning session for example, briefly recite the approach and accomplishment and actualise their visualizations. Rays of light stream out from the five deities (the main deity and the four Taras in the retinue) to invoke Hook Tara's wisdom mind. Actualise the pacifying activity visualization while mainly reciting her mantra and recite the three others briefly at the end of the session. After sunrise, practise mainly Noose Tara's mantra and so on in the same way.

• • •

Drupchö

During a Chimé Phakmé Nyingtik drupchö for example, if it is an ordinary, simple drupchö, we may recite the main ten-syllable mantra one thousand times during each session. Accordingly, we should also recite three hundred mantras of the combined practice, the jnanasattva and the nirmanasattva, one hundred for each of the four Taras and just twenty-one recitations for each of the four activities.

If you perform the practice mainly for long-life accomplishment, recite the ten-syllable mantra three hundred times and the mantra of the combined practice one thousand times since it is the mantra and clear visualization of the long-life accomplishment, while the other mantras are as before. The rest is the same as before.

• • •

Mantras for Daily Practice

When you practise the daily sadhana to maintain the continuous flow of the practice, you can recite only the approach mantra and omit the accomplishment and activity mantras. As a main mantra of approach, the mantra of the combined practice is also very good. Having said that, to practise more elaborately by reciting and visualizing briefly the accomplishment and activity is not only *not* a fault but is very good, since approach is the foundation that comes at the beginning of approach, accomplishment and activity. So after the approach, it is good each time to practise some accomplishment and also a little bit of the activity.

• • •

The Quicksilver that Accomplishes All

The "quicksilver that accomplishes all" is the substance of alchemy and rejuvenation (*chulen*), white like an autumn moon, shining bright as the sun, sparkling and gleaming with all kinds of auspicious patterns like svastikas and coils of joy and symbols turning to the right. Its power is such that whoever it touches can be transformed so they then possess the strength of an elephant, the life span of the sun and the moon and an indestructible body with the vigour of a sixteen year old. If it touches iron, the iron is transmuted into gold. If it is scattered on a dead, withered tree, the tree will immediately burst into life and grow leaves, flowers and fruits. So in your meditation, imagine these forms and images gathering as the blazing, brilliant splendour of great bliss.

. . .

The Great Practice Torma

Although a yellow scroll revealed as an earth terma and deciphered by the great tertön Chokgyur Lingpa is the source of a detailed presentation of the structure of practice focusing on the great practice torma,[113] this text is only recited during drupchens and is not necessary otherwise. First you need to study the drawing of the torma very closely, otherwise the preparation and building of the torma will be difficult.

. . .

Shrine Set-up

In general, when you do the practice, lay out an image of the mandala if you have one, or make a mandala with heaps in number equal to the number of deities in the mandala made of grains. You mainly need a kapala filled with pills, and since it is a good practice support specific to this practice, you don't necessarily need the practice torma. The offering torma is the usual blazing jewel (*rinchen barwa*) torma. You can also have a single torma instead of the practice and offering tormas, to which you apply the four considerations and so on.[114] This torma should be in the bejewelled form (*rinpoche ngawa*). The long-life torma should be made of flour of unparched barley grains (*tsampa*) kneaded with alcohol shaped into a usual vase and surrounded with pills made of dough, all painted in red.

Kaya ayushah dhadzati shtantu

The Visualization for the Mantra Recitation of the Phases of Approach, Accomplishment and Activity of Chimé Phakmé Nyingtik

by Dilgo Khyentse Rinpoche

I. VISUALIZATION FOR THE MANTRA RECITATION IN THE APPROACH PHASE

Visualize yourself vividly and clearly in the divine form of Jetsun Arya Tara. In your heart is the jnanasattva Amitayus, brilliant white, alone without a consort and with all the sambhogakaya adornments. In his heart on a white lotus blossom sits a hollow sphere composed of the sun below and moon above, within which stands the core[115] seed syllable TAM, and around it the ten vajra syllables arranged in a clockwise direction. Keep your mind focused attentively on this and recite the mantra.

Reciting the mantra invokes and inspires the wisdom mind of Amitayus, and from the syllable TAM and the mantra mala, limitless and inconceivable rays of light radiate and pour out from the jewel on the ushnisha of Jetsun Arya Tara's head. Within the expanse of this light appears the nirmanasattvas, the emanations Ushnisha Vijaya, their bodies dazzling white in colour. Their right hands in the gesture of granting refuge are poised on their right knees and form the threatening mudra as they hold a hook in a gathering manner. Their left hands at the level of their hearts in the mudra of supreme giving hold a long-life vase from which they pour a stream of nectar. Their feet are loosely crossed in the sattvasana, and they preside on a lotus blossom and moon disc seat. In a blaze of light and dazzling rays, countless emanations of Ushnisha Vijaya like the specks of dust in sunbeams stream out uninterruptedly above, below and in every possible direction.

They go to the deities of the root mandala, the four Taras and the four gatekeepers, as well as to the buddhas and bodhisattvas of the whole of space and time, the yidam deities of the six classes of tantra, the hosts of dakas and dakinis in the sacred places and the ocean-like throng of dharma protectors bound by their solemn vajra pledge and gather the blessing, capacity and strength of all their inconceivable qualities of wisdom, love and power. They go throughout the whole outer, inanimate environment of this world, gathering the vital energy of its five elements. They go to the living inhabitants within and gather the vital energy of their longevity, merit, prosperity and wealth, charisma and excellent auspicious signs both spiritual and worldly.

All these wonderful qualities combine to form the substance of alchemy and rejuvenation (*rasayana*) called the "quicksilver that accomplishes all". White like an autumn moon shining as bright as the sun, it sparkles and gleams with all kinds of auspicious patterns like svastikas and coils of joy and symbols turning clockwise. Its power is such that it can transform whoever it touches so they possess the strength of an elephant, the life span of the sun or moon and an indestructible body with the vigour of a sixteen year old. If it touches iron, it is transmuted into gold. If it scatters onto a dead and withered tree, it will immediately burst into life with leaves and fruit and flowers.

So imagine these forms and images gathering as the blazing, brilliant splendour of great bliss and dissolving into your body[116] and into all the practice substances, long-life pills, amrita, rakta, torma and offerings. As a result, imagine that blessings, radiance, energy and power all shine out in glory like flowers bursting into blossom after the rain. As you visualize this, recite just the ten-syllable vajra mantra.

At the end, maintain the same visualization and recite the mantra that combines approach, accomplishment and activity all in one. When reciting the mantra of the jnanasattva Amitayus, you keep up the same visualization while the core syllable TAM transforms into a HRIH, around which his mantra is arrayed. In the case of the emanation Ushnisha Vijaya, visualize that in her heart in the centre of a locket formed of the sun and moon is a DROOM with the mantra mala arranged around it.

II. VISUALIZATION FOR THE MANTRA RECITATION
IN THE ACCOMPLISHMENT PHASE

From the forms of all the deities of the mandala, the light of wisdom streams out and returns as before, making the quicksilver-like substance composed of the vital essence of the entire inanimate and animate worlds dissolve into the principal deities and their entourage. Through this, their bodies experience the full intensity of uncontaminated great bliss; their speech resounds in the stirring, inspiring majestic tones of invincible vajra-like mantra like bees swarming around a broken hive and their minds rest in serene equanimity in unchanging samadhi, the supreme enlightened intention of pacifying, increasing, magnetising and subjugating.

As a result, imagine that basic impure phenomena—the five skandhas and five elements, sense-fields, sense organs and objects—are all awakened into the mandala of the complete "three vajra seats" of the five families of Tara. The great wisdom mandala of all-pervading purity where enlightened body, speech, mind, qualities and activity are inseparable is activated in the everlasting flow of inexhaustible adornment.[117]

Visualizing vividly the core syllable of each of the four Taras—TAM, DROOM, HRIH and HUNG—in the centre of a locket formed of the sun and moon resting on a lotus blossom, recite the mantras of the three principal deities and the four Taras.

III. VISUALIZATION FOR THE MANTRA
RECITATION IN THE ACTIVITY PHASE

The visualization during the mantra recitation for the three principal deities is to imagine that compassionate rays of light stream out from the three deities and invoke the four Taras to rest in serene equanimity in the enlightened intention of the four activities. Then rays of light from the four Taras' samadhi of pacifying, increasing, magnetising and subjugating invoke the four emissaries at the four gates who accomplish the enlightened activities. They in turn emanate white, yellow, red and black emissaries that fill the whole sky and stream out like particles of dust in sunbeams. Without any limit to their action, they provide whatever beings need by means of the four activities: illness and harmful influences are pacified, long life and merit are increased, the three realms are magnetised with the four types of aspiration and enemies and obstructors are utterly destroyed—these are the four ordinary activities. Then harmful actions and obscurations are pacified, the power of rigpa is increased, the wind-mind is mastered and dualistic grasping is utterly destroyed—these are the four enlightened activities. Consider that they are all brought to completion. Jamyang Khyentse Wangpo said that you should do the peaceful recitation before daybreak, the recitation for increasing at sunrise, the practice for magnetising at twilight and the wrathful recitation at night.

Vajrasattva Mantra Recitation

from *The Confession and Fulfillment of Vima Ladrup*
as arranged by Jamgön Kongtrul Lodrö Thaye

A

Upon a lotus and moon on the crown of my head

Is the glorious guru, Samantabhadra in the form of Vajradhara,

Greatly blissful Vajrasattva,

White and luminous, holding a vajra and a bell.

Adorned with silks and jewel ornaments,

He embraces his consort, his self-radiance.

Blazing with the major and minor marks,

He abides with his two legs in vajra posture.

From the mantra garland circling

The syllable HUNG upon a moon disc in his heart,

Light emanates making offerings to the buddhas and their heirs,

Purifying the obscurations of all beings,

Placing the world and beings in the state of great vajra bliss.

The light returns into the mantra as a stream of amrita,

Which now pours forth a stream of nectar, an abundant flow of bodhichitta.

As it enters through the aperture of Brahma on top of my head

And fills my body, it purifies illnesses, negative influences, negative actions and obscurations,

And grants me the empowerments and accomplishments.

Concentrate on this visualization and recite the hundred-syllable mantra as many times as you can.

At the end, you can do the confession and promise more elaborately by reciting the Rudra's Lament, *"OM Great compassionate one, the conqueror Vajrasattva . . ."*[118] *and so on. Or more simply, you can say the usual prayers, "O protector! In my ignorance . . ." and so on as follow.*

O protector! In my ignorance and delusion
I have gone against and corrupted my samaya.
Guru protector, be my refuge!
Chief of all the mandalas, vajra holder,
Embodiment of great compassion,
Chief of all living beings, in you I take refuge!

I confess all my impairments of the root and branch samayas of body, speech and mind. I implore you: let my negative actions, obscurations, wrong doing and downfalls—all my flaws—be completely cleansed and purified!

At these words of mine, Vajrasattva is pleased and smiling, grants me the purification of all my negative actions and wrong doing. Granting his forgiveness, he melts into light and dissolves into me. As a result, I rest in the natural state free of object, thought or word as my mind merges inseparably with his wisdom mind.

APPENDIX 4:

The Meaning of Sundok and Tenshuk:

The Traditional Long-Life Ceremony

by Tulku Orgyen Tobgyal

According to the Tibetan calendar, tomorrow is the fourth day of the sixth month of the Water Sheep year in the seventeenth cycle and the anniversary of Buddha's turning of the wheel of the dharma for the first time. We are currently in the middle of a Chimé Phakmé Nyingtik drupchen. Our main reason for doing this drupchen is to spread the teachings of the Buddha far and wide and to promote the well-being and happiness of all sentient beings. But we also do it for ourselves, so that we may be free from illness, live long lives and quickly attain the state of omniscience free from suffering—enlightenment. A very special feature of the Chimé Phakmé Nyingtik is that it is the supreme practice we do to protect all the great holders of the teachings and to lengthen their lives. It's a terma, so it contains the vajra words of Guru Rinpoche, Vimalamitra and Shri Singha. We therefore have many important reasons for performing the drupchen of Chimé Phakmé Nyingtik here in Lerab Ling. Perhaps our greatest reason for doing it is to ensure the long life of Sogyal Rinpoche. So it has become a kind of tradition that every year within the framework of the Chimé Phakmé Nyingtik drupchen, we offer Sogyal Rinpoche a long-life ceremony. This ceremony has two aspects: the tenshuk to request that he remains with us for a long time and the sundok to turn back the summons of the dakinis. Here in Lerab Ling, our tradition is to practise both.

SUNDOK

The sundok, or turning back the summons of the dakinis, is a ceremony we do for great practitioners who are holders of the teachings. These great masters choose to be reborn in this world from Akanishtha as a result of their aspiration prayers and great compassion and sentient beings' karma, to fulfill their vision of spreading the teachings of the Buddha and helping all sentient beings by bringing them true happiness. These great masters are the expression of the two wisdom kayas. They are great practitioners who have accomplished the level of Vajradhara, the Lord of the sixth family, whose manifestation is determined by wisdom, karma, the world with which they are connected and samaya and who are leaders of the dakinis. When they appear in the world to help sentient beings, they come in the form of a nirmanakaya—a *tulku* in Tibetan.

In Jamgön Kongtrul Rinpoche's autobiography, he describes going to a pure land and visiting a large palace inside which were billions and billions of dakinis, all making offerings to a stupa that had been built to enshrine the corpse of a great master. Jamgön Kongtrul asked the dakinis whose relics were in the stupa and was told that they were those of Pawo Töpe Dumbu Tsal, the chief of the dakinis, lord of mahasiddhas and an incarnation of the Lord of Secrets, Vajrapani. This is who they were making offerings to. The dakinis also said that from time to time, Pawo Töpe Dumbu Tsal would appear in this world with the express purpose of helping receptive beings and that he also visited other buddha fields to help those living there. But at the same time, he would manifest in the form of relics which do not speak and that whenever his emanation returned to the stupa, it dissolved into the relics. Pawo Töpe Dumbu Tsal would then turn the wheel of the dharma for the dakinis and accomplish infinite enlightened activities for their benefit.

> "How long does he stay in the buddha realms?" asked Jamgön Kongtrul.
> "At most, one hundred human years," replied the dakinis.
> "Where is he now?" he asked.
> "In Tibet," they said.

This indicates that Pawo Töpe Dumbu Tsal was the basis from which Jamgön Kongtrul himself manifested.

So when the incarnations of these great beings—tulkus—are reborn in this world, if their students have broken samaya or circumstances work against them and they cannot help sentient beings or they are faced with obstacles or negative influences, the wisdom dakinis invite them to return to the pure realms. They also summon these great beings at the end of their lives once they've completed their activities in that world. If a great master's life span is already exhausted and he has also completed his activities, then the sundok practice won't help. But if a master has not yet completed his activities and their life span is not exhausted, by doing a sundok practice to ask the dakinis not to summon him, any obstacles to his life can be eliminated. This is why we're doing a sundok, to turn back or reverse the summons of the dakinis.

The person who leads the practice and offers the sundok should be a vajra master who is confident in their realization of the view and in meditation, with the assistance of worldly dakinis of the five families. These worldly dakinis will help the master remain in this world after the wisdom dakinis' invitation has been repelled. Great masters who have attained a high view and meditation must increase the three gatherings and the three blazes related to the channels, inner wind and energies, and to do that they rely on dakinis whose nature is wisdom—they are the most important. Of the many groups of five we talk about in Buddhism—the five wisdoms, five aggregates, five elements and so on—the most important are the five categories of wisdom dakinis. A great vajra master will invite the wisdom dakinis of the five families by using the power of various substances, mantras, mudras and samadhi and by making outer, inner and secret offerings to them. The offerings include tormas, serkyem and offerings of praise. He also requests that the dakinis carry out the activities necessary to help the master live a long life so that he is able to remain in this world for a long time.

The teachings of the Secret Mantra Vajrayana are rich with skilful means and we use the power of these skilful means to make an effigy of the master to whom the tenshuk is offered. The effigy is then blessed with substances, mantra and samadhi before it's sent away. Only then is the vajra master himself invited to sit on a lion throne marked with a vajra. We visualize the vajra master as Amitayus and invite Amitayus to merge as one with him, then make offerings. Amongst the offerings we make are substances that have been blessed by the vajra master through the practice—in this case, the Chimé Phakmé Nyingtik—for example the long-life vase, long-life torma, long-life pills, long-life alcohol and so on. Then the practice of summoning longevity is performed. This is all part of the sundok practice, then you do the tenshuk.

TENSHUK

As we want the master to remain in the world for long time, we must pray to him to ask him to stay. Praying is extraordinarily important. For example, it was only when disciples of the Buddha Shakyamuni prayed to him and asked him to remain longer in the world that he extended the length of his own life. Therefore, praying and requesting is very important. And to support our request, we offer a mandala. Just saying the words without making an offering to show you mean what you say is like the western custom of just saying "thank you" when someone has done something for you and not accompanying your words with a meaningful gesture.

Once the mandala has been offered, you must offer representations of the enlightened body, speech, mind, qualities and activities. To request that the master's body remains forever stable and unchanging, you must offer an enlightened body. As the Bhagavan Buddha Shakyamuni said, "In this World of Endurance, in Sukhavati, there is a buddha whose 'life is infinite' (which is the meaning of Amitayus). Not only is his life never-ending, but he has the ability to eliminate all of life's obstacles." So by offering a statue of Amitayus, what you are doing is asking the master to live as long as Amitayus lives. So we also pray, "May you live as long as Buddha Amitayus."

For example, in our ordinary perception, in the World of Endurance, the Land of Great Bliss has existed for many kalpas, long before this world. Buddha Shakyamuni spoke about Sukhavati for two weeks to explain what it is like and paint a clear picture of the features of this pure land. So basically, that's the reason we offer this particular representation of the body.

Just the body of the master isn't enough really to help beings. To truly help, he must be able to turn the wheel of the dharma. So we must also offer a representation of enlightened speech since speech is the main enlightened activity buddhas use to help sentient beings. Since the Buddha's inexhaustible wheel of ornament of enlightened speech appears in the form of letters and syllables, the representation we offer is a book.

Buddhas manifest the three aspects of enlightened body, speech and mind, of which the main aspect is mind. The support for enlightened mind—the unmoving primordial purity of dharmakaya—is the stupa. Of all the representations of the Buddha in this world, the most sacred and important is the stupa. Enlightened mind is the ability to relate completely and precisely to the wisdom of the Buddha.

The enlightened body, speech and mind can be divided into different groups of enlightened qualities. The qualities of the Buddha are his abilities to fulfill the wishes of all sentient beings exactly as they conceived them. These qualities are everywhere and everlasting, and we offer the vase as a symbol. According to Indian lore, there's a wish-fulfilling vase that can manifest everything that we may wish for.

The symbol of enlightened activity is the vajra. The vajra represents immutability throughout all four times and is the symbol of the continuously turning wheel of enlightened activities. Vajras have a hub in their centre. When the hub is surrounded by four vajras, one in each of the four directions, it is described as a crossed vajra. The central hub represents the fundamental nature of all phenomena and manifests as the four types of activity—pacifying, enriching, magnetising and subjugating—which can be divided further to make twelve aspects and so on.

Each support of body, speech, mind, quality and activity is offered with a katak the colour of its respective buddha family. To say a prayer or make a request, you must use your voice, you must speak. Since Rigpa students are experts at long-life practices because you recite so many long-life prayers again and again, you should know the meaning of such prayers which should be recited at that point.

In any case, the person who makes the request shouldn't be faking it, it should be genuine and come from the depth of his or her heart. If you're just mouthing words without thinking about what they mean, you're little more than a sweet talker. If you don't agree with what you are saying but still say it, that's deception. Mind is the most important aspect, so we must make our request with deep, heartfelt conviction. For the mind to be pure, you must confess and purify all the thoughts that make your mind busy, all your negative thoughts and actions, all breakages of samayas and all kinds of pollution. Be sure to purify through confession practice. Basically, to be able to make this request, the students' devotion and samayas must be utterly stable. If you pray with a completely pure mind, there's no doubt that your prayers will be granted. As it is said, all the qualities of the Buddha arise from aspiration prayers. Therefore, praying is extremely important.

In order to express the unstained purity and stability of our mind, we hold a katak of white silk. White is a colour that hasn't been changed, hasn't been distorted—it's completely clean.

When we offer this prayer to the glorious protector, the glorious guru whose nature of mind is compassion, he is moved by our request and replies, "If it will help sentient beings and the teachings of the dharma, I will remain in this world for one hundred and eight years or more."

This long-life ceremony will work if we create the perfect circumstances—the perfect place, the perfect teacher, the perfect assembly, the perfect teaching and the perfect time. Then it will help.

So this is what we now need to do. But if we do it just because it's what we do every year, it will become another empty tradition and there will be nothing extraordinary about it—like eating dinner every night. Therefore, you should know and understand what must be done and then actually do it.

After the great teacher agrees to live for one hundred and eight years or longer, we must celebrate! Why? Because it means the teachings of the Buddha will remain in the world and will spread. So we celebrate all the happiness and well-being that will result from those teachings. And we also celebrate for ourselves because the lama is the source of everything good. As he is the source of all the good circumstances we experience in this life and in the next, the lama's long life is very positive and very important to us. This is why we thank him for agreeing to remain by offering a mandala. And if we'd like to, we can also make other offerings. If you don't have anything to offer, just to rejoice is already extremely good. We celebrate by drinking tea and eating rice; that's the celebration. Actually, eating rice is an Indian way of celebrating, not Tibetan. When Tibetans have a party, they eat meat.

Gendun Chöpel wrote that before the Buddha's teachings came to Tibet, Tibetans would celebrate by killing a yak then drinking its blood and eating its meat. But we don't do that anymore. Now we eat rice and drink tea. When people are happy, they sing and dance, don't they? Even animals run around, leap up and down and wag their tails when they're happy. They also make a noise, for example when a sheep is happy—perhaps because it can see its father or mother—it *baas*. Therefore, there's no reason not to chant.

I felt it was important to say all this today so that tomorrow during the ceremony, you will be able to recognize the different stages of the practice. I don't expect you to remember everything, but if you can just remember ten percent, it would good.

APPENDIX 5:

Advice for Offering a Short Tenshuk

by Tulku Orgyen Tobgyal

Question: Rinpoche, how do we do a tenshuk ceremony slightly simpler than following Jamyang Khyentse Wangpo's tenshuk ceremony manual called "Sweet Droplets of Amrita from the Mouths of Siddhas"?[119]

Do the Chimé Phakmé Nyingtik, and at the point where you all enjoy the tsok, the lama to whom you wish to offer the tenshuk should join you. As an offering, ask him to sit on the throne, then immediately meditate on Amitayus. If you like, you can do the self-visualization and descent of blessings mentioned in the text, but you don't have to. Do the practice for summoning longevity,[120] offer the long-life vase, pills and nectar, offer the mandala and then the supports of enlightened body, speech, mind, qualities and activities and finally the long-life prayers. This is how you practise.

Should you want an even shorter practice, follow the Sutrayana approach to tenshuk. Invite the lama and the moment he sits on the throne, offer a mandala and representations of enlightened body, speech and mind— omitting the offerings of enlightened qualities and activities—and recite the long-life prayers. These days, this is how short tenshuks are offered to His Holiness Dalai Lama and other great masters.

For a really short long-life ceremony, once the lama is sitting on the throne you should present the seven-branch offering from *The King of Aspiration Prayers: Samantabhadra's "Aspiration to Good Actions"*,[121] then offer the mandala, representations of enlightened body, speech and mind and long-life prayers. It's simple enough. I don't need to keep going on and on about it.

Actually, the text Jamyang Khyentse Wangpo composed will guide you through the long-life ceremony used for important lamas as well as for other people. In the text, Khyentse Wangpo indicates how to do a long and elaborate practice, a medium-length ceremony and a short one. He also tells you how to do it with or without a sundok. It's all there in the practice in the small print. You're asking me all these questions, but you haven't yet looked at the text! The other questions you ask don't make any sense at all. This one for example, "Can you conduct the ceremony without a vajra master?" What can I tell you? All these activities must be led by a vajra master.

Setting up the Mandala of Chimé Phakmé Nyingtik

According to *A Drop of Moonlight Nectar*
by Jamgön Kongtrul Lodrö Taye

by Ane Chökyi Drolma

ESSENTIAL ARRANGEMENT

For an essential shrine you will need the following substances and articles.

Shrine

—A Chimé Phakmé Nyingtik poster or thangka consecrated in the proper way
—A Chimé Phakmé Nyingtik mandala to place under the torma
—A Chimé Phakmé Nyingtik torma, or a simple white offering torma
—Kapalas containing amrita and rakta
—A tripod as support for the kapala or the small bowl
—A kapala or a small bowl containing the white pills made of the 12 substances or, if that is not possible, of tsampa with amrita
—A red cloth to cover the white pills, folded 8 times (if possible)
—A set of offering bowls and lamp
—A container to keep the remainder for the duration of the recitation

The torma can be in front or behind, whatever is easier. Offering bowls can be in front or around, whatever is most convenient.

Seat

—Kusha grass to make a crossed vajra
—Rice for the svastika

You'll also need vajra, bell and damaru.

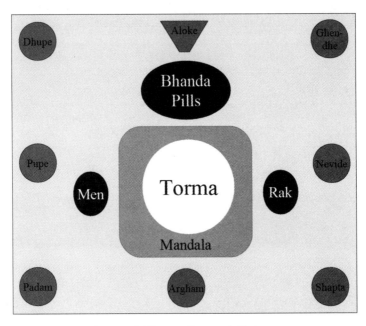

Approach Phase—Essential Shrine

For the accomplishment phase:

—Place a phumba containing the twenty-five substances[122] with a
white cloth tied at the neck to the right of the kapala
—To the left, put a stand made of precious substances that contains
the long-life torma
—Refresh amrita, torma and rakta

The arrangement for the activity phase is the same.

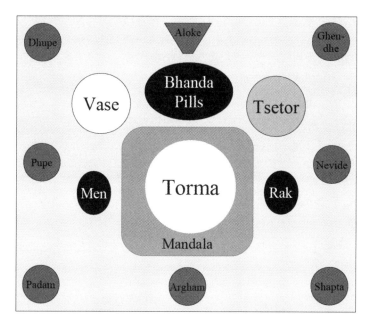

Accomplishment Phase—Essential Shrine

ELABORATE

If you want to make your shrine more elaborate, the following is recommended by Ngawang Tsultrim, the ritual master at Trulshik Rinpoche's seat Thubten Chöling, but it must be understood that the essential shrine set up is complete.

Shrine

—Picture of the protectors
—Photograph of your master
—*Lebum* (activity vase), plus a piece of red cloth for the neck (The lebum can be placed on the practitioner's table.)
—*Tsebum* (long-life vase)
—*Dadar* (long-life arrow)
—Long-life nectar, which is amrita in alcohol or dry, inside a kapala

Furthermore, you can also add:

—Statues of the deities, if you wish to do so
—Text of the practice
—Stupa and crystal

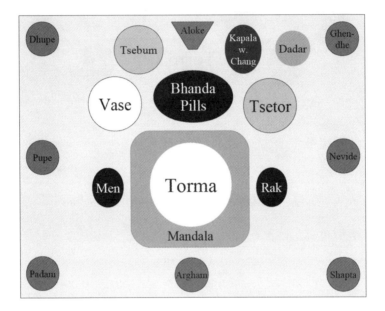

Elaborate Shrine

NOTES

1. www.all-otr.org.
2. https://www.lotsawahouse.org/topics/chime-pakme-nyingtik/.
3. https://www.siddharthasintent.org/resources/practice-resources/.
4. "The Life of Jamyang Khyentse Wangpo". https://www.lotsawahouse.org/tibetan-masters /orgyen-tobgyal-rinpoche/biography-khyentse-wangpo. "The Life of Jamyang Khyentse Chökyi Lodrö". https://www.lotsawahouse.org/tibetan -masters/orgyen-tobgyal-rinpoche/biography-khyentse-lodro.
5. See Appendix 1, page 306.
6. "Tantra of the Union of Sun and Moon" (*nyi ma dang zla ba kha sbyor*) in volume 4 of the *Seventeen Tantras* (*rgyud bcu bdun*), Adzom Ed., text Ma, page 8a, line 3.
7. Nagarjuna, *Root Stanzas of the Middle Way,* chapter 24, verse 19, lines 1–2.
8. "'The Melody of the Auspicious Conch,' The Life Story Supplication to the Incarnated Great Tertön Chokgyur Lingpa", in Schmidt, M., *Precious Songs of Awakening,* Rangjung Yeshe Publications, 2014.
9. Śāntideva. *The Way of the Bodhisattva,* Chapter 7, verse 14, page 99.
10. This teaching forms our Chapter 1, pages 17–22.
11. Khenpo Petse taught the *Secret Essence Tantra* from 13 to 29 August 1997 in Lerab Ling when Tulku Orgyen Tobgyal was visiting.
12. Orgyen Tobgyal added that a detailed explanation of this would involve a great many things, for example the basis of purification, the methods of purification and so on. For a short presentation, see for example Shechen Gyaltsap IV, "Illuminating Jewel Wisdom", pages 133–136. Khyentse Chökyi Lodrö related them to the palace; see page 98.
13. See note 19 below.
14. "Dilgo Khyentse Rinpoche gave an incredible commentary on the Chimé Phakmé Nyingtik that fills an entire volume, and it's all about Dzogchen", Orgyen Tobgyal said.
15. "Essence of Wisdom Nectar", in Jamyang Khyentse Wangpo et al., *The Great Accomplishment Ritual of the Heart Essence of Deathless Ārya Tārā,* Appendix 6, pages 173–182.
16. "Greatly Increasing Wisdom", in Jamyang Khyentse Wangpo et al., *The Great Accomplishment Ritual of the Heart Essence of Deathless Ārya Tārā,* Appendix 7, pages 185–196.
17. "'Treasure Trove of Wisdom'—the framework liturgy for the great accomplishment ritual", in Jamyang Khyentse Wangpo et al., *The Great Accomplishment Ritual of the Heart Essence of Deathless Ārya Tārā,* pages 53–117.
18. Also see note 65 below.
19. Wish-Fulfilling Wheel's consort is sometimes said to be the long-life deity Amitayus, sometimes Avalokiteshvara whose name he bears (see note 89 below). Amitayus is the dharmakaya of the lotus family, and Avalokiteshvara the sambhogakaya of the lotus family, so they are not like two different individuals. In his teachings, Tulku Orgyen Tobgyal sometimes mentions Avalokiteshvara like here, sometimes Amitayus and sometimes both.
20. The translation I used is weaved into Tulku Orgyen Tobgyal's explanations on Chapter 4, pages 42–58. You can find a very similar translation on lotsawahouse.org (https:// www.lotsawahouse.org/topics/chime-pakme-nyingtik/), and another translation in *The Great Accomplishment Ritual of the Heart Essence of Deathless Ārya Tārā.*

21 See note 19 above.

22 Assembly of wisdom deities, I invite you. Please come!
    I offer you outer, inner and secret offerings.
    I praise your body, speech, mind, quality and activity.
    I confess careless transgressions and errors.
    MAHA AMRITA BALINGTA RAKTA KHAHI

23 See Chapter 8, Explanation of *Activities for Uncovering Primordial Wisdom,* the Root
    Sadhana of the Chimé Phakmé Nyingtik, pages 109–184.

24 See lotsawahouse.org (https://www.lotsawahouse.org/topics/chime-pakme-nyingtik/).

25 See Chapter 6, *A Drop of Moonlight Nectar,* pages 80–88.

26 Patrul Chokyi Wangpo, "The Melody of Brahma Reveling in the Three Realms: Key
    Points for Meditating on the Four Stakes that Bind the Life Force" in *Deity, Mantra,
    and Wisdom,* Snow Lion, 2006, pages 81–96.

27 Padmasambhava, Jamgon Kongtrul, Jamyang Khyentse Wangpo and Chokgyur Lingpa.
    Light of Wisdom, Volume 1–5. Translated by Erik Pema Kunsang. Kathmandu: Rangjung
    Yeshe Publications, 1995–2013.

28 From the *Perfection of Wisdom in Eight Thousand Lines.*

29 See for example Padmasambhava and Jamgon Kongtrul. *Light of Wisdom, Volume 2*
    pages 87–106. Khyentse Chökyi Lodrö also mentions about them in his commentary,
    pages 97–106.

30 See note 19 above.

31 See note 59 below.

32 Buddhist cosmology understands the sun and the moon to be devas who are beings who
    have a very long life.

33 In Mahayoga there are two approaches: meditation on an aspirational level (*mos sgom*),
    and the flawless perfection of perpetual contemplation (*nges rdzogs*), which is the fast
    path of great practitioners who don't need to go through the stages of approach, accom-
    plishment and activities.

34 See note 16 above.

35 The Sanskrit phrase translates as, "Homage to the guru, the sublime Tara!"

36 Glorious root lama, precious one,
    Dwell on the lotus-seat on the crown of my head,
    Look upon me with the grace of your great compassion,
    Grant me the attainments of body, speech, and mind!

37 From *The Vajra Root Verses, from the Heart Essence of Venerable Tara,* a term revealed by
    Jamyamg Khentse Wangpo.

38 The three means of gratification or the three ways of pleasing or serving the teacher
    (*mnyes pa gsum*) are 1. offering our practice, 2. offering service with body and speech and
    3. material offerings.

39 Tib. *Drolme Zabtik,* or more commonly known as the *Zabtik Drolchok.*

40 See Appendix 3.

41 Jamyang Khyentse Wangpo wrote two texts; the translation of the shorter can be found
    online, on www.lotsawahouse.org.

42 "Mudra" here refers to the deity's form. HUNG is the seed of that form and has the
    nature of awareness rather than sound. (We are grateful to Khenchen Pema Sherab for
    clarifying this point.)

43 A "torana" is a decorative tympanum or archway found in Indian architecture. Sometimes, it is found above the doors and is then very much similar to a tympanum. In other cases, however, as with the torana of the Sanchi stupa, it is more like an arc de triomphe. The Tibetans translated the term as *tabab* (*rta babs*), literally the "place of dismounting a horse".

44 See Appendix 1, page 303.

45 These are the shravakas, pratyekabuddhas, bodhisattvas and buddhas.

46 From *Taking Care of Students, From the Mind Treasure of the Profound Essence of Tara* (*Drolme Zabtik*).

47 See note 73 below.

48 The idea is that these three recognitions are "carried over" from meditation into post-meditation.

49 Ibid.

50 This refers to the 18th chapter, which is said to have been added later.

51 The Chimé Phakmé Nyingtik sadhana, *Activities for Uncovering Primordial Wisdom.*

52 Cycle of practices focusing on Vimalamitra known as *Vima Ladrup.*

53 A "three parts kapala" is a skull cap showing bone sutures delineating three areas. There are one-part, two-part, three-part and so on, up to nine-part kapalas.

54 See page 184–186.

55 Such as making tsatsas, reading the sutras like the *Heap of Auspiciousness, Dispelling Darkness in the Ten Directions, the Eight Auspicious Ones, Long-Life Sutra,* offering tormas—the "four times one hundred", water torma, and so on.

56 "Intervening deity" refers to a deity that is not the actual deity of the sadhana being practised, but a deity that accomplishes specific activities from time to time in the practice.

57 See note 73 below.

58 Jamgön Kongtrul here repeats Jamyang Khyentse Wangpo's original instruction (see Appendix 1, page 303). It should be noted that on some thangkas of the Chimé Phakmé Nyingtik, including the one used as a practice support by Jamgön Kongtrul, it is the opposite: the right is at the level of the heart and the left on her knee. When I asked him, Trulshik Rinpoche laughed and said it doesn't really matter, and that he himself practises as indicated on the thangkas.

59 The "vajrasana" is the full lotus posture of male deities, and the posture when seating across them is the "sattvasana", seating with legs crossed in a loose way.

60 Even though Jamgön Kongtrul wrote, "Ho In the assembly of the Sublime Lady. . .", the first line of the confession section in the sadhana reads "Ho In the mandala of the Sublime Lady. . ."

61 The twenty-five ingredients that are prepared to make the content of the phumba are comprised of five sets of five substances. They are five medicines, the five grains, the five precious substances, the five fragrant substances and the five essences. (Most of the five sets have a different listing, so for further detail see Rigpa Shedra's on-line encyclopaedia, www.rigpawiki.org.)

62 That is, before receiving the siddhis when the accomplishment mandala is still there.

63 This is most certainly a reference to Jamyang Khyentse Wangpo's answers to questions about Chimé Phakmé Nyingtik that form the basis for Jamgön Kongtrul's *Retreat Manual,* and that we have translated in Appendix 1, page 195.

64 The translation is the previous chapter, Chapter 6, pages 115–128.

65 Tulku Orgyen Tobgyal, in answer to a question, said that if you want to do a retreat on the Chimé Phakmé Nyingtik, you need the elaborate empowerment. You cannot do the retreat just by receiving the short or medium-length empowerments which are long-life blessings.

66 See note 53 above.

67 See note 54 above.

68 The Tibetan word "*nyenpa*" implies familiarization, associating with or approaching and is sometimes translated as "approach". As His Holiness Sakya Gongma Trichen and Alak Zenkar Rinpoche have explained, in the past the approach practice mainly involved focusing on the visualization of the deity during the session, and the mantra was recited in between sessions. Nowadays however, mantra recitation is the standard practice to measure deity meditation. Most of our sadhanas advise us to recite a certain number of mantras for the different phases of the practice such as approach, close approach, accomplishment and great accomplishment. This is why some Buddhist practitioners today use the word "recitation" or talk about "doing accumulation" when referring to the *nyenpa* which is sometimes translated as the "approach or recitation practice" and also means doing a sadhana retreat, as is the case in this instance. Some rinpoches advise their students to use the word "*nyenpa*" in this context.

69 "RAM YAM KHAM In the state of emptiness . . .", and the Akaro mantra are additions to the sadhana text.

70 See note 19 above.

71 The "four Taras" here are the four Tara gatekeepers. Jamgön Kongtrul doesn't mention the visualization of the four Taras in the immediate retinue at this point; he explains it with the visualization for the accomplishment phase, in the mantra recitation section.

72 See the Chimé Phakmé Nyingtik section on lotsawahouse.org. Also in *The Great Accomplishment Ritual of the Heart Essence of Deathless Ārya Tārā*, Appendix 1, pages 119–122.

73 Orgyen Tobgyal explained on another occasion that when the mantra doesn't turn, the syllables are "arranged clockwise". When you meditate on the approach, the syllables are in a fixed position; you visualize the mantra like the moon and stars reflecting in a lake. When the mantra revolves around the seed syllable, it should turn clockwise to accomplish the activity as explained in the *Secret Essence Tantra,* and to do that the syllables must be placed counterclockwise.

74 See note 60 above.

75 See note 61 above.

76 For Jamgön Kongtrul's commentary, see Padmasambhava, Jamgon Kongtrul, *Light of Wisdom, Volume 1,* pages 68–82. Guru Rinpoche's root text is page 9 of the same publication.

77 See note 68 above.

78 See *A Drop of Moonlight Nectar,* which forms Chapter 6, pages 115–129, of this publication.

79 This is the root terma of the *Vima Ladrup,* which is also part of the Chimé Phakmé Nyingtik terma cycle.

80 See *Light of Wisdom, Volume 1,* pages 36–40.

81 From Tsangpagyare's *Aspiration.*

82 Mipham Rinpoche explains the meaning of empowerment as follows: "The Sanskrit word for empowerment is *abhiṣiñca.* Etymologically, *abhi* means "manifest" and *ṣiñca* means "to scatter" or "to pour". The profound ritual of mantra empowerment washes,

or scatters, the stains related to the disciple's body, speech, mind and to all three and establishes, or pours, an extraordinary capacity into the disciple's being, whereby he or she may develop the wisdom that will ripen the body, speech, mind of the disciple and their combination into the four vajras." (*Luminous Essence*, page 89.)

83 See Chapter 11, pages 289–297.

84 Dilgo Khyentse Rinpoche said in *The Wish-Fulfilling Jewel* (page 38), "When we make the prostration, touching the ground at five points—with our forehead, two hands, and two knees—we should think that in this way we pay homage to the five buddha families, and in this way we transform the five poisons (anger, attachment, ignorance, pride and jealousy) into the five wisdoms."

85 In answer to a question, Rinpoche explained that in this case, music must involve instruments being played. Drum or *gyaling* are musical instruments, but they need a player for a musical offering. Two stones hit together can constitute music offering.

86 See for example Jigme Lingpa. "Ladder to Akaniṣṭha", pages 31–40.

87 On page 69, although Jamyang Khyentse Chökyi Lodrö speaks of twelve prongs, he doesn't say anything different: as usual a crossed vajra is made of two intersecting vajras, hence the name; it means that the four halves of the two vajras, which Orgyen Tobgyal calls "prongs" here, extend in the four directions. Each of these halves have three prongs, according to Khyentse Chökyi Lodrö's usage of the term, amounting to twelve prongs. Brocades showing such crossed vajras are often seen at the front of high lamas' thrones.

88 See note 19 above.

89 Orgyen Tobgyal used the Sanskrit Nateshvara, the Lord of the Dance. On another occasion he explained that all Hindus believe that the world was brought into being by a creator. For Buddhists, this world came into being as a result of Noble Avalokiteshvara's compassion, so to us, Avalokiteshvara is known as the Lord of the World, or the Lord of the Dance. For Indians, the great and mighty lord of this world is called Nateshvara, who is a dancing god. They say that as long as Shiva Nateshvara continues to dance, our world will endure; but if he stops dancing, the three realms of existence will cease to exist immediately. That is why Nateshvara, or Lord of the Dance, is another of Avalokiteshvara's names.

90 See on lotsawahouse.org (https://www.lotsawahouse.org/topics/chime-pakme-nying-tik/), and "The White Tara Offering Garland" in *The Great Accomplishment Ritual of the Heart Essence of Deathless Ārya Tārā,* pages 119–120.

91 See note 28 above.

92 "The Melody of Brahma Reveling in the Three Realms: Key Points for Meditating on the Four Stakes that Bind the Life Force", in Jigme Lingpa et al., *Deity, Mantra and Wisdom,* pages 81–96.

93 Orgyen Tobgyal explained the nine principles of mantra in Lerab Ling, on 23 August 1997: 1) *Mantra as Deity.* If we verbally recite a mantra such as OM VAJRA KILI KILAYA SARWA BIGHANAN BAM HUM PET whilst contemplating its meaning, then the ultimate fruition will be that we come face to face with the yidam deity Vajrakilaya in a vision, or that we recognize the nature of our own mind to be inseparable from his. This means that the deity and the mantra are inseparable. The first principle is therefore "understanding mantra to be the deity". 2) *Mantra as Mandala.* If you recite a single mantra such as the Vajrakilaya mantra and you accomplish the practice of that yidam deity, then because all buddhas are in their wisdom nature one, you simultaneously accomplish the practices of all other deities who are inconceivable in number and

appear in all manner of forms, some of them peaceful, some wrathful. If you recite the mantra of the chief deity in a mandala, then that encompasses all the many other deities surrounding the chief deity who belong to the same mandala, and so the second principle is "understanding the mantra to be the mandala". Mantra is recognized as identical to the mandala. 3) *Mantra as Offering.* If while reciting the mantra you use your concentration to visualize rays of light emanating from and gathering back into your heart centre, you will be able to please the buddhas with offerings, and then, as their blessings and accomplishments are received, all your negative karma, turbulent emotions and habitual tendencies will be purified. Thus, the third principle is "mantra as offering". 4) *Mantra as Blessing.* As you verbally recite the mantra and mentally reflect on its meaning, you receive its blessing and are infused with the blessings of the wisdom, love and power of all the buddhas and bodhisattvas. Since it has this power to confer blessings which lead you to become inseparable from the buddhas and bodhisattvas, the fourth principle of mantra is "mantra as blessing". 5) *Mantra as Accomplishment.* Then as you recite the mantra, it brings you accomplishment: the supreme siddhi of the great seal (mahamudra) and the eight common siddhis. Since they all come about through the power of the mantra, the fifth principle is "mantra as accomplishment". 6) *Mantra as Enlightened Activity.* As you are repeating a single mantra such as the Mani mantra, you can perform various visualizations and thereby carry out all kinds of enlightened activity, whether it be pacifying, enriching, magnetising or subjugating; so the sixth principle is "mantra as enlightened activity". 7) *Mantra as Shunyata.* With the ultimate fruition of mantra recitation, all grasping at entities and conceiving of them as impure is cut through, the meaning of shunyata is fully realised and everything is seen in the light of pristine primordial awareness. Since it has the power to bring about this realization of shunyata, the seventh principle of mantra is "mantra as shunyata". 8) *Mantra as Purification.* Reciting mantra has the power to purify all the impairments and breakages of samaya that can affect a practitioner of the Vajrayana. Therefore, the eighth principle is "mantra as purification". 9) *Mantra as Similar to a Wish-Fulfilling Jewel.* To put it simply, mantra recitation is an effective means for fulfilling all our wishes. If there is something you desire, then by keeping that in mind as you recite the mantra, your wish will come true. Every kind of activity—pacifying, enriching, magnetising and subjugating—can be accomplished merely by the power of reciting a mantra. Not only can those activities connected with the dharma be accomplished by means of mantra, but also activities that are unrelated to the dharma can also be affected simply through the power of mantra. Therefore, the ninth principle of mantra is "mantra as similar to a wish-fulfilling jewel".

94 See note 73 above.

95 They are mentioned in the *Tantra of Magnificent Lightning* (Tib. *ngam lok*) that Jamyang Khyentse Chökyi Lodrö quotes: see page 108.

96 See page 122 above.

97 "Essence of Wisdom Nectar", in *The Great Accomplishment Ritual of the Heart Essence of Deathless Ārya Tārā*, Appendix 6, pages 173–182.

98 See note 19 above.

99 See on lotsawahouse.org (https://www.lotsawahouse.org/topics/chime-pakme-nying-tik/). Also in *The Great Accomplishment Ritual of the Heart Essence of Deathless Ārya Tārā*, pages 33–35, where it is translated as "invocation of longevity".

100 Orgyen Tobgyal explains that when they are not under control, they deteriorate. It is because they deteriorate that we get older every day. Once they are brought under control, they do not deteriorate.

101 See "'Treasure Trove of Wisdom'—the framework liturgy for the great accomplishment ritual", in *The Great Accomplishment Ritual of the Heart Essence of Deathless Ārya Tārā*, pages 53–117.

102 See previous note.

103 Because Orgyen Tobgyal quoted the whole text, the complete translation of this text is weaved into his explanations. For an alternative translation, see *The Great Accomplishment Ritual of the Heart Essence of Deathless Ārya Tārā*, pages 100–101.

104 The five essences are the purest, subtlest aspect of the five elements.

105 Karma Rinchen Dargye. *"yongs rdzogs 'chi med snying thig dang 'phags ma'i snying tig gi gtor ma'i pra khrid 'chi med 'dod pa 'jo ba'i dga' ston ldeb"*.

106 Orgyen Tobgyal is probably referring to the *The Garland of Offerings of the Sixteen Vajra Goddesses—The Lute of the Gandharvas*, an offering prayer from the Longchen Nyingtik cycle that features each of the sixteen offering goddesses in some detail. A translation can be found in Rigpa's Rigdzin Düpa practice books. They are also described briefly in Shechen Gyaltsap, "Illuminating Jewel Mirror", page 120.

107 *Dagams* here refers to half-spheres that fill the vase.

108 For the four main ways to relate to tormas, see above page 187.

109 See note 105 above.

110 See note 33 above.

111 See note 59 above.

112 See note 73 above.

113 See note 103 above. *Heart Essence of Complete Immortality* (Chokgyur Lingpa. *The Collected Discovered Teachings (gter Ma) of Gter Chen Mchog Gyur Gling Pa / Gter Chen Mchog Gyur Bde Chen Gling Pa'i Zab Gter Chos Skor. Gnas-brtan dgon-pa.* 39 vols. Paro: Lama Pema Tashi, 1982, vol. 31, p.377–379.)

114 Orgyen Tobgyal mentions them briefly, page 187.

115 *Thugs srog*: the core, or vital essence or heart (*snying po srog*); what is central, or main (*thugs srog shing*).

116 Literally, skandhas, dhatus and ayatanas, or aggregates, constituents and sense fields.

117 There are three levels here: 1) the coarse forms (*rnam pa*) of our real body, the skandhas and so on, 2) their transformation into the mandala of Tara and 3) the ultimate nature of this wisdom mandala. Often the "everlasting flow of inexhaustible adornment" refers to qualities and enlightened activity.

118 There exist several translations. See for example https://www.lotsawahouse.org/words-of-the-buddha/lament-of-rudra.

119 There is an unpublished translation by Rigpa Tranlsations.

120 See note 99 above.

121 For a translation see for example *The King of Aspiration Prayers* on lotsawahouse.org. (https://www.lotsawahouse.org/words-of-the-buddha/samantabhadra-aspiration-good-actions)

122 See note 61.

BIBLIOGRAPHY

Dilgo Khyentse Rinpoche. *The Wish-Fulfilling Jewel: The Practice of Guru Yoga According to the Longchen Nyingthig Tradition*. Shambhala Publications, 1999.

Jamyang Khyentse Wangpo, Jamgon Kongtrul, Chokgyur Lingpa and Jamyang Khyentse Chokyi Lodro. "The Great Accomplishment Ritual of the Heart Essence of Deathless Ārya Tārā". Dzongsar Jamyang Khyentse Rinpoche and Siddharta's Intent, 2019.

Jigme Lingpa. "Ladder to Akaniṣṭha". In *Deity, Mantra, and Wisdom: Development Stage Meditation in Tibetan Buddhist Tantra*, translated by Dharmachakra, 1st edition., 21–79. Ithaca, N.Y: Snow Lion, 2007.

Jigme Lingpa, Patrul Rinpoche and Getse Mahapandita. *Deity, Mantra, and Wisdom: Development Stage Meditation in Tibetan Buddhist Tantra*. Translated by Dharmachakra TranslationCommittee. 1st edition. Ithaca, N.Y: Snow Lion, 2007.

Karma Rinchen Dargye. *"yongs rdzogs 'chi med snying thig dang 'phags ma'i snying tig gi gtor ma'i pra khrid 'chi med 'dod pa 'jo ba'i dga' ston ldeb"*. In *The Treasury of Revelations and Teachings of gter chen mchog 'gyur bde chen gling pa*, Vol. 31 (ki), pages 385–403. Bir: Lama Pema Tashi, 1985.

Mipham Rinpoche. *Luminous Essence: A Guide to the Guhyagarbha Tantra*. Translated by Dharmachakra Translation Committee. Ithaca, N.Y: Snow Lion, 2009.

Nagarjuna. *The Root Stanzas of the Middle Way: The Mulamadhyamakakarika*. Shambhala Publications, 2016.

Padmasambhava, Jamgon Kongtrul, Jamyang Khyentse Wangpo and Chokgyur Lingpa. *Light of Wisdom, Volume 1*. Translated by Erik Pema Kunsang. 2nd edition. Kathmandu: Rangjung Yeshe Publications, 1999.

Padmasambhava and Jamgon Kongtrul. *Light of Wisdom, Volume 2: A Collection of Padmasambhava's Advice to the Dakini Yeshe Tsogyal and Other Close Disciples*. Translated by Erik Pema Kunsang. Hong Kong: Ranjung Yeshe Publications, 1998.

———. *Light of Wisdom, Volume 3: Teachings on the Secret Empowerment*. Rangjung Yeshe Publications, 2018.

———. *Light of Wisdom, Volume 4*. 4th edition. Rangjung Yeshe Publications, 2001.

Padmasambhava, Jamgon Kongtrul, Jamyang Khyentse Wangpo, Chokgyur Lingpa and Tulku Urgyen Rinpoche. *Light of Wisdom, Final Volume: The Conclusion*. Boudhanath: North Atlantic Books, 2013.

Patrul Rinpoche. "Melody of Brahma Reveling in the Three Realms: Key Points for Directing the Practice for the Four Nails That Bind the Life Force of the Practice". In Jigme Lingpa et al., *Deity, Mantra, and Wisdom: Development Stage Meditation in Tibetan Buddhist Tantra*, translated by Dharmachakra, 1st edition., 81–95. Ithaca, N.Y: Snow Lion, 2006.

Śāntideva. *The Way of the Bodhisattva*. Translated by Padmakara. Shambhala Publications, 2011.

Schmidt, Marcia Binder and Michael Tweed, eds. *Precious Songs of Awakening: Chants for Daily Practice, Feast, and Drubchen*. Translated by Erik Pema Kunsang. Hong Kong: Rangjung Yeshe Publications, 2006.

Shechen Gyaltsap IV and Kunkyen Tenpe Nyima. "Illuminating Jewel Wisdom. A Brief, Clear, and Comprehensible Overview of the Development Stage". In *Vajra Wisdom: De-*

ity Practice in Tibetan Buddhism, translated by Dharmachakra Translation Committee. Boston: Snow Lion, 2013.

"The King of Aspiration Prayers". Accessed 12 January 2021. https://www.lotsawahouse.org/words-of-the-buddha/samantabhadra-aspiration-good-actions.

"The Life of Jamyang Khyentse Chökyi Lodrö". Accessed 12 January 2021. https://www.lotsawahouse.org/tibetan-masters/orgyen-tobgyal-rinpoche/biography-khyentse-lodro.

"The Life of Jamyang Khyentse Wangpo". Accessed 12 January 2021. https://www.lotsawahouse.org/tibetan-masters/orgyen-tobgyal-rinpoche/biography-khyentse-wangpo.

INDEX